The Travels of Elkanah Watson

The Travels of Elkanah Watson

*An American Businessman in the
Revolutionary War, in 1780s Europe
and in the Formative Decades
of the United States*

JEREMY DUPERTUIS BANGS

McFarland & Company, Inc., Publishers
Jefferson, North Carolina

LIBRARY OF CONGRESS CATALOGUING-IN-PUBLICATION DATA

Bangs, Jeremy Dupertuis, 1946–
The travels of Elkanah Watson : an American businessman in the Revolutionary War, in 1780s Europe and in the formative decades of the United States / Jeremy Dupertuis Bangs.
p. cm.
Includes bibliographical references and index.

ISBN 978-1-4766-6245-9 (softcover : acid free paper) ∞
ISBN 978-1-4766-2336-8 (ebook)

1. Watson, Elkanah, 1758–1842. 2. United States—Description and travel. 3. United States—History—Revolution, 1775–1783—Personal narratives. 4. Europe—Description and travel. I. Title.

E164.B32 2015   973.3092—dc23   [B]   2015024369

BRITISH LIBRARY CATALOGUING DATA ARE AVAILABLE

© 2015 Jeremy Dupertuis Bangs. All rights reserved

No part of this book may be reproduced or transmitted in any form or by any means, electronic or mechanical, including photocopying or recording, or by any information storage and retrieval system, without permission in writing from the publisher.

Cover image: *Elkanah Watson* (1782), oil on canvas by John Singleton Copley (Princeton University Art Museum/Art Resource, New York)

Printed in the United States of America

McFarland & Company, Inc., Publishers
Box 611, Jefferson, North Carolina 28640
www.mcfarlandpub.com

To Caleb and Sheila Crowell

Table of Contents

Preface 1

Introduction 3

One. The Colonies 7

Two. France 41

Three. Belgium and England 74

Four. The Netherlands 111

Five. America 145

Six. Final Journeys 184

Chapter Notes 195

Bibliography 203

Index 207

Preface

When I transcribed the seventeenth-century documents in the collections of the Pilgrim Society, Pilgrim Hall Museum, in Plymouth, Massachusetts, twenty years ago, I read through the Watson family papers. These mostly concern other members of the Watson family than Elkanah who is the subject of this book. Among them, however, I found a copy of *Men and Times of the Revolution*, Winslow Watson's book about his father. The exciting events recounted in this largely forgotten work inspired my interest in Elkanah, whose careful retention of notes, diaries, receipts, newspaper clippings, and ephemera from his travels provided riches of documentary evidence from which a less ponderous re-telling of his travel adventures could be constructed.

My thanks go to Peggy Baker of the Pilgrim Society for introducing me to the society's extensive collections beyond the topic of the first-generation Pilgrims. I also want to express my appreciation to the staff of the New York State Library and Archives, where Elkanah Watson's own papers form a major collection. Their assistance during four rushed visits to Albany made my work there efficient and productive. The most important material for Elkanah Watson's biography is found in the Albany documents, many of them unpublished. These include the original diaries of his travels, which proved to be more detailed and exciting than the edited versions that formed the sources for what appeared in *Men and Times of the Revolution*.

A generous grant from Caleb and Sheila Crowell allowed me to make my initial acquaintance with the Elkanah Watson papers. Without their subvention, my work could not have taken form beyond enthusiasm for what Winslow Watson had already written. My thanks go also to Chad Moncy, who through the years has sent me numerous items of significance to Elkanah's life, enlarging my familiarity with the existing literature in ways unlikely to have been possible for someone living in Holland.

All quoted material is from Watson's notebooks or, less often, the published version (*Men and Times of the Revolution*, 2d ed. 1861), unless attributed to someone else taken from some other specified source.

Introduction

"It was in the spring of the year 1894 that all London was interested ... by the murder of the Honourable Ronald Adair under most unusual and inexplicable circumstances." Sherlock Holmes decoyed the murderer, Col. Sebastian Moran, into attempting to kill Holmes but instead fooled him into shooting at an exact and lifelike sculptured bust. "It was a wax-coloured model of my friend," explained Holmes's assistant, Dr. Watson, "so admirably done that it was a perfect facsimile. It stood on a small pedestal table with an old dressing-gown of Holmes's so draped round it that the illusion from the street was absolutely perfect."[1]

Another perfect facsimile interested all London in the autumn of 1782. News spread that the great diplomat and philosopher Benjamin Franklin had come in person to the city to negotiate America's independence and end the Revolutionary War. But the curious were fooled by a lifelike wax bust, draped in Franklin's own clothing, and made to move by remote mechanisms so that the illusion of the great man working at a desk, seen across a room, was absolutely perfect, at least for a brief moment. The prankster responsible for this deception was the young American merchant Elkanah Watson. But who was Elkanah Watson?

Elkanah went everywhere and met everybody, it seems; yet his own name has been practically forgotten. A few people remember him as the founder, developer, and promoter of the American county fair, an outgrowth of his public exhibition in 1807 of his Merino sheep, the first two to be imported into western Massachusetts. His early interest in the development of canals in New York State accounts for some notice in every history of the Erie Canal. But his vain sense of injury expressed in demands for credit as the inventor of the idea to build such canals in western New York has aroused a negative response. A recent historian of the Erie Canal proclaimed that "if ego alone were enough to get things built, Elkanah Watson might have made a canal across the continent."[2] Canals were not his only hobbyhorse—all sorts of ideas for civic improvement flowed from his pen, and some were transformed into reality, such as paving the main street of Albany, New York. Referring to his involvement with architectural design, Watson is described as "a man of resolute ego."[3] Another author judged that "Watson would surely rank high among the social climbers of history."[4]

Elkanah first attracts our attention as an apprentice working for the Providence, Rhode Island, merchant John Brown, but that was scarcely an indication of low social position. What better way to learn the practical aspects of international commerce, so that he might eventually take over the shipping business of his father, which extended from Europe to the Caribbean? Elkanah was very well connected in Massachusetts society. Descended from one of the Pilgrims, growing up in Plymouth, he was, for example, related to the playwright and historian Mercy Otis Warren, to the loyalist Judge Peter Oliver, and to anyone named Winslow.

In September 1777, John Brown, the wealthy supplier of ammunition to George Washington's army (as well as a major participant in the slave trade), sent young Elkanah Watson from Providence down to Charleston, carrying 50,000 new American dollars sewn into the lining of his coat. The money was to be invested in goods that could be shipped to Europe, avoiding the British harbor blockade at Newport and Providence. With the proceeds, military supplies could be obtained and shipped back to America. Elkanah, inspired by Tobias Smollett's fictional account of the adventures of Roderick Random, began to keep a diary, a practice he maintained in one form or another for the next half century. On returning from South Carolina, Elkanah wanted to join the army. Instead, encouraged by his father and the Browns, he moved to France, delivering communications from Congress to Benjamin Franklin in Paris. Elkanah set up a shipping agency in Nantes, actively engaged in entrepreneurial business and in supplying the needs of America's revolutionary army. In the course of four years in Europe, he described his travels in France, England, Belgium, and The Netherlands, where he met most of the leading politicians and scientists of the period—not only French officials such as Vergennes (the Foreign Minister, to whom he brought messages from Congress) and Tallyrand (who later worked for him in exile at Albany during the French Revolution) but, more importantly, all the Americans in Paris who surrounded Franklin, such as Tom Paine (for whom Elkanah acted as interpreter), Henry Laurens (with whom Elkanah later traveled in England), and the first American sculptor, Patience Lovell Wright (who created his wax portrait of Franklin). In England he met pro–American voices, such as Edmund Burke, Richard Price, and Joseph Priestly. He also met James Watt, the Prince of Wales, and the widow of the Anglo-African composer Ignatius Sancho. Famously, he commissioned a portrait of himself from John Singleton Copley, on which the painter added a depiction of the American flag the very day when King George III recognized American independence. In The Netherlands, John Adams acted as his guide. Elkanah became acquainted with the consortium of bankers who provided loans that financed the Revolution. Out of patriotic and familial piety he visited Pilgrim sites in Leiden, the city where the founders of New England's first colony had spent years in exile before 1620.

All of this went into notebooks. Elkanah also corresponded with major politicians and was a guest at their houses. He visited Robert Morris in Philadelphia on his way to stay overnight at Mount Vernon, where he presented George Washington with anti-slavery books given him in London by their abolitionist author, Granville Sharp. He exchanged letters with Thomas Jefferson and James Madison; and, when he thought of improvements for the projected new capital city of Columbia (now Washington, D.C.), he sent them along to Pierre l'Enfant, sure the architect would want to think about them. Alexander Hamilton and Aaron Burr were both guests in Elkanah's house in Albany, New York.

Elkanah was inspired by French, English, and Dutch canals to praise the economic benefits and promote the necessity of building waterways from the Hudson River to Lake Ontario and Lake Erie, and, in the opposite direction, to Lake Champlain. For several years he became a gentleman farmer in western Massachusetts, where the Berkshire Agricultural Association that he founded became the origin of America's county fairs. Elkanah proudly thought this his greatest accomplishment.

Yet, without himself being aware of it, Elkanah Watson initiated a new genre of literature—the travel book in which an American describes Europe to an audience of people unlikely to share the experience except through reading. His *A tour in Holland in MDCCLXXXIV / by an American*, published anonymously in 1790, marks the beginning of a peculiarly American variant of the tales of the Grand Tour that had been part of English literature for nearly two hundred years. Washington Irving, Jacob Abbott, Mark Twain, Joseph Pennell, and Henry James would add their contributions, but Elkanah Watson had been there first. Elkanah's journeys extend from north to south in America; they include his voyages in France, England, Belgium, and The Netherlands; and they cover his experiences from the Atlantic coast to Detroit in Michigan, and from upper New York State north to Montreal. That part of his life forms this book.

The Elkanah Watson papers in the State Library at Albany, New York (a town in which the Watsons lived for many years), provide a great variety of material from which to reconstruct his travels—diaries kept at the time, receipts, letters received and copies of those sent, newspaper clippings, engravings, official reports of his commercial activities, and several series of revisions of his journals that he made with the hope of publishing them in some form. At one point, he sent a version to be read by his friend, the painter and author John Trumbull. Finally, in 1854, his son issued a much edited version of Elkanah's life, with the title *Men and Times of the Revolution*.

Elkanah took as his literary models Smollett and Sterne, and he admits to having altered the journal texts to improve the philosophical content—observations on human nature characterized by the sententiousness of the time. In one notebook, he commented, "This Journal was received & corrected from the original after my Return from Europe.[5] I off necessity interlarded with some remarks after a more enlarged View of men & manners, than at the Juvenal year in which the ... wrote. The two preceeding volumes of travels in America are the naked unvarnished effusions of simplicity & inexperience, deprived of the advantages of a liberal education to have enabled me to embellish my stile even with the common rules of grammer, in consequence should the publication of my travels ever be contemplated, they wil require so much p ... ing & polishing to bring them to the standard of scholastic criticism as to change the colour & stile of the original. It will therefore be advisable merely to correct bad spelling, bad grammer and eraze ... certain words but leave the stile in its naked deformity."

Spellings have generally been corrected. I have recast the content, but the narrative is entirely derived from Elkanah's written or published texts. I have added passages excluded in the printed version prepared by his son and I have contributed explanation and comment, while yet inventing nothing—for example, a description of the battle of Yorktown as reported by an eyewitness in the French fleet. This gives us the information that came to Paris and was reported to Elkanah's friend Benjamin Franklin. Quoted conversations are taken from Elkanah's reports of them. I have attempted to present Elkanah's experiences in the immediacy of his initial impressions, set in a context that clarifies what has now become unfamiliar, without the pompous platitudes of past polemics that mar the version edited in the middle of the Victorian era, but retaining the phrases of Elkanah's time that characterize his prejudices and sometimes jar against modern conformities and expectations.

Elkanah Watson was a Whig—and proud of it. His attitudes now arouse incredulous response: how could he judge the Indians incurable drunkards when it was his rum sold to them that got them drunk? Why were they inevitably lost while he became a campaigner for temperance as a means to draw back from his own addiction to the same rum? How did he reconcile his revulsion with the reality of slavery in the South with his own employment in the firm of a major Northern slave trader? How is it that his only response to the Haitian Revolution was to see an opportunity to develop the market for maple syrup—a move that might eventually bring an end to dependence on slave-made cane sugar, but which also meant personal profit for Elkanah? What made him such a firm believer in progress? The journals give some answer, but much remains mysterious. Proud of his own innovative ideas, Elkanah does not seem to have identified in himself something quite new—the practice of uniting his experience of his surroundings in a grand interpretation of history and nature as a providential narrative of nationalist expansion. Everything he noticed was part of national progress, or, if not, could be dismissed as an unfortunate hindrance. We no longer think in the same way, without questioning the inevitability of outcomes whose advantage for some included the opposite for others. Elkanah fascinates us with the unabashed self-confidence that created America.

Elkanah Watson chronicled the sights and events of America's Revolution, of the political and social changes in the post-war period, of the War of 1812, and of the great population shift westward that followed the dispossession of the Six Nations at Fort Stanwix (Elkanah was there when the treaty was signed in 1788). His travels form an exciting counterpoint to the broader narratives of American beginnings, familiar to many people through textbooks about pre–Civil War American history. Anyone who enjoys the exhibits and events of a county fair can thank Elkanah. He should be remembered by anyone with an interest in the development of transportation and trade. But what he wrote down for memory's sake cries out to be recalled as well—the sights of America and Europe when America as a nation was a new idea.

ONE

The Colonies

A Revolutionary Youth

Elkanah Watson learned in elementary school to march resolutely through brush and woodland. He could keep silent in swamps. He knew how to prime, load, and pretend to fire his imaginary flint-lock musket. Step back at the right time. Move forward. March in rank and file. The well-disciplined children of Plymouth, Massachusetts, paraded and sang each year on December 22 to honor the landing in 1620 of their Pilgrim ancestors fleeing the oppression of tyrants. Elkanah had learned division and multiplication, reading and writing, but martial exercises promised to be more practical. The Revolutionary War could be felt coming. Elkanah's teachers, Alexander Scammel and Peleg Wadsworth, foresaw a future commanding real soldiers in a war they thought inevitable.[1] Others were unsure. Elkanah's father (also named Elkanah) decided that, war or not, his boy needed training to prepare for a future in the family business—international shipping. His ships brought American exports to Liverpool, Hamburg, the Caribbean islands, Surinam, and even St. Petersburg, returning with exotic luxuries to sell. Most ships from Plymouth went out for cod. Seventy-five fishing schooners anchored in the harbor, while village notables drank toasts to their illustrious ancestors, recalling the Pilgrims' "virtue, their patience, their fortitude, and their heroism."

Plymouth, its 2,500 craftsmen, fishermen, merchants, farmers, and housewives, talking themselves into standing up to tyranny, was too small.

Elkanah needed broader experience; the best place to get it was as an apprentice to Rhode Island's leading merchant and manufacturer, the Watsons' friend John Brown.[2] Brown's family business produced candles and oil from the whaling out of Nantucket, besides the manufactures of their iron works. They imported sugar and molasses and exported rum and tobacco, together with many other commercial ventures, including the African-Caribbean slave trade. In September, 1773, at age fifteen and no longer the schoolboy known as "Crazy Elk," Elkanah began training in commerce at Providence.[3]

Everyone of substance knew the Watsons. They were related to, married to, or at least acquainted with most of southern New England's best families. Their large wooden house up the hill above the wharves could offer hospitality to guests. Young Elkanah's ancestors had owned what was known as Watson's Hill. He was proud to be a descendant in the seventh generation from the Pilgrim Edward Winslow, *Mayflower* passenger and third governor of Plymouth Colony. Through the connections established in subsequent generations he could now call himself cousin to important members of both the Tory and the Whig political par-

Leyden Street, Plymouth, Massachusetts (steel engraving from W. H. Bartlett, *The Pilgrim Fathers*, 1853).

ties. His father was a leading Plymouth Whig. In 1772, the Town of Plymouth appointed him to be one of the new Committee of Communication and Correspondence, to keep in touch with Samuel Adams, the chief revolutionary of Boston, and to coordinate resistance to arbitrary British demands.[4]

In late 1773, tea delivered by ship to New York and Philadelphia had been sent back to England, unaccepted and unopened. In Boston, many people demanded that the same be done. Plymouth's citizens thought themselves "in duty and Gratitude bound ... to aid and Support" the Bostonians and pledged "at the hazard of our lives and fortunes ... to defend them against the violence and wickedness of our Common Enemies"—stirring words that for the meantime boiled down to a refusal to drink tea.[5] Massachusetts' Governor Thomas

Hutchinson resolved to ignore opposition and have the tea landed. According to one refined Plymothian, Mercy Otis Warren, "this drug had become almost a necessary article of diet, the demand for teas in America had become astonishingly great, and the agents in Boston, sure of finding purchasers, if once the weed was deposited in their stores, haughtily ... determined ... to receive and dispose of their cargoes at every hazard."[6]

Parliament in London had decreed the tax without consulting any representatives from New England. That act treated the colonists as people without the rights England's Glorious Revolution and the Bill of Rights had guaranteed to all Englishmen around eighty years earlier. The tax on tea was a test—once accepted and paid, the precedent for further taxation without representation and without limit would be established.

Outraged citizens from the city of Boston and nearby towns gathered in the South Meeting House (a church) where John Hancock proclaimed the ancient English right of representative government and Samuel Adams called for action. After noisy arguments but a failure to agree on any plan, the agitated crowd adjourned as evening fell.

Less than an hour later, men disguised as Indians carrying axes and clubs marched to Griffin's Wharf where they climbed on the ships and in three hours emptied into the ocean all the chests of tea—more than three hundred. Only they themselves knew who they were; and no individual could be sure who all the others were behind their war paint. English warships moored nearby rested unresisting, perhaps unaware. Just after, Boston lay dark and silent as if nothing had happened. Thousands of pounds of tea flavored the mud at the bottom of the harbor. Would the tea's owners, merchants who were not the government, be compensated? By whom, if the actors remained anonymous? Guesses about the expected punishment spread as quickly as the news of the impetuous action.

A year earlier, at Providence, other men had dressed up as Noble Savages, too—romantic wild symbols of stern virtue resisting tyranny. Refusing taxes imposed without representation, they captured and burned the king's excise-collecting schooner, the *Gaspée*. John Brown, who was a member of Rhode Island's revolutionary committees and a deputy to the province's legislature, had decided on the attack and was one of the leaders. But the English found no more than rumor to justify their suspicions against him. Nonetheless, the government was intent to punish this and an increasing number of other treasonous insolencies. Brown might be free to walk around Providence, but Hancock's and Adams's caper would not go unanswered.

Even before newspapers could publish their stories, reports of Providence's and Boston's simple and sudden solution to the impasse on taxes reached towns throughout New England. The Committees of Correspondence wrote letters that brought people in towns throughout the colonies the latest news. The committees also spread information about actions or ideas conceived to regain lost freedom. Loyalist supporters of the British colonial administration attempted to disown the actions of the committees and to keep the town governments from advocating open rebellion.

In Plymouth, customs tax collector Edward Winslow (another descendant of Elkanah's forefather of the same name) had attempted to present a petition to the town meeting (council) objecting to the majority's resolutions against the government, but that same majority voted to refuse to allow his sentiments even to be read. By March, 1774, the Committee of Correspondence reported that tea was still making its way into town. Elkanah's uncle, William Watson, and two others were appointed to see to it that resolutions against selling or drinking tea were obeyed. People discovered to be selling teas would be shunned and "considered as an Enemy to the rights of America and the Constitution of this Country."[7]

Something more needed to be done. Plymouth Rock, the town's most powerful symbol, had become the metaphoric gateway to a new world for the Pilgrims in 1620.[8] Now the stone would be promoted to new significance, elevating spirits at least for a while. Twenty yoke of oxen combined their efforts to try to move the boulder left alone on the beach by retreating glaciers. Plymouth Rock was to be placed beneath the Liberty Pole in front of the Meeting House at the top of the hill. Above it a flag would wave defiantly, calling for "Liberty or Death." But the increasing pressure of the screw-jacks used to hoist the rock onto a carriage strained unseen weaknesses. The rock split. Half remained in the coastal muck. The other half progressed in slightly diminished triumph to become a symbol of the British empire cracking and disintegrating.

Stores of gun powder were established in places around Boston like Concord. A co-ordinated revolutionary army did not yet exist, so there were no guards. Unconnected militias practiced locally three times a week, paid a small amount by the town meeting for showing up. In Providence, Elkanah joined one of the new companies of boys who drilled, fitted out in fine uniforms of red with yellow facing. Towns bought guns and ammunition. "Liberty Companies" of farmers- and tradesmen-turned-soldiers began to form in all the towns, electing their own officers without general organization.

Governor Hutchinson responded by ordering more than a thousand professional soldiers to parade through Boston to Jamaica Plain and back through Dorchester, flaunting the superior numbers of trained men that he as governor had at his command. English officers were sure the resistance would collapse when confronted with hundreds of practised professionals. General Thomas Gage, Boston's military commander, stationed a company of guards in Marshfield close to Plymouth, prepared to occupy the restive home of the Pilgrims. The threat of a company of Minutemen commanded by Peleg Wadsworth, and inevitable armed insurrection if the British army entered Plymouth, convinced the soldiers to turn around and evacuate by sea to Boston.

In April, 1775, General Gage ordered a night-time march of troops to capture the supplies stored at Concord and to try to catch Sam Adams and John Hancock, who were reported to be at Lexington.[9] Guards were sent out early in the evening to prevent express messengers from alerting the colonists, but a warning had gone out five minutes earlier. Paul Revere and William Dawes escaped, riding away in the night to warn the country. The soldiers started out soon after, unfamiliar with the route. Edward Winslow, Jr., son of Plymouth's royalist tax collector, guided the English along roads he knew well. But hearing about the army's movement, anti–English messengers sped to call up the militias of more distant towns. News reached Providence in the afternoon on April 19. The Liberty Companies prepared to march but discovered they did not have enough ammunition. Working through the night, Elkanah cast bullets and rolled powder into cartridges so the soldiers could depart in the morning.

Seventeen-year-old Elkanah Watson was a cousin of Tory Edward Winslow, Jr., who had guided the British army to Lexington. Elkanah marched with his company of youths from Providence towards Lexington on the 20th. On the way, news reached them that six men had died in the battle the day before. Thirty armed militiamen and forty onlookers had been attacked by more than eight hundred regulars, who shot at the retreating Americans.

At Concord, more were killed but a direct confrontation was evaded. Minutemen arriving from nearby towns managed to attack the British soldiers from behind walls and fences lining narrow roads. On their way out of Lexington, the soldiers plundered and torched unprotected houses and shops when families tried to find safety in the fields and woods. In the face of rising militia strength the regulars retreated through Charlestown to Boston before Elkanah's reinforcements from Providence reached the scene. The siege of Boston began, and, with it, the war.

Militias surrounded Boston peninsula and made the royalist garrison's supply and communication impossible except by sea. The English used boats to send soldiers towards the militia's strongholds as if to attack them but really attempting to confiscate cattle still in the fields. An attempt in May to bring in hay from one of the Boston Harbor islands failed when rebellious farmers burned over seventy-five tons. Later, British raiders stole cattle and supplies from the farms of Martha's Vineyard and the Elizabeth Islands to feed the troops. Reinforcements for the garrison arrived by sea, bringing the numbers to around six thousand—more mouths to feed. Townsfolk in Boston were put on rations.

Throughout New England, townsmen argued about how to prepare. Sandwich organized

Watson rousing Plymouth (engraving by Thwaites after Benson J. Lossing, in *Men and Times of the Revolution*, 2d ed., 1861, p. 19).

watchmen along the coasts of Cape Cod.[10] Plymouth bought fifty "Good Guns and Bayonets for the towns use" as well as two drums, and the council also decided to build a breastwork for firing the municipal cannon as well as to "procure thirteen hundred of cannon shot of various sizes." A little later the town meeting bought almost all of a gunpowder shipment that had just come from the West Indies. And finally, they considered appealing to the General Court for help building a fort overlooking the harbor to defend the town.[11]

In Providence, boredom settled down on Elkanah Watson. After the excitement of preparing for, but missing, the battle of Lexington and Concord, his work in Brown's store reduced itself to a continuum of unfulfilling tedium. Friends joined the army, flocking to surround Boston. Everyone else marched away, it seemed, but Elkanah's father and his boss refused to release him from the indentured term of training and employment. He itched to get away to do something for liberty more important than minding the store. His chance came soon.

John Brown had contracted to supply the rebel army with flour. When sailing with the shipment from Newport in the second half of April, his ship was captured and he was sent to Boston in chains—suspected for his part in the burning of the *Gaspée* in 1772. He was indeed guilty, but proof was lacking. Elkanah hoped to get help to intercept the loaded flour ship as it came around Cape Cod, before it got Brown to Boston's jail. He galloped on horseback across from Providence to Plymouth.

Calling "Fire, Fire," Elkanah aroused Plymouth's citizens at two in the morning. His urgency convinced Plymouth's Committee of Safety to arrange a sortie with two lumbering fishing schooners. Each vessel carried a couple of small cannon and a crew of thirty to forty men. Elkanah's pride in this exciting adventure was strengthened by the thought that these ships sailed away from Plymouth Rock, somehow acting to defend the freedom his ancestors had sought on these shores so long ago. A twenty-gun warship chased these hastily organized rebel sailors back into Plymouth harbor after a week and a half of ineffectual cruising. Having no commission, the Plymothians would have been hanged as pirates if caught. Elkanah could at least claim in later years that he had sailed on the first American vessel to oppose the British flag in this war. The war settled into the waiting, watchful routine of siege.

Brown was released not long after arriving in Boston. His brother Moses, a well-known Quaker convert, evidently convinced the authorities that they had no warrant for John's arrest and no proof for their accusation. Moreover, Moses promised to temper Rhode Island's anti-government activities in exchange for his brother's release. Elkanah, on the other hand, had promised nothing and was willing to fight. With his militia company, he marched around the streets of Newport to guard the American general Charles Lee, who was visiting Providence and wanted to survey English naval strength in Newport's harbor. But the ambiguous position of Rhode Island at that moment meant the youths' military display provoked no response from the British fleet. Marching in uniform, fully prepared for battle, even though daring and provocative, remained a form of inactivity.

After Lexington the lack of ammunition and powder crippled attempts to plan strategy. By June, the Continental Congress appointed George Washington to command the militia companies and unite them into some sort of shape as an army. When he arrived in early July, Washington discovered that the army at Boston was running out of bullets. John Brown sent one of his ships out from Providence to try to intercept a shipment of gunpowder and shot from London. Luckily, supplies on hand in town could be sent to Washington immediately. For some time Brown had been bringing gunpowder as a return freight from Europe. He asked young Elkanah to conduct wagons carrying a ton and a half of powder to General Washington in person at Cambridge.

Elkanah presented his letters of introduction while General Washington was in the midst of reprimanding a subordinate officer. The commander's stern and authoritative character impressed the youth. Here was a leader who could bring order out of the undisciplined chaos of amateur enthusiasm. Washington redirected the powder to an arsenal at Mystic (also called Medford), where Elkanah was relieved to note the supplies on hand. "Sir, I am happy to see so many barrels of powder here," he said to the officer receiving the shipment from Providence. "Those barrels are filled with sand," the officer whispered, "to deceive enemy spies."

The English were running out of supplies as well. In October, Captain Henry Mowat appeared with four ships in the harbor of Falmouth (in Maine, now called Portland) to confiscate munitions, demand submission to the king, and, in the face of insubordination, to punish. He gave people a short time to evacuate their houses before his ships bombarded the town. Then he landed soldiers who set fire to all the buildings. Mowat proclaimed his orders to reduce all harbor towns to ashes and announced that he was sure New York and other ports had already been destroyed.

In November an American ship captured guns and ammunition from a British supply ship. This booty replenished the needs of Washington's army while limiting the tactical choices for the British soldiers in Boston. The regulars now had to be even more careful to conserve what they still had.

On Thursday, the 23rd of November, a day of Thanksgiving was celebrated in the army camp with a grand supper of turkey and goose.[12] Routine returned, with the occasional random death from the exchange of shells, and with the fear of infection when a soldier in camp caught smallpox.

The stalemate of balanced forces shifted in the rebels' favor with the arrival of over fifty cannon in late January to be installed in earthwork emplacements on the hills of Dorchester, capable of bombarding the defenses of Boston. Benedict Arnold and Ethan Allen had captured these guns when the rebel forces they led had overrun Britain's Fort Ticonderoga on Lake Champlain near the Canadian border. A young soldier, Henry Knox, took advantage of freezing weather to drag the artillery on sledges three hundred miles across mountains and rivers. The trek took two months, and another month was spent getting the barrels mounted on gun carriages and set up aimed at Boston.

Sporadic shots started the second day of March, with a full bombardment throughout the second week. Stormy wind and torrential rain prevented a counterattack by the Boston garrison. By the middle of the month, the English decided to retreat and abandon Boston. On March 17, nearly ten thousand British soldiers withdrew in a hundred and twenty ships, also carrying away over a thousand loyalist women and children. That same day, Americans ventured onto Bunker Hill, discovered it abandoned, and then felt safe to re-enter Boston.

General Sir William Howe, the final English commander at Boston, withdrew to Halifax in Nova Scotia. General Sir Henry Clinton, however, sailed south towards New York and Virginia. The American general Lee moved rapidly overland to fortify New York, arriving there before the English fleet, which continued past without seriously attacking the city. Washington, more slowly, moved towards Virginia. He passed through Providence on April 5, escorted by local companies of infantry and grenadiers, together with the cadet company of young men that included Elkanah.[13]

Clinton's goal, however, turned out to be Charleston, South Carolina. In May, 1776, he arrived with many ships off Cape Fear to await seven regiments straggling over from Cork, Ireland, but dispersed by storms. Tories from inland North Carolina expected to join Clinton. Rebel action blocked them. The English offered freedom to run-away slaves who would fight their former masters. Unprepared and scarcely armed, the freed men provided little military help, but their exodus from plantations raised fear of inland revolt at the same time as the English naval attack.

Assaults on American fortifications on Sullivan's Island began on June 28. The battle for Charleston lasted twelve hours. When the British withdrew, they left ships grounded on sandbanks or positioned too far away for effective bombardment. Ignorance and bad luck defeated the British more than any sort of American military superiority, but the result nonetheless encouraged Americans up and down the coast to hope that they could prevail against great naval superiority.

Shipyards rushed to construct coastal defense boats. The Congress authorized confiscation of trading vessels arriving from Britain. The last surviving hopes for avoiding war vanished. In May and June, towns instructed their representatives to urge the Congress to end the uncertainty and choose independence.[14] The official declaration came on July fourth.

A surge of self-confidence invigorated the newly independent country, but reality did not rush to confirm the citizens' image of freedom. "By the declaration of independence, dreaded by the foes, and for a time doubtfully viewed by many of the friends of America, every thing stood on a new and more respectable footing, both with regard to the operations of war, or negociations with foreign powers."[15] There were no ambassadors yet, let alone offers of help from foreign countries—rather the contrary. Reinforcements of Hessians and other mercenary regiments arrived to strengthen the British army.

Assuming there would be an attack to capture a major port, George Washington moved thousands of soldiers onto Long Island hoping to defend New York by preventing the German troops from landing. Using Staten Island instead, English and Hessian soldiers rapidly moved onto Long Island where they routed the Americans, forcing them to retreat to New York City, with loss of men, artillery, and other equipment. Washington next had to abandon the city itself, which the British occupied on October 22.

Preparing for extended action, Elkanah and over a hundred other cadets from Providence had themselves inoculated against small pox. They wanted immunity from infection during encampments like those around Boston. The process was innovative and dangerous. Scabs from infected small-pox sufferers were rubbed on surface scratches to produce a minor case of the disease that could result in immunity to later infection. Often this worked; some patients, however, became seriously ill; a few would die. Small-pox hospitals stood in isolation, to prevent the disease's spreading in case the controlled infection failed. Meals were limited and the doctors thought it best for their patients to be cold, lest heat increase the power of the illness. Years later, Elkanah recalled that "Our sufferings were severe."

News arrived of Washington's retreat from New York into New Jersey. Some of the soldiers recently protected from smallpox were infected with fear of defeat and discussed emigration to any place beyond British tyranny. Elkanah, however, while visiting Plymouth, heard an American army officer bring encouraging descriptions of Washington's resolute confidence in eventual victory. Hope had not fled, but the moment of victory grew indeterminate. A week later, Parson Chandler Robbins climbed his pulpit in Plymouth's Meeting House to read news of Washington's capture of the Hessian regiments guarding Trenton the day after Christmas. Courage revived.

The British still controlled Staten Island, Manhattan Island, Long Island, and Rhode Island (now called Aquidneck Island to distinguish it from the state). They occupied Newport and blocked trade to and from Providence. Elkanah's cadet company was stationed at Pawtucket north of Providence, but sentinel duties in winter without even sight of an enemy once again proved tedious and without glory. Elkanah complained. His father again refused permission to leave the cadets and join the army. Moreover, his indenture to work for John Brown had not ended. The year 1777 wore on, bringing news of victories in New Jersey and Connecticut, still without change for the people of Providence and surrounding areas. Suddenly, Elkanah's dull routine ended forever.

From Providence to Charleston

John and Nicholas Brown, brothers and business partners, had a contract to supply the rebel army with munitions and other supplies. Their ability to obtain New England goods that they could ship out and sell in France was, however, severely restricted by the British blockade of Newport and Provincetown. They managed to send a shipment of sugar to their agent in Charleston, South Carolina, Nathaniel Russell.[16] With the proceeds from the sale of the sugar, plus a promise of further payment, Russell could load the ship with rice and indigo, products that had a ready market in France. The cash from sale in France could be re-invested in merchandise sent back to America and sold on arrival to produce a profit for the venture. This long-term complicated system for transferring money also enabled them to import munitions such as gun powder needed by the revolutionary army. This ship, the *Live Oak*, disappeared at sea. Russell demanded speedy payment in new Continental paper money to make up the difference, not wanting to wait for eventual profits when Brown's other ships returned from Europe.

Elkanah would travel overland from Providence to Charleston carrying over twenty-six thousand Continental dollars newly issued by Congress sewn in to his clothing (an amount he later remembered as fifty thousand).[17] The near quilted effect of a sturdy long-coat could conceal almost anything, as long as no one suspiciously felt the weight or investigated the stiffness when the cloth folded. Elkanah would cover the entire length of the war action, endangered by royalist soldiers along the coast and by loyalist settlers in large regions of countryside. Southern roads were beset by highwaymen—"mostly women," he was warned.[18] He might hope to escape attention by appearing to be an innocent and inexperienced youth. Aged nineteen, he was.

Elkanah crossed the wooden bridge over the Naragansett River and rode out of Providence on September 4, 1777, with a pair of pistols in his holster and a sword hanging at his side. The diary he resolved to keep would record the character of the people and the features of the land amidst the events that made him feel a participant in actions so significant, so revolutionary the whole world would watch.

Elkanah rode steadily to the west towards Connecticut. In the rough hilly country, venerable farmers harvested grain in fenced fields. Cows chewed their cud. Trees cast shadows from fall foliage finally forsaking green for brown, red, and gold. The distant war might not exist except for the absence of strong, young men in the fields to help their fathers.

On the far side of the Connecticut River, Hartford seemed respectably prosperous with three hundred houses. But, having been asked who he was and where he was going every time he stopped to feed and water his horse, Elkanah decided to avoid the town's gossips and spend the night farther along, at Wethersfield, a much smaller settlement.

Riding into New Haven at eight in the evening the next day, he immediately found lodging at Bier's Tavern. "What may I call your name? If I may be so bold!"—the usual questions rushed to meet him. "Where are you a going? What is your business?" Elkanah decided to match the next impudence with rudeness. In the morning he viewed the town and wrote down that there were nearly four hundred houses, two brick-built colleges, two meeting houses (Church of England and Presbyterian), and a "state house" with six cannon defending it. The idea that a notebook with such information might brand him a spy to anyone suspicious of his trip and his motives did not yet occur to him.

Elkanah rode next to Puk's tavern at Milford, where he had the chance to practice his newly resolved impudence. "Mrs. Puk made up to me and asked where I might be from. Why mam! I was last from Jerusalem." "Ah," she responded, "the Jerusalem we read of in scripture?" "Yes." She wasn't through: "Where might you be agoing now?" "If the wind holds fair, I intend shaping my course for Heaven in the morn." She realized he was ridiculing her so "shut

Elkanah's first map of his travels (detail) (from the Elkanah Watson Papers, courtesy New York State Library).

her clamshell" and went back to preparing food for the guests. He noted that the village had around ninety houses spread over a large area about three miles long. There was "1 church and one presbitarian meeting House and also 1 Baptist meeting house."

From Milford he rode on to look up his grandmother in Fairfield. Her house was filled with visitors. Unrecognized, he was simply given a chair in the circle of guests. One of the women was Elkanah's aunt. She couldn't recall his face, since his last visit at age eleven. After embracing the nearly forgotten youth, his relatives introduced him to other visitors. Among them Elkanah met General Gold Silliman, a local rebel hero during a British attack on Danbury a few months earlier.

Noticing odd movements from a warship off the coast, Elkanah expected an English attack. At dawn, a cannonshot and ringing bells sounded the alarm. Elkanah jumped out of bed and into a closet—accidentally, he said later. He had been searching for the chamber door, not trying to hide. When the second alarm shot was heard three minutes later, he was still upstairs. His grandmother urged him to escape. To be discovered with all that money would be disastrous. Instead of listening to her advice, Elkanah ran outside to the alarm post.

Five hundred English soldiers had landed at a farm three miles away. Militiamen marched to battle them; but the English re-embarked without conflict. They had come ashore only to steal cattle and stores.

Elkanah stayed nearly a week in Fairfield, then moved on towards Danbury. In April, the British resupplied their army by capturing Danbury's stores of powder intended for the Americans. The English in control of New York then began pushing towards Philadelphia, capital city of the rebellion.

Avoiding New York, Elkanah crossed the Hudson at King's Ferry by Peekskill. A messenger brought news there of the British victory against Washington's army at the battle of Brandywine Creek. Unsure of his safety and not knowing the sympathies in the countryside, Tory or rebellious Whig, Watson headed towards Morristown in New Jersey, three days' ride from Peekskill. At Morristown, Watson met a friend from earlier years in Providence—Captain Jeronemus Hoogland, now at the age of twenty-one, experienced and weathered, commanding the 3d troop of the 2nd regiment of Light Dragoons. Elkanah also met two young men intending to travel to Charleston in South Carolina, just as he was. Elkanah bought a sulky (a two-wheeled carriage, considered the most practical way for a single person to travel) and joined the other two carriages. The three men hired a servant to accompany them.

After passing Princeton's college, they reached Trenton. People pointed out where George Washington had accepted the surrender of the Hessians last January, reminding the travelers of American victories. But in the next town, Burlington, a messenger announced the occupation of Philadelphia by British troops just two hours earlier. Their route had to change—shifting north to Bethlehem and down through Reading, Lancaster, and York. Elkanah would miss one of his intended goals—conveying eleven hundred dollars to Josiah Hewes of Philadelphia for Nicholas Brown.[19]

Suddenly, at the far side of the Delaware River, they were arrested as British spies. Elkanah's notebook aroused suspicion. America's first spy, Nathan Hale, had been hanged by the British in September, 1776; there could be no doubt that Americans would happily put a noose around the neck of any English spy. Elkanah protested his patriotic innocence and convincingly named the American politicians he knew. However beautiful virtuous patriotic death might be, Elkanah's value to the country lay not in the intelligence he collected but in success conveying the secret funds to Charleston. No one noticed the exceptional padding in Elkanah's coat. He and his new friends were released the next morning.

Elkanah had never before seen log cabins like those in the mountainous country around Bethlehem, where they rested two days at the Sun Inn. In the same hotel, the Marquis de Lafayette was recuperating from a wound to his leg suffered at the battle of Brandywine Creek on September 11.

That major British victory had left the rebel army in disarray with over a thousand casualties and the loss of eleven of their fourteen cannons. Philadelphia was exposed to capture and fell on the 26th.

Lafayette and Watson were the same age, nineteen. The Frenchman was soon to command a division of Washington's army and achieve lasting fame, while Elkanah continued his trip southwards in useful obscurity.

Accustomed to the weatherboarding of New England's timber-frame houses, Elkanah paid attention to Bethlehem's stone buildings. One served as a school for young women, a novel idea for him. Elkanah noticed further that German girls worked in the fields here, something women did not do in New England.

A rope bridge over the Lehigh River confronted Elkanah with the first technological innovation among many he carefully recorded throughout America and Europe. A system of ropes and a pulley propelled a boat across the water; the bow and stern being attached to the rope, the current pushed the boat quickly across by pressure against the stern with the bow pointed upstream.

On October 4, they reached Ephrata, where they could hear the artillery being fired by Washington in the battle of Germantown. Fog obscured the battle, and a few American units ended up firing on each other. One regiment was surrounded and forced to surrender. Other Americans, after killing and wounding many opponents, fled from greater numbers of Hessian and English soldiers. Despite this disorganized disaster, the ability of the American army to come together again after the Brandywine defeat and make a serious attack on the English brought renewed hope. Lafayette praised Washington's tactical skills in planning an attack that surely would have ended the war, had the American peasants and craftsmen been practised soldiers. Time would bring experience and improvement, the rebels hoped. Elkanah, on the other hand, was endangered and needed to move farther away from Philadelphia and the British.

Ephrata, contrasting with everything familiar to him, almost drove thoughts of the battle out of his mind. Elkanah described the settlers as a "most eccentric and remarkable sect of fanatics." They baptised by immersion ("dunking") and called themselves "Dunkers." Their dress was a long monk-

The Marquis de Lafayette (pointiliste engraving and etching signed [Jean-Baptiste] Verité).

like garment with a sash and a woollen hood. Believing themselves in communion with "ethereal spirits," they had withdrawn from the world. The sexes lived in separate houses, remaining separate also in church. They ate only "vegetables and roots, except at their occasional lovefeasts," events that inspired outsiders to imagine sexual excess. Their half-timbered houses and religious buildings looked like a German village, far from familiar New England's clapboard houses. The travelers, leaving, "heard the brethren chanting their melodious hymns, in plaintive notes that thrilled our souls."

Lancaster, Pennsylvania, presented a peaceful, pleasant scene of a thousand houses set in idyllic farmland of hills and valleys. But factories here produced the rifles used by the American army. Elkanah rode on to York, where the Congress had retreated when Phildadelphia fell to the British. Secret sessions were held every day, protected by Washington's army camped at Valley Forge in the country between York and Philadelphia. From Congress, Elkanah obtained a passport for the remainder of his journey, to use if arrested again as a British spy.

The travelers cut through a wilderness region of Maryland, which Elkanah thought was "infested by a semi-barbarian population." The three men managed to rescue another traveler who had been attacked by one of the locals.

Virginia, reputedly civilized, shocked Elkanah beyond words. Stopping for a meal and lodging at a "highly respectable house," Elkanah saw "for the first time, young Negroes, of both sexes, from twelve even to fifteen years old, not only running about the house, but absolutely tending table, almost as naked as they came into the world." Some young women seated at the table "appeared totally unmoved by this scandalous violation of decency." Elkanah never had to think much about slavery before; here it was in front of him. Perhaps he had also never had such opportunity to see adolescent bodies, disturbingly presented nearly nude in captive vulnerability. He was the apprentice of one of the country's major slave traders. John Brown, with wide-ranging commercial interests, was a forthright advocate of slavery and, with his brother Nicholas, was involved in kidnapping Africans and selling them into slavery in the West Indies. This took place far away from Providence. Was the money that supported the war for independence tainted? Whose independence from what? Their brother Moses had left the family business when he became a Quaker and an outspoken abolitionist. According to John, the government had no business meddling with commerce and private property.

Elkanah was shocked, but what assaulted his sensibilities—slavery—was an essential, if hidden, part of his own life: working for John Brown, his own career was to some extent based on slavery, however distantly. And he had grown up with servants. His father had owned at least one slave, Caesar, mentioned in 1771 as having been granted his freedom in 1758.[20] Elkanah's attitude to slavery tended towards abolitionism, but ambiguity remained.

From Leesburg they drove south in the pine forests towards Fredericksburg. In the moonlit night the only inn they found was a "wretched ordinary, filled with a throng of suspicious characters." Tom the servant rode on ahead. Late at night he galloped back to warn them, "'O massa, I see the devil just this minute flying in dem woods!'" Mr. Scott, one of Elkanah's companions, went with Tom to discover the apparition among the trees. Soon he called out, "'I have got the devil, or some dead Tory fast by the leg; a man in gibbets!'" At a tavern five miles farther they learned that the man they had found hanged was a slave. He had murdered his master and then been lynched. Elkanah's next comment in his diary is that on the approach to Fredericksburg, "we passed many elegant plantations, whose owners appeared to enjoy the splendor and affluence of nabobs." He added, "My New England feelings were constantly aroused and agitated by the aspect of slavery in this land of freedom." Moving on, at Fredericksburg he was impressed by the efficient production of the arms factory, where slaves made the weapons needed for the revolt against tyranny.

When they reached New Castle, one of the travelers wanted to buy a slave and his horse to accompany them further. Another, who had just intruded himself on the party, objected that the owner couldn't sell the "boy" out of the "colony" (to go out of Virginia). Elkanah retorted that there was no truth to that claim, perhaps believing that he, at least, could treat a slave well, without yet completely rejecting the system. Or maybe he was focussing only on the literal state of the law, with no thought to the injustice of slavery. After almost starting a fight, Elkanah decided to part company with the others when they reached Williamsburg.

Four more days of riding along sandy roads crossing few hills brought them on the seventeenth of October to Virginia's capital, Williamsburg. Elkanah drew a map of the town which he estimated was three quarters of a mile long. A single street connected the brick college of William and Mary on one end with the State House at the other. At one side stood the former palace of Lord Dunmore, now Governor Patrick Henry's, and on the opposite side, the munitions magazine. The city contained around three hundred twenty houses, mostly wooden. He was told that the strikingly elegant marble monument portraying the "Late Lord Burtertout" in his "usual garments" had cost 700 guineas. In the Council Chamber he spent the afternoon of his second day in town studying maps, including one eighteen by fifteen feet showing London and the countryside around.

Elkanah had "a snugg Little Room in the Rolly" Tavern, where he relaxed with his flute and his journal, as well as books and "a Case of Instruments." After attending church services with the landlord of the Raleigh on Sunday the 19th of October, they toured the palace, "supposed to surpass anything of the kind in America." Elkanah was particularly interested in the ice house behind the garden. Ice and snow brought in the winter by wagon stayed cool throughout the summer and into the next fall in an underground chamber shaped like "half of an egg standing upon the End." Elkanah's guide was the ice house's architect.

Continuing towards Charleston with a new companion, Captain Harwood, Elkanah commented that Jamestown's interest lay only in past history. Here in 1607 adventurers established the first English colony in America. Here Pocahontas was said to have protected the colonists from "famine and treachery." Nothing was left but venerable ruins. No village had become a town. The James River at this point was two and a half miles wide and thirty feet deep. That information in his notebook could seem suspicious (although the river's width, at least, was available in published maps). At Suffolk on the Nansemond River officers arrested the travelers as suspected spies. Showing their passports to a magistrate and taking, or re-taking, the oath of abjuration renouncing allegiance to the king achieved their release. A fee to the magistrate for his exertions accomplished wonders of jurisprudence.

Level roads in pine woods that skirted the western edge of the Great Dismal Swamp brought them in a couple of days to Edenton in North Carolina. People told them the swamp provided cover for "concealed royalists and runaway Negroes," who "often attacked travelers," and not long before had murdered someone.

A ferry carried them twelve miles across Albemarle Sound in the evening. They landed up a small creek overarched with branches filled with singing birds. Eleven miles farther, on the road to Bath, they came upon a place to stay after dark, Colonel Blount's plantation. Hounds aroused in the night attacked them as they dismounted. "Half-clad Negroes, who came flying from their huts," shooed the dogs away. The next day as they were on the move again, the pack of hounds with huntsmen crossed the Bath road in front of them, running after a deer. Elkanah confided to his journal that he "could not suppress a sigh at the fate of the inoffensive hunted animal."

After they crossed Pamtico Sound at Bath (now called Pamtico Sound), sandy roads took them farther south through pine scrub with an occasional tar burner's hut among the trees. At dusk they reached the Neuse River, two miles wide at that point. Crossing despite the late hour, they were caught in a storm and nearly lost their bearings. Elkanah finally saw a light to guide them to the ferry house on the far shore. They rode further in the drenching rain to Newbern, whose inns were full. Several turned them away, but one finally let them crowd in. In the morning, Watson followed Harwood into town but soon met his friend who was rushing down the street, half shaven. He'd gotten into an argument with the barber and knocked him down. Elkanah advised Harwood to clear out of town fast. They could meet later.

The road in the sandy pine woods became indistinct—clearings and various small meadows seemed to be possible continuations of the route. Elkanah got lost among swamps and forests of tall straight pines and had to spend the night in the open, far from any sign of a road. His horse grazed nearby. While reharnassing and hitching up the horse to the sulky, he noticed a bear ambling along not too far away. Two days later, the sense of isolation lifted as he found the road again and caught up with his new friend.

Together Harwood and Watson crossed the New River and rode into Wilmington, a town guarded by two forts and with two sixteen-gun ships in the harbor along the Cape Fear River. They spent the night there. Next day, Brunswick, just upriver from Fort Johnston which guarded the river entrance from the Atlantic, was nearly deserted from fear of invasion by sea. They found a place to stay. The feeling of emptiness increased the day following, when they rode for miles without seeing any settlement or even a single hut until they came upon an abandoned hovel to shelter for the night. Wrapping themselves in blankets, they slept on its dirt floor after feasting on sweet potatoes they'd found and a wild opossum they'd shot. But they had nothing to feed the horses and the grazing was sparse.

The next day was different. Crossing a dangerous mud-flat, they rode along the sands of Long Bay—sixteen miles long. A view of ships off the coast shifted to birds soaring over the dunes to the west. There were even porpoises playing in the surf, "rolling up their black backs on the surface of the sea." A group of men with horses and carriages they seemed to see swimming in the sea turned out to be a mirage; changes in the air dispelled the mirror effect. Hours later they met the travelers they had seen in the mirage, now approaching them on the beach—General Lachlan McIntosh and his suite going to join Washington's army in the north.

McIntosh brought the exciting news that the English general Burgoyne and all his army had been taken prisoner—news confirmed by a printed announcement just issued at Charleston. Burgoyne's army had failed in its attempt to separate New England from the colonies to the south. Surrounded by Americans at Saratoga in northern New York, the English general was forced to surrender on October 17. Six thousand British soldiers laid down their weapons while Americans played "Yankee Doodle." Watson and Harwood, out of touch and imagining no improvement to the long list of American failures, now rejoiced, tossing their hats and cheering. That evening they brought the good news to William Alston, one of South Carolina's richest planters. Music and madeira accompanied the celebration long into the night. "All considered this glorious event as deciding the question of our eventual Independence."

They were warned of the danger of runaway slaves as they prepared to pass through swamps on the way to Winyaw Bay. Suddenly in the second swamp, their way was blocked by "fourteen naked Negroes, armed with poles." These highwaymen fled when Harwood rushed at them yelling and waving one of Elkanah's pistols, while Watson came up in the sulky aiming at them with the other pistol of his pair. The travelers reached Winyaw Bay without more danger.

Across four miles of flowing water, "four jolly, well-fed Negroes" rowed the ferry. Below the clear, starlit sky, these "poor fellows amused us, the whole way, by singing their plaintive African songs, in cadence with the oars."

From Georgetown, where they spent the night, the travelers rode southeast across to Santee Island and farther on the way to Charleston, which they reached on November 18. The trip had taken seventy days—days of danger, novelty, excitement, and tedium.

Elkanah's first task was to deliver the money he had been carrying in his coat, as well as to make some plans for his business with Nathaniel Russell, the merchant and shipper who had moved from Rhode Island to Charleston in 1765 and was John Brown's consignee. Personal news that Elkanah brought from the Browns to Russell was compared with more recent information that had arrived by sea-post, and possibilities for investment and European trade were sketched. Elkanah could help organize the details, but he would need to become familiar with local merchants, plantation owners, and products for sale.

Having made contact with Russell, on Sunday Elkanah and Captain Harwood re-crossed Cooper's River to check on their horses they had left stabled for the winter at the plantation of a Mr. Towsend. For the first time Elkanah saw a grove of orange trees. The fruit proved as tasty as any he'd had before from the West Indies.[21] Back in his hotel (At the Sign of the Three Legs, in King Street), Elkanah found a message asking that he contact a woman who hoped for news from her friends in Providence. Some friendly chat led to an invitation to stay at her place, so he moved his belongings into "a snugg little retired Chamber" in Stoll's Alley down by the harbor, away from the noise of the main streets. As suspicious newcomers in town, both Watson and Harwood were summoned to take the oath of abjuration again, this time from an impertinent magistrate who enjoyed the privilege of his office to cause annoyance and charge a fee.

Besides fulfilling his obligations for the Browns' business, Elkanah experimented in buying and selling on his own. First he bought forty hogsheads of rum that he soon sold for a profit that covered his traveling expenses. He thought he could double his capital within a few months, but trade in winter was variable if not entirely stagnant, so he decided not to speculate very much as yet. The British attempting to prevent trade at Charleston captured and burned one of the Browns' ships in December. Others got through the blockade, so the attempt to acquire profits needed for the war was not entirely thwarted. Elkanah had work enough to arrange cargoes for his master. But business was slow, leaving time to get acquainted with Charleston's society. He received invitations to dine at various gentlemen's houses. After dinner, "I find it a universal custom for the young lady of the family to pleasure us with a tune on the harpsichord, spinet, or guitar—in concert with their harmonious, enchanting voices."

At festive Christmas time, the militia patrolled the streets, ready to quell any rebellion and quick to check excess enthusiasm from the throngs in the streets—crowds of "unhappy Africans that are in bondage" who came in from the country. Allowed two or three days of recreational liberty in town just once a year, under severe watchfulness from the ever-present guards, they knew they would soon return to slavery. Two weeks later, Elkanah described a contrasting gathering, "a brilliant assembly" of the wealthiest people of Charleston. "The splendid appearance of the ladies and gentlemen added to the elegance and grandeur of the music (the musicianers being elevated in a gallery of a very considerable height, and the hall arched, it echoed nearly like distant thunder)." Such a perfect "quintessence of politeness" exceeded anything Elkanah had ever witnessed before. Lacking full-time business concerns, he decided to acquire some of this culture by studying French and learning to play the violin.

Cries of "Fire! Fire!" in the early morning of January 15, 1778, woke Elkanah from deep sleep after an evening of polite society. He rested against his pillow once more. For the last four or five nights, such alarms had turned out to be false every time. Beating drums joined the shouts, then church bells. Increasing noise soon formed the background to shifting orange-shadows on the wall opposite his window. Men banged on the door. "Turn out! Turn out! The town is on fire!" A bakery had gone up in flames in Damnation Alley.

Elkanah rushed into his clothes and ran down to the bay, but, seeing the fire was on the north side of town, slowed to a walk to reach the Exchange. His stock was only four doors away from the flames. He ran back to warn his landlady that the whole town was in danger, then took a boat and rowed quickly to the storehouse where the Browns' property was threatened. Almost despairing, Elkanah found "the whole back roof of the store in flames, the doors and windows locked and barred, and the house wherein the key was left reduced to a heap of rubbish." Nearby sailors from Marblehead, Massachusetts, stood, just watching. Elkanah begged for help. They "battered in the doors and windows, entered the store (by this time the back side of the house and roof were just falling in, and indeed we are surrounded upon every side with the cracking of flames." Elkanah knocked open a brandy keg and distributed a dram to each of the sailors, inspiring them to surprising speed. "Just as the flames were bursting in upon us, we almost cleared the store and quitted, but the drams had by this time animated my sailors to such a desperate pitch that they swore 'by God' that I should lose nothing, and imprudently against my entreaties rushed close into the flames and brought everything safely off at the expense of scorching themselves." A few seconds later the building collapsed.

Whores driven from their burning house in Damnation Alley emerged from the night and started stealing the salvaged property. Elkanah collected what he could and had it taken on board a sloop from Connecticut, guarded by the first mate. All kinds of boats crowded with frightened refugees from burning homes filled the harbor. Some had not escaped. The charred body of a woman burnt to death while trying to save her property from the inferno seared an image in Elkanah's memory: avarice the cause of death.

Elkanah and the sailors next went to help the landlady remove what could be saved. Just as he sat down to rest afterwards, someone rushed in, "Your roof is on fire!" Sparks carried in the wind had brought the flames across town. The sailors had left. Elkanah saved his own trunk by carrying it on his back. All along Main Street one side was burning. Despairing young women and children wandered dazed. A large building exploded; the force knocked Elkanah to the ground. He found a large, elegant house set back from the street. The doors were open, yet everyone was gone. In a grand parlor, Elkanah found a closet with its key in the lock. He stowed his trunk, pocketed the key, and returned to the job of fire-fighting.

The haughty indolence of southern gentlemen shocked Elkanah. "From their infancy," he judged, they have "ever been perfect strangers to putting their delicate paws to anything that has the appearance of labour ... scarcely one of them will ... seize a bucket, but stand like so many nabobs with their canes and hangers under their arms, beating and bruising the poor Negroes to exert themselves, who work as composed and easy as though they were digging upon a plantation." New Englanders had done far more to rescue property than had these southerners, he thought. But, returning to the sloop, he discovered the first mate was emptying John Brown's barrels of brandy into bottles. Elkanah knocked him to the deck, then had to fight off the captain, who "coming aboard, fell afoul of me without reason."[22]

In the morning, still exhausted and smudged with soot, Elkanah returned to where he had locked away his trunk. The house, it turned out, belonged to Governor John Rutledge. A young man answered his knock on the door, but when Elkanah told his story, asking for his trunk, this servant refused, put off by the shabbiness of the filthy man standing before him, probably, he thought, another thief aroused by the opportunities presented by the disaster. "Whose trunk?" he said, with tones of unapproachable superiority. "My trunk," Elkanah responded. "That's likely, indeed!" was the answer, as the servant turned on his heels and disappeared into the house.

Elkanah tapped again with the door knocker. The Governor came this time in person. Elkanah bowed, although this brought no return gesture. He let the governor know that during the danger and disruption of the fire he had locked his trunk in the governor's parlor closet, taking the key; he begged the governor's pardon. All Rutledge could say was "I know nothing of you or your trunk and shall deliver you nothing." With resentment and a sense of injustice, Elkanah returned to the ship of Captain Sheldon, had a meal, and then went once more to the governor's house, again to no good result. Some other plan had to be carried out.

Elkanah borrowed a clean coat, bought a new hat, and then got a haircut and shave. Yet again at the governor's house, instead of frowns and disdain the servant gave him a welcome and conducted him to the governor who welcomed him: "Sir, your servant! Please to walk in, Sir! Will you drink a glass of madeira?" After some pleasant conversation, Elkanah raised the matter of his trunk. "There was somebody here this forenoon," said Rutledge, "I suppose you sent after it, but I did not like to give up the trunk to him." "Why, Sir," said Elkanah, "that person (you speak of) was myself, and the reason of my appearing in such a ragged situation must be entirely attributed to the severe struggles I was obliged to grapple with, by means of the horrid conflagration." After apologies and compliments, Rutledge ordered a servant to carry the trunk to Watson's lodgings, where Elkanah was finally able to reward the servant, change his clothes, and re-arrange his things for a return to normal living.

Normal life in Charleston could not return for years. More than two hundred fifty houses had been destroyed. Property not burnt had been stolen. The homeless needed housing. The "smashing, breaking, and roaring of the flames, the hails of sparks and flakes of fire, and houses blowing up ... conveyed a distant idea of Hell."[23]

The fire destroyed Elkanah's business plans, but he still sought products he could buy to ship to Europe. Markets and commerce in the city were disrupted. Towsend's plantation, however, had indigo ready. Elkanah crossed the river in a barge rowed by slaves. Waiting an hour for their master to arrive, the slaves horrified Elkanah with stories of cruel treatment in miserable conditions. One of them had not eaten for two days. Elkanah gave him a new two-dollar bill. Elkanah considered these stories "sufficient to move a man of sensibility to the most affecting sensations." When they reached the far side of the river, Elkanah distributed alms to each of the rowers before going up to Towsend's plantation mansion, where he managed to buy a wagon-load of indigo. He was able to add rice, deerskins, and tobacco before sending the wagon under armed guard north to Brown in Providence. After two weeks of stagnation, with little to buy and no warehouses to store anything while waiting for ships, Elkanah decided to make better use of his time by exploring farther south, into Georgia and Florida.

An Excursion into Georgia

Elkanah and Henry Bromfield of Boston drove sulkies, and Mr. Clark from New Haven rode his horse Rocinante.[24] They had hired a servant named Silas to accompany them, who was "mounted upon an elegant horse, with a brace of pistols and a fine dog" named Watch. Leaving Charleston on January 29, a hot day, they rode south, going past elegant plantations in fine gardens that overlooked the Ashley River. Owners had recently converted marshland into rice production. Beyond the Ashley they continued through balmy evening weather to the far side of the Stony River, where they settled down for the night at McCrea's Inn.

At ten o'clock a noisy fight in the room next door suddenly brought Elkanah out to see what was happening. A "great raw-boned fellow, with his eye balls glazed," loomed over a short "one-eyed ragamuffin" to challenge him to a fight. The two began a contest of kicking and gouging. "The little fellow knocked the big one's head about the room, as the saying is, like a beggar's can! Finally he plunged him into the fire." Elkanah and his friends pulled the ruffians apart, the taller one with "the blood gushing out of both ears and nostrils in a flood, and his face mangled beyond conception for so little time." The landlady swore that the cause was the "big fellow's eating a great quantity of beans, which made him offensive to the company, ha! ha! ha!" The hotel was no better than this entertainment—dirty sheets, filthy rooms, and a wealth of fleas and bed-bugs.

Level straight roads took them past plantation fields with peas in bloom. These signs of prosperous increase made the war seem very distant. Near the river, in the midst of the village of Ashepo's dozen houses, shops, and brick church, they stopped at Huwes Tavern. Seated on a log by the door was "a company of those hideous inhumane, blood-thirsty savage warriors, the Indians, touched off in the highest taste, with their faces painted, andc." The landlord identified them as the famous warrior commander Little Carpenter (Attakullakulla), together with his wife and some of his principal advisors, as well as several other chiefs of tribes, all on their way to Charleston "to confer with the governor to strengthen the chain of union and friendship with the states."[25] The landlord called Little Carpenter a "civilized sensible man, and perfect master of the English language, however savage his appearance." Elkanah and his friends bowed deeply before the Indians, who were "all smoking their great wooden pipes, with their elbows supported upon their knees." Little Carpenter had been in London many years earlier. He returned Elkanah's gesture, but the others, unacquainted with English custom, merely looked the newcomers over and continued to smoke. Little Carpenter, King of the Cherokees, made space next to him on the log and shared his pipe with Elkanah while interrogating him for an hour about the way the war was going.

After their horses had rested, Elkanah and his friends resumed their journey. For four or five miles, large mansions set hundreds of yards back from the road up shaded avenues grandly contrasted with "little villages of Negro huts" surrounding them.

At the shore of the Combee River, they stopped for the night at McGraw's inn. Sitting down around a welcoming fire, they ordered some tubs of water to scrub themselves clean of the mud they'd gotten when they freed one of the horses from a bog by the river. Unexpectedly the sheets were clean, and each traveler had his own bed with curtains. "Travelers generally prefer sleeping alone," Elkanah observed. Cheap inns expected several people, all clothed, to fill the available space on each bed. Mr. Clark did some horse trading with McGraw, leaving Rocinante to "linger out a miserable life in this pine corner of the globe."

The first of February held mixed showers and thunder. They lodged at a ferry house on Port Royal Island where the owner, a Mr. Williams, "has several buxom lasses, which in some measure compensates for the want of provisions." Elkanah thought his flute-playing might be a novelty, so played some medleys, which succeeded in "soothing them into transports of joy." When he stopped, they gathered around him and begged for more, like "a flock of pigeons would around their bait." To some quick tunes, they "jumped up and capered round the room." Elkanah commented that he couldn't recall "ever spending a more jovial evening than at the expense of these ignorant uncouth buckskins."

Port Royal Island produced rice and indigo, besides some cotton. Elkanah sketched the stages in indigo production. In the evening, warmed by pine knot fires, slaves sat around their huts plucking cotton seeds out of the fibers. After exploring the island, the travelers returned to the mainland by the same ferry and proceeded farther south towards Savannah. Around noontime, just after crossing the bridge at Stony Creek, they saw what looked like an inn. They rode up to the door and ordered some servants to rub down the horses. Elkanah stepped inside and demanded a bowl of "Sangria and the best dinner the house afforded." After dinner, they ordered a decanter of the best madeira. Elkanah called for the bill and took out his cash to pay for the meals. "What bill?" the man they supposed to be the landlord asked. "Your demand, Sir!" responded Elkanah. "Do you mean to insult me, Sir?" he replied. "By no means, Sir! But I must insist upon your explaining yourself." "Why," said he, "do you think I receive pay for entertaining gentlemen? I disdain it." "Why, indeed, Sir," responded Elkanah, "that is a general custom at taverns." "Taverns, Sir! I keep no tavern!" Elkanah was scarcely able to compose an apology for having mistaken this man's private home for a public house. His companions made things worse. They tried to insist on making payment. Eventually their angry host calmed down. The travelers again apologized, being sure when they left to tip the servants so that there could be no complaint for the extra work.

A level road through sparsely settled low country brought them by sunset to an inn operated by a Mrs. Adamson, whom Elkanah described as a "great Irish ghoul." She promised them an excellent supper, but what they got was "insipid trash, rice bread, and rank bacon and eggs." Only someone extremely famished could stomach this the way it was cooked and served, "by an old weathered, dried-up, wrinkled, crooked, decrepit, sore-eyed Negro woman, bordering somewhere nigh a 100 years of age. We observed several times, as she was crawling to and from the table, large drops of head-matter, slush, gravy, or something of that nature drop from her hollow eyes upon the table, and perhaps into the dishes." Disgusted, they told the landlady that they "could not, consistent with civilized people, think of eating anything she had yet provided."

"Oh, by my soul," she said, "It is as good victuals, I assure you gentlemen, as you will meet with in this whole country."

They persisted in refusing to eat that meal. She argued but ended up bringing a dish of coffee that she brewed herself in their presence. For food they prepared some sweet potatoes of their own.

After they had finished eating, the ancient servant crawled into their room to make the beds and lay a fire. An hour's inconsequential labor resulted in a room filled with smoke. Mrs. Adamson grabbed Elkanah's riding whip and rushed into the room, knocked the old woman down, and began to beat her fiercely. Elkanah and his friends broke down the door and threatened to call in authorities to protect the old woman. Mrs. Adamson "swore by J[esus], she had a right to kill her own Negro, if she pleased!" Instead of murder, however, she called in a few slaves who dragged away the injured woman "to the Negro house like a dog."

Old Silas, their own Mulatto servant and no slave, was about forty-five years old. He had lived since a baby in New England, where, according to Elkanah, "the Negroes are generally treated with tenderness." He exclaimed that "he wished the Lord would soon deliver him from

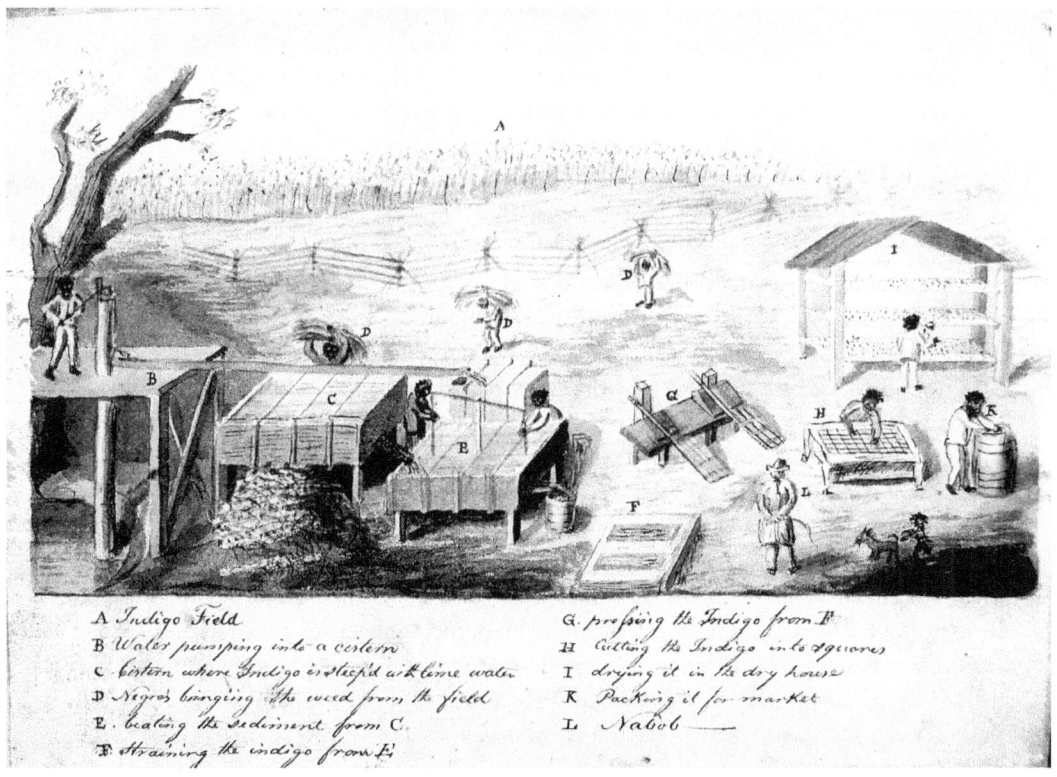

Indigo production, drawn by Elkanah Watson (from the Elkanah Watson Papers, courtesy New York State Library).

this wicked, cruel country." They barricaded the door for protection and all slept in their clothes.

When they left the next morning, Silas inquired among the slaves and learned that the woman who had been beaten was still surviving.[26]

Approaching Savannah on February 6, at Zubly's ferry by Purisburg, they were surprised to meet the Rev. John Joachim Zubly himself, coming away from the city with his son. Zubly had been Savannah's most renowned preacher, a Presbyterian. His pamphlets supporting the American cause were read not only in the colonies but also in England. At the second Continental Congress in Philadelphia in 1774 he had represented Georgia, arguing for moderation. He demanded representation in Parliament for the colonies, but he hoped for reconciliation rather than revolution. In a sermon from 1775 to the Provincial Congress of Georgia (published as a tract in Philadelphia), Zubly preached that "a people that claim no more than their natural rights, in so doing, do nothing displeasing unto God; and the most powerful monarch that would deprive his subjects of the liberties of man, whatever may be his success, he must not expect the approbation of God, and in due time will be the abhorrence of all men."[27] Moreover, Zubly proclaimed that the idea "that government and tyranny are the hereditary right of some, and that slavery and oppression are the original doom of others, is a doctrine that would reflect dishonor upon God; it is treason against all mankind." His audience could hear a criticism of the king but they did not interpret this as an inexorable call to free their slaves. Zubly wrestled with biblical attitudes towards established authority. "The Christian religion, while it commands due respect and obedience to superiors, nowhere requires a blind and unlimited obedience on the part of the subjects; nor does it vest any absolute and arbitrary power in the rulers." Then he remarked, "We should fain obey our superiors, and yet we cannot think of giving up our natural, our civil and religious rights, nor acquiesce in or contribute to render our fellow creatures or fellow citizens slaves and miserable." Once again, his listeners understood that as a Presbyterian he opposed the claims of the Church of England to privilege and established superiority, and that as a colonist he objected to laws and taxes unjustly imposed. But they were not inspired to free their slaves, no matter how repugnant Zubly thought participation in enslavement would be to their freedom-loving souls. In contrast to human laws, "the law of the Lord is perfect" (Psalm 19:7), Zubly quoted, and he repeated that "the Gospel is the law of liberty"—referring to James 2:12 ("So speak ye, and so do, as they that shall be judged by the law of liberty"). No one, he thought, "can transgress [the law of the Lord] with impunity." And as a Calvinist believing that the world with all its social hierarchy was predestined to be as it was, he could not avoid a literal application of Romans 13: 1–2 ("Let every soul be subject unto the higher powers. For there is no power but of God: the powers that be are ordained of God. Whosoever therefore resisteth the power, resisteth the ordinance of God: and they that resist shall receive to themselves damnation"). Zubly's unavoidable conclusion was unpalatable to the rebels: "Never let us lose out of sight that our interest lies in a perpetual connection with our mother country." According to Zubly, a Christian was not permitted to rebel against the king, nor could a faithful Christian "acquiesce in or contribute to render our fellow creatures or fellow citizens slaves."

Zubly's fellow citizens of Savannah, in rebellion against the king and not wanting to hear that slavery was sin, had that very day banished him and his son from Georgia and had confiscated Zubly's property, including his library of over a thousand volumes. The books were eventually tossed into the Savannah River. Indignant and depressed, Zubly nonetheless impressed Elkanah with his interesting and instructive conversation, and the sincerity of his evening prayer vindicating "the rectitude of his intentions."

Slave labor worked the rice plantations they toured near Savannah. Sowing around the first of April, weeding from the beginning of June when the shoots were six to eight inches high, opening the sluices from canals to flood the plants up to the fragrant blossoms, refreshing the stagnant water, then at the end of August draining the fields, napping and stacking the rice like wheat in New England, then threshing, then placing the rice in blocks that held about half a peck and that are lined up in rows so that large iron pestles operated by horse-driven cog wheels could pound the rice all at once, then sieving and winnowing three or four times—all this was the work of slaves. Trying to figure this out, Elkanah mused, "Indeed considering the immense Expense attending making a rice Plantation from a wild swamp, and the difficult process of cultivating the rice for markets; and the great expense of stocking a plantation with Negroes andc., I say! From these circumstances I am surprised to think what capital fortunes the planters accumulate barely from a dollar and a half per hundred for this insipid commodity."

On arrival in Savannah, Elkanah and his companions sought out George Walton, who was among the signers of the Declaration of Independence and later became a General, then, briefly, governor of Georgia. Elkanah had letters of introduction to him, as well as to the New Englander, Commodore Oliver Bowen, and to other gentlemen. They were welcomed into "the delightful society of the city." The travelers found lodgings with a Mrs. Minus. After dinner, her daughter provided evening music on the guitar, while other musicians played harpsichord and fiddle. Not only the lodgers but other visitors joined the audience as well. One evening an unidentified voice of angelic quality (as Elkanah perceived it) chimed in from outside. When Elkanah got up to look out the door he could see no one. Eventually the singer was discovered—a ragged Continental soldier who had come along with one of the officers sitting around the table with the gentlemen indoors.

On Sunday, in order "to have a general view of the Savannah ladies," they attended morning service, where the Rev. William Piercy preached. They "returned back again to [their] lodgings without any apparent stabs to the tranquility of either of us." Not only were they disappointed in their quest for aesthetic satisfaction among the women, they concluded that the church as a whole was "by no means elegant, and rather upon a decline." Piercy, an Episcopal minister, had been sent out by Selina Shirley, Countess of Huntington, to manage the Bethesda Orphanage that she had inherited after the death of the evangelist George Whitefield in 1770.

Sunday evening, Elkanah and his friends were invited to a meeting of The Smoking Club. Old Smokers sat in a circle "intrenched under a thick cloud of smoke of their own raising." All present stood up for separate introductions to the visitors. Then each newcomer was given a long pipe and told that the rule was for "every person to smoke while they continue in their company; but if that was not agreeable to suck an empty pipe rather than appear singular." The tobacco smokers dissipated by ten o'clock. "Such harmony and unreserved agreeable sociability stimulates this whole happy society; that I shall ever wish to be seated in life, in some place where there is a society of a similar nature established." For the moment slavery could be ignored.

From Savannah Elkanah and his friends made a short excursion to visit the Rev. Piercy's

Bethesda Orphanage founded by the Methodist minister George Whitefield in 1740. Whitefield had raised funds for the charity during his preaching tours in England and America, awaking a great deal of religious intensity whose emotional enthusiasm was directed towards financial support for this institution. A fire in 1773 had destroyed the main building, but two others remained. The Northerners were particularly interested in meeting a young woman named Miss Baker, whose beauty and accomplishments had been praised by people they met in Savannah. When she eventually appeared, Elkanah judged that the trouble to travel to the orphanage was "doubly compensated. Without vanity," he wrote, "I think her appearance, both in features and the freshness of her countenance, by far out-vies any lady I have seen south of Virginia." After dinner, Miss Baker and Mrs. Piercy sang duets accompanied on the harpsichord. "The mutual and reciprocal pleasures that each of this happy pair endeavours to cultivate together; the truly enchanting echoes of their soft music and the angelic perfections of the captivating Miss Baker, was such as thrilled to our very souls and began almost to lead us to imagine our selves suspended into another world, surrounded by angels and that the objects before us were not mortal, but ethereal."

The song's words "soothed our breasts into the most delicate agreeable sensations":

> Nature when She form'd a man,
> Gave a Soul for Love's designs;
> Love with Life at first began,
> and Possessed his Infant mind.
> When upon the breast he Lay,
> Love began to grow within;
> With his milk he Every day,
> Suck'd the soothing passion in.
> First a feeble spark it glow'd,
> Glow'd and brighter still became;
> Beauty, full soon bestow'd,
> Youth, Increas'd it to a flame,
> Till by age, and weakness worn,
> Half Extinguish'd it shall Lie;
> Thus was Every mortal born,
> Once to Love, and Once to die.[28]

At the Rev. Piercy's suggestion they traveled south to view the Vernon River, but Piercy had learned that British soldiers and allied Indians had approached within six or seven miles. He counselled them to return to stay overnight at the orphanage instead of continuing past the Ogeechee River into Florida. The Piercys and Miss Baker again sang by the harpsichord, inspiring Elkanah to imagine a future of such bliss: "The mutual tender affections for a dear pledge of their love and the harmony and happiness their eyes proclaimed almost enraptured us with the idea of matrimony. About 10, the front door was wide opened and the servants summoned to attend prayers, by a little bell, that tolled, tink! tink! tink! for at least 15 minutes in the piazza. This collected 10 or 15 Negroes and children around the door in the piazza. Mrs. Piercy seated herself by her beloved husband; and after the religious ceremonies were subsided; they concluded by an anthem in concert with the harpsichord. Soon after this we were conducted to bed, where I laid a long time meditating with pleasure the agreeable occurrencies of the day before I fell asleep."

This touching scene of religious ceremonies where the slaves were welcome reflects a brief period of economic tranquility. When debts were pressing in 1773, however, the Rev. Piercy had offered to sell all the slaves and send the profits to their owner, the Countess of Huntington, whose portrait now looked down benevolently on the pious exercises, "drawn at full length by an Italian in London, and executed to admiration and as natural as life."[29] Did the offer to sell the slaves aim pointed irony at the countess? Was it a test of her religious sincerity and commitment to the orphanage? Or did the minister merely display crass insensitivity to humanity?

On Friday the 13th of February, the trip back to New England started with a detour to visit the plantation of George Hall, Esq. On a slope overlooking a little creek, the house was a small palace set in a beautiful garden with formal gravel walks separated by mossy beds. Beyond the house more gardens had been laid out with a great deal of planning and labor. At the foot of the garden by the creek stood a grove of laurel trees. Following their stroll in the gardens, "Esquire conducted us across a parterre, or cause-way into his valuable plantation, and then to the buildings where the miserable blacks were executing the different processes of preparing his rice for market." A combination was needed "of insensibility and base immodesty to withstand the shock. Around a large pile of straw was seated blacks of both sex clawing upon the insipid trash rice boiled barely in river water, without salt or any other nourishment." Without betraying their feelings, they asked "Esqr. Hall" if the slaves were "allowed any other sustenance." Carelessly half-laughing, he said, "not anything but rice, and sometimes a few potatoes" except for a little meat at Christmas. All they had to drink was "stagnated ditch water." Not only were they nearly starved, they had almost no clothing. "None of them had anything else but an old piece of coarse cloth round their middles, and some scarcely that." Elkanah thought better treatment would bring health and enliven their spirits, but as it was, "from their emaciated manner of living they are the most stupid, dejected, broken, dead-hearted race of mortals that exist." Lenient and tender treatment would be advantageous to "these miserable fellows," and it would also "discharge a debt of humanity and conscience." No one deserved this, according to Elkanah. But politeness evidently restrained the New Englanders from upbraiding the plantation owner. They were his guests for the night. After breakfast in the morning Esquire Hall courteously accompanied them on their way back to the Savannah River.

On the 14th, after riding for three hours, they breakfasted at Vanbiber's Tavern at Pocotaligo, a "fine, large, and gentle" house with "a handsome landlady and two or three pretty girls," and within sight of the private gentleman's residence they had a week earlier mistaken for a public tavern. The fine gentility contrasted with the slavery. "Every day fresh scenes of cruelties and obduracies that the unhappy Negroes are obliged to grapple with, presents to us. Some we see entirely naked. Others, cruelly whipped for the most frivolous offences and some almost famish with hunger, On short such hardened inhumanity would disgrace the most savage barbarians; At Vanbiber's in particular, there was a young wench chained by the leg with a large heavy chain to the end of which was riveted a 56 [lb.] weight. Everywhere she moved this weight she of course was obliged to drag with her; This punishment had been inflicted four months. Commonly we see them with a large piece of Iron round their Legs, but still beat to labour. Women, as well as men indiscriminantly. The white women in general seem not only deprived of the tender impulses of humanity, but of every glimpse of modesty, as it is very common for us to see their own sex nigh as naked as they entered the world."

Rather than taking the most direct route back to Charleston, they decided to see several more mansions and plantations. At Lynn's Tavern, a boxing fight broke out, following customary rules of behavior unknown to the Northerners, who were surprised to see all the men who had been fighting a few minutes before gather around the fire in friendship as if there'd been no fight at all. Boxing represented the height of discourse, preceded usually by an agreed-on preamble of kicking, biting, and gouging. Spectators could join in. Fights only became important if something serious happened, like an eye gouged out.

Mr. Lynn was proud of his tavern and of his family, describing every detail in glowing terms. "Here," says he, "Gentlemen, I live as happy as heart can wish by my shoul. There is nothing that I want but I have; you see I have got a fine house and as fine gardens as ever was in this whole would; and I'll tell you shentlemen, I do assure you I have got my parn full of the pest poultry that ever was. I have got a fine fishing pond, and plenty of Negroes, and why should one be after wanting more? And by my shoul besides all this shentlemen, I do assure you I have got fourteen bastards in this very country: and I keep four as fine whores as any lord in England, all in this niberhood, besides one I always keep aloft, locked up in my own chamber. I have 3 as fine boys by her, as you'll ever see; l faith, and to convince you I'll fetch them down to you this very moment."

He left, then returned with three little boys in neat clothes. "There shentlemen, did you ever see finer boys, in all your Lives? These I do assure you, I had by that very whore up chamber." This citizen's frankness startled the New Englanders even more than his peculiar accent. But were the five women slaves, or did they form some less expectable polygamous congregation? Elkanah doesn't comment.

They stayed overnight, but kept their clothes on, boots and all, as armor against the fleas. They barricaded the door in case the locals turned rambunctious. The next night's lodgings were no better, although familiar—the same McCrea's where they'd enjoyed bedbugs and fleas on the earlier stage of their excursion. Breakfast was miserable, cooked by the landlady in moments between snorting her snuff. Riding late at night, their route had taken them through a forest fire, fanned by a rising wind. "Gigantic pines, blazing and crackling, covered with fire to their tops, were falling with tremendous crashes in every direction." After that, even the dubious comforts at McCrea's had represented shelter.

Charleston was scarcely any safer. Since the great fire had destroyed countless houses, robbers stalked the night streets, stealing hats, watches, money, even murdering. Recently a member of the Free and Accepted Masons was robbed and killed after a lodge meeting. Citizens walking in the morning found his body, naked, mangled, and propped up as if seated in a mud puddle. Elkanah, who heard of this and claimed to know nothing about the Masons, nonetheless at Charleston joined the group, which he was told was based on virtue and religion.[30] With all the experience of a youth from New England who had now traveled to Georgia, he judged the rites supremely impressive. "Should I live to the age of Methusehlah, and one half of my life employed in roving into the different parts of the world, I am confident that I should never encounter any scene that could possibly exceed this." He was not at liberty to describe the splendid secrets, reserved only to "brothers." Throughout the civilized world, Masonry's support came from "the most wealthy and virtuous members of society." So he was told. That Masonry was "generally derided by the ignorant" was a puzzle, since, he believed, the most active members were often men of high character.

Charleston offered other attractions besides arcane fellowship. Girl-watching allowed for elevated assessments: many of the town's women Elkanah considered elegant and accomplished, although often sallow-complexioned and without the rosy cheeks of New England's beauties. The town itself was splendid and stylish. Rich planters could afford a life of "almost Asian luxury." Poor people were still looking for places to live after their houses had burned down.

Slavery, Idealistic Visions and Valley Forge

To return to New England, Elkanah obtained a passport from Governor Rutledge, addressed "To all whom it may concern." The handwritten document stated merely that "Mr. Elkanah Watson is permitted to go from hence to Pennsylvania. (signed) J. Rutledge, Charleston, So. Carolina, March 1778." Elkanah traveled again with Mr. Bromfield, as well as a Mr. Gibbs of Philadelphia and Captain Paul Hussey of Providence, besides old Silas and his dog Watch. The departure from Charleston took them past the fort on Sullivan's Island whose construction of spongy palmetto wood had absorbed the cannonballs of the English naval attack in 1776 without giving way.

North of Charleston, large regions between the towns remained scarcely settled. Roads in the pine forests were sometimes no more than paths identified by "blazes" or chops through bark to expose wood on the tree trunks along the route. Near Lockwood's Folly, Captain Hussey became lost in the woods one night, bewildered in swamps. Striking flint to steel he lit a fire of pitch-pine for warmth then had to defend himself against wolves attracted by the light.

At Wilmington, Elkanah wrote a letter to a business friend from Charleston, Jonas Clarke, who must have shared Elkanah's disgust for slavery. "I have just witnessed a scene too affecting for a mind of sensibility, especially to one whose feelings and sympathy for our fellow mortals are not blunted by habit. It was a sale of a parcel of unhappy Africans, drove in like swine from the country for the highest bidder; a poor wench in an agony of despair clung to her little girl, and begged for no other favour but to have her child sold to the same master as Herself; but these unfeeling sons of barbarity were deaf to her cries, and thus wrested her only comfort perhaps forever from her sight. How revolting to humanity!" Mother and child went to separate buyers. "The husband and residue of the family were knocked off to the highest bidder." In the presence of this tragedy, Elkanah's lofty sentiments about the brotherhood of mankind collided with the harsh and unfeeling economics of the slavery on which southern refinement reclined. Where was the universality of mankind he'd just pledged when joining Charleston's Freemasons?[31]

The countryside changed. Rice gave way to peach orchards and tobacco, then corn and peas with tobacco, then hogs with tobacco, always more tobacco. On the way to Williamsburg from Halifax, Virginia, horned snakes infested the creeks and swamps. Thinking a coiled snake dead, and intrigued by the pattern of its scales and the famed poisonous horn on its tail, Captain Hussey flicked his whip as a test. Immediately aroused, the snake prepared to lunge, with flashing eyes and its tongue flickering forward from its flat head. Hussey sprang back. The snake writhed then slid away. Hussey relaxed while the others laughed at his mistake. So poisonous was this type of snake, they were told, that, when sap was rising, a tree could be killed with one sting.

A dull-witted ferryman rowed them across the James River. War or peace, snakes or no snakes, people needed to cross the river. Elkanah calculated the river's commercial importance—thirty thousand hogsheads of tobacco had been shipped from here each year before the beginning of the war. Free from conflict, he could foresee profits returning along the James, the Hudson, the Delaware, the Potomac rivers.

Revisiting Williamsburg, they did not stay long but continued northward. At Hanover Court House a local election inspired brawling. A "wretched pug-nosed fellow" insisted on swapping watches. A "wild Irishman" wanted to swap horses, and, when refused, threatened to start a fight to punish Elkanah for not treating him "like a jintleman." Nearby, two fat men fought furiously, gouging each other and pulling hair. Crudity contrasted with civility.

At Fredericksburg Elkanah was impressed by George Washington's mother, who was pointed out to him—"a majestic and venerable woman." People proudly showed the house where Washington was born, opposite the town.

In Alexandria he delivered funds from the Browns to American agents of a French company of munitions suppliers with whom they traded in Europe—Pliarne, Penet, and Compagnie, of Nantes.[32] (Elkanah later moved to Nantes where he thought he could take advantage of this commercial contact.) Although the road from Fredericksburg to Alexandria was "frightfully bad," Elkanah looked around him and saw a glorious future replacing the undeveloped and tawdry circumstances of present-day reality. Overlooking the Potomac River, his prophetic vision revealed a "cluster of noble buildings, over topped by gilded spires; the streets alive with merchandize, and the bustle of the sons of commerce; the masts on the river representing a forest; and the semicircle of hills, which enclose the plan of the city, embellished with pleasant gardens and villas. When I arrived at this point; I saw at Mount Vernon, in anticipation, a magnificent tomb, erected by the United States; in which was deposited the ashes of the immortal Washington, now in his glory." A believer in inevitable progress, Elkanah returned again and again to edit and embellish his diaries in the light of hindsight.

But reality intruded itself on his idealized imaginings. Slavery, he thought, had contributed to a "prevailing indolence ... the poor white man had almost rather starve than work, because the Negro works."

From Alexandria, via Georgetown, they headed for Baltimore, a town of around six thousand. On April 14, they re-entered Pennsylvania and rode through pleasant farmland that had been "richly improved by the industry of its Dutch and German population." Elkanah commented in his diary that "the inhabitants are a medley of various nations, but principally Dutch and Germans, and about ⅕ Quakers, to whose examples of piety, frugality, and industry this state owes its astonishing progress, from a wild state of Nature, within less than one century." From the Susquehanna to the Schuylkill River, their road took them over rolling hills. Well-farmed valleys presented neat and careful agriculture that inspired Elkanah to contrast North and South. "Here, we witness the impulses and results of honest industry, where freemen labor for themselves. There, we see the feeble efforts of coerced labor, performed by the ennervated slave, uninspired by personal interest, and unimpelled by a worthy ambition."

Chance and stormy weather brought them to take refuge in the home of a well-to-do farmer. He was hospitably kind, intelligent, and sensible. His library was fine; he was conversant on most topics. "His house was spacious and neat, and well supplied with the comforts and substantials of life. Independence, wealth, and contentment were conspicuous in every thing." He epitomized Elkanah's conception of the ideal "virtuous, affluent, and intelligent republican freeman."

When they entered the winter quarters of the American army, camped above the Schuylkill River at Valley Forge, officers from Rhode Island welcomed Elkanah. The visitors took a day to attend reviews of troops and look into the arrangements and circumstances of the army. Conditions were shocking: "the poor devils are half naked, and what is worse, they have been half starved half the winter." Log huts with canvas for doors and sometimes tenting covering the roof were crowded and unsanitary. There were no wells; water came from rivers and streams polluted by the presence of the soldiers themselves. Daily military exercises taught tactical movements and discipline. At a distance Elkanah saw General Washington who was passing through the camp on horseback. Loyalty to his leadership and a firm belief in the cause of independence held the army together despite the inadequacy of the food and the severity of the camp conditions.

Departing, they were kept waiting at the new army bridge over the Schuylkill by armed guards who had to be convinced that they were not British spies just come from surveying the camp. The countryside around Valley Forge was filled with Tories. Their threatening presence endangered the roads leading away from the army. In the dark, an officer rode up to Elkanah and his companions and commanded them to halt. "We did so, and trembled too for our fate." Discovering they were friends, the officer told them he had just "disarmed and wounded a Tory highwayman, cruising the road." Just five miles from the army encampment, the inn Elkanah and his friends finally reached was crowded with boisterous soldiers and suttlers. They paid a soldier to guard their horses through the night, and attempted to get some sleep in the jammed lodgings—Elkanah between two drunken teamsters.

The next night they arrived again in Bethlehem, Pennsylvania. Around midnight, Hussey poked Elkanah awake. The two travelers heard "a distant band of musick—the serenity of the night, all nature hushed into a profound silence, with the excellence of the musick, excited me in a kind of solemn sensation I cannot express," wrote Elkanah in his journal, expressing the search for sensation that every young romantic pursued. "We dressed and proceeded immediately to the chapel, with some buxom lasses out of the country. The organs welcomed our arrival, and as soon as we entered at one door, the sisters ushered in at another, two and two, making a ghostly figure in their white caps. The band continued playing for some time; then the priest mounted the pulpit and gave us a short German prayer, followed by an anthem; after which, the Moravian men, followed by the women, march in solemn processions, two and two, to the burying ground, the spectators fetching up the rear. I was surprised to observe the exact symmetry of this burying ground. It is handsomely paled in, forming a square, and the graves laid off with as much neatness and regularity as the beds in a garden. They are about eight inches high, flattened on their tops, and on the center of each lies a flat stone 18 inches square, on which is inscribed a short epitaph of the name, age andc. of the deceased, in German. To return to the procession: they entered this magazine of Moravian bones, with solemn pace, just at the dawn of day; the musick in unison with their pace—the whole body forms a square round the burying ground, with hats off—Moravians and spectators. It began just then to rain, from a small cloud, which rather incommoded our skulls. A dead silence prevailed, till the sun began to peep over the horizon—then the musicians entered in the spacious alleys, between the graves, playing a pathetic concert; while the priest was busily employed, reading aloud the inscriptions upon the grave stones—then commenting—then

General Washington at Valley Forge (lithograph by R.R. in *Views from Nature* [American Tract Society, ca. 1860], p. 15).

praying—their eyes all devoutly fixed upon the heavens the whole time. In short the solemnity of the scene, animated by the refulgent beams of a warm morning sun; affected us so sensibly that we seemed to realize the day of judgement; when all mankind are to be summoned from their graves. The whole concluded with a prayer. They then fell in again two and two, returning in the same manner they came. This ceremony was in celebration of the resurrection of our Saviour. Our curiosity satiated, we left Bethlehem on our way to Easton, where we arrived at noon."

Riding through New Jersey, they met various units of soldiers marching to join General

Washington at Valley Forge. The region they were passing through had deteriorated from the constant troop movements. Supplies were scarce; fields untended. In one inn, the travelers found no beds, only a "pile of oats, with no covering but our clothes." In the parlor a woman with smallpox sat by the fire to try to sweat it out. Elkanah, inoculated against the deforming disease in an unheated barrack where no fire had been permitted, insisted that the woman's blankets be unwrapped and that she move away from the fire in hopes of increasing her chances of survival.

After eight months of travel, on April 29, 1778, Elkanah entered Providence, Rhode Island, again. The trip had brought him through ten provinces along routes totalling around two thousand seven hundred miles. Summarizing his observations, he foresaw a great and blessed future for America, where everything would be bigger and better. "What are called mountains in Europe are hills in America; rivers are reduced to brooks; trees to bushes; and lakes, to ponds. In short, the map of the world presents to view no country, which combines so many natural advantages, is so pleasantly diversified, and offers to agriculture, manufactures, and commerce so many resources, all of which to conduct America to the first rank among nations. This I prophesy. It must be so. In contemplating future America, the mind is lost in the din of cities, in harbors and rivers, crowded with sails, and in the immensity of its population."[33]

Elkanah also looked at the town of Providence with new eyes. He could now describe his town as if in an encyclopedia of the new and mighty nation he predicted would arise—the Wonders of America. Once an unimpressive village, in four decades Providence had become an emporium notable for "the industry, enterprise, and activity of its citizens." Divided by the Providence River, the town held around six hundred houses, most of them wooden, and, according to Elkanah, many of them elegant.

Providence's merchants were, he reflected with an obvious nod to his boss, among the most intelligent in America. A third of the town lay west of the river, with broad streets. The east side rose on the banks of a hill, with a street a mile long lined by houses on both sides. Parallel streets terraced the hill. On the hilltop stood "a magnificent brick College, built by subscription, four stories in height, and the largest building in America.... From its roof, a vast extent of country round may be seen: the town and vessels at foot, and a most delightful range for the eye for three miles down the river, encompassing Naragansett Bay and its pleasant islands.... Besides the College there are several churches and an elegant brick state house, well situated upon the second street, and a large brick market house. The steeple of the new Baptists' meeting house is said to be the most perfect piece of architecture in America. Connoisseurs, however, condemn it, for being too massy at the top."

But Elkanah detected present decline as well as future promise. Horse breeding around Naragansett Bay had nearly become extinct. "Here is another proof of the fatal effects of Negroes; in the last generation, every farmer in Naragansett must have his Negroes. The present generation have consequently degenerated into indolence and drunkenness." Was his sentiment directed against slavery, or against the people enslaved?

Not only was what he saw changing with experience, his own appearance had altered. On arrival at John Brown's house, no one recognized him and once again he had to prove who he was and re-establish his credibility.

Home Again—Plymouth and Providence

The British still occupied Newport; Providence's trade by sea was blocked. His task for the Browns completed, Elkanah decided to include more of New England in his travels, but first he would go home. Crossing the bridge at Taunton, whose river-side situation inspired Elkanah to predict a rising industrial success from expanding ironworks and ship-building, he continued through scrub pine forests to his birth-place, Plymouth. "Here our forefathers first landed among savages in an inhospitable region in the winter of 1620."

From the high hill above Plymouth some years earlier, Elkanah had seen British warships bringing three regiments of soldiers to command and subdue Boston's "rebellious spirit." Now he saw "a glorious prospect of Cape Cod and the Atlantic to the horizon." And now on this hill behind the meeting house he visited his mother's grave, surrounded by those of ancestors and relatives. These few days revisiting places where he had played as a child, recognizing "every tree, rock, and bush," were in later memory the happiest days of his life. He pondered the arrival with years, of cares and anxiety. Memories greeted him—three years earlier, in the winter, for example, news had reached Plymouth that the army was exposed to great suffering because of cold weather. Elkanah's father had immediately gone home and ordered that all extra blankets be brought together and delivered to the Committee for Correspondence to be forwarded to the army besieging Boston. That left only a single blanket for each family member's bed. The beds of home were now mere memories. Strangers lived in the house where he had grown up. They weeded what had once been his father's garden. Elkanah's notes about the town pretend the detachment of a visiting stranger. "The town is regularly laid off in four or five streets, and containing about 100 wooden houses. The harbor is bad. They carried on a small foreign trade, but pursued the cod fishing extensively." From his diary one would never guess that the foreign trade was his own father's trans-oceanic shipping business.[34]

North from Plymouth, Elkanah traveled through Milton and Roxbury, towns bombarded in the siege of Boston.[35] He rode into town across Boston Neck, "a tongue of land which joins the town of Boston to the continent." Twenty-five thousand people lived in Boston. From the beacon on the hill behind the town one could see a wide view of the ocean and the harbor, with its thirty-six islands, and the countryside extending to the west. The Long Wharf extended into the harbor nearly half a mile long, lined with warehouses and stores.

Elkanah continued north along the coast to Marblehead and Salem, "once the seat of the detestable witch excitement" and now a major center of shipping. At Dracut he crossed the Merrimack River into New Hampshire. Looping back to Boston, he followed the roads that the British had used to retreat from Lexington into the city. Besides contemplating the events that had started the war, Elkanah visited "the old brick college of Cambridge, which is the most ancient literary institution in America, and from which the rays of science have been widely spread throughout New England." He also spent an hour at Bunker Hill. "My mind's eye witnessed the British veterans twice repulsed by the sons of the Pilgrims, determined to be free, and with scarcely any weapons but their fowling pieces.... A spectacle of such deep and thrilling interest, America, and perhaps the world, never before witnessed." His mind continually filling with patriotic hyperbole, Elkanah returned to Providence and to his work for John Brown, although, trade being blocked, there was not much to do.

In early summer Elkanah was approached by his mother's uncle, the once outspoken Plymouth Tory Edward Winslow, Sr., who was now ostracized and kept strictly watched in the midst of a town predominantly rebel in sympathy. The war had reduced him from wealth to deprivation. His son, however, had risen in the British army after guiding the soldiers to their attack on Lexington. Since 1776, Edward, Jr., had been Aide to the commander of the army occupying Newport and the island of Rhode Island, opposite the Whig stronghold, Providence. The elder Winslow and one of his daughters arrived in Providence in June, 1778, to ask Elkanah to try to contact General John Sullivan, who led the American military forces there. Winslow wanted permission to arrange a meeting with his son on one of the islands in Narragansett Bay. Elkanah first proposed this idea to John Brown, then discussed it with General Sullivan's Aides, and finally spoke to the General in person. Elkanah succeeded in arranging the meeting. General Sullivan received a promise that Winslow would speak of nothing but private matters not related to the public circumstances.

A message sent to Newport under a flag of truce included an unsealed letter written by Edward Winslow in Plymouth to his son, proposing a time and location for the reunion—Providence Island midway between Newport and Providence. An American officer who was appointed to conduct the father to the meeting invited Elkanah to join them. Both parties approached the island from opposite directions in specially identified long boats. Father and son and sister embraced in silence on the beach. Edward Winslow, Jr., recalled that officers and soldiers from both sides were present, as well as "sailors of both denominations and Negroes—not a heart among them that did not melt."[36] Elkanah Watson recorded that "the highest-toned feelings of the human heart were stretched to the utmost tension, and overtasked nature seemed exhausted." From then on, into 1779, Elkanah served as a go-between to convey personal supplies from the son to the father. Whig relatives complained, but Edward Winslow and his family expressed gratitude. Later they emigrated to Nova Scotia where the British government granted them and other loyalists land in compensation. The Winslows abandoned one of Plymouth's finer mansions, but they took with them a few family mementoes including ceremonial pikes once carried when their ancestor, the Pilgrim colony Governor Edward Winslow, had presided over Plymouth's court in the 1630s. The Pilgrim heritage so important to Elkanah was fragmented by the fortunes of revolution.

Such intensely felt local experiences dominated Elkanah's mind at the moment, but distant transactions were to be of greater lasting effect. General Burgoyne's surrender at Saratoga proved the seriousness of American military action. That victory implied to England's opponents in Europe that the revolution could succeed. On February 6, 1778, France, represented by the Count de Vergennes, and the United States of America, represented by Benjamin Franklin, Arthur Lee, and Silas Deane, concluded a treaty of commerce and of military assistance. America now had an ally against Great Britain. Probably attempting to prevent war with France, the British sent a commission to America to offer terms to resolve the conflict and end the war. Their proposals to Congress in June were rejected, as were secret attempts at bribing congressional leaders to support the English. In advance of the arrival of large-scale support from France, the British withdrew from Philadelphia and retreated to New York. A French fleet commanded by Admiral d'Estaing showed up in July to help the Americans, expecting to shut up the English by blocking the harbor at Philadelphia. D'Estaing sailed next to Sandy Hook, where Americans expected him to meet the English fleet there in a battle for New York. Instead, after a week and a half of inaction, d'Estaing sailed north to Newport, Rhode Island, arriving with about seven thousand soldiers in twelve warships. Soon nearly ten thousand American troops came together on land, under Generals John Sullivan, Nathanael Greene, and LaFayette, with General John Hancock in charge of the Massachusetts militia. Elkanah again took his place in the Providence militia in the center of serious battle.

The army landed on Rhode Island and set up a temporary camp, waiting for the French to land. Commanded by Robert Pigot, the British pulled back into Newport, bringing in all livestock from the surrounding area, and destroying houses and other hindrances to defensive fire from within the town. In the American camp Elkanah noticed the presence of James Otis, Jr. When an elected representative at the Massachusetts General Court, he had for many years spoken famously in support of American independence and against slavery. James was the brother of Mercy Otis Warren, the historian and playwright. In 1769 in an argument about politics, a customs official hit him on the head with a sword, causing brain damage and intermittent insanity until his death in 1783. Elkanah, describing the action at Rhode Island, commented that "James Otis, a martyr to the cause of liberty, was there, a strolling lunatic about the camp. The great and fervid mind, that first grasped the idea of independence, was then a melancholy ruin."

The British retreated from Newport as the Americans came to attack and occupy it, waiting for the French to join them. Suddenly a small British fleet approached the harbor and the French turned to drive these ships out to sea. The next day, one of the worst storms ever experienced that time of year threw further military planning into chaos. Two days of tempest drove both fleets apart with severe damage. The English sailed for New York. The French admiral's ship had been dismasted in the hurricane. The French dragged up north to Boston for repairs, leaving the American army defenseless from the sea. From Elkanah's viewpoint, it seemed any British attack could have captured the entire American army. Delayed, the British came back and attacked, engaging in battle near Quaker Hill. The Americans retreated in disorder. Elkanah's unit ensconced behind a stone wall withstood an attack by Hessians but in the night escaped to the mainland without loss, not even abandoning their cannon. General Clinton arrived the next day with four thousand British soldiers and a fleet to match. Newport was again occupied and Providence remained blockaded.

Elkanah's life returned to an unsatisfying routine. Daydreams of advancement through gallant action in the militia evaporated in the hot boredom of reality as an apprentice. Again, release from his employment so he could join the army was refused. Three years older, he was back where he'd started, but now he had some experience in buying and selling. He began investing on the side in cheese, tobacco, lime, and whatever else came to hand, selling at small profits and acquiring capital that gave him hopes of future fortune.[37]

Two

France

At Sea—to France

Elkanah Watson celebrated his twenty-first birthday on January 22, 1779. "Disappointed in the expectations I had formed in respect to my establishment in life, I was induced to embrace proposals made to me by Mr. Brown and others, to proceed to France in association with them." Elkanah once again was to travel with their capital and carry out business for the Browns. He'd be their agent in France to coordinate the acquisition and shipment of munitions and other supplies for the revolutionary army. He would also convey messages from Congress to Benjamin Franklin, America's ambassador in Paris.[1]

Captain Simeon Sampson commanded the small ship *Mercury* when she departed Boston harbor on August 4, 1779. Designed for speed, shipwrights at Plymouth built her quickly for the American navy. Sampson, twice Elkanah's age, came from Plymouth, too. He had been captured twice—once by the French in 1762, and again by the British in 1776. Among the *Mercury*'s crew, Elkanah discovered former schoolmates from Plymouth. That they were now employed at a lower level than once had been their schoolboy expectations inspired Elkanah to ponder the vagaries of fortune. Here he was, one of four passengers on their way to France and, in his case, he hoped, prosperity. There they toiled as they would continue to toil, having once, he imagined, been equal in advantages and potential. Yet a few months earlier he had been despondent about his own prospects.

The *Mercury* waited off Nantasket for favorable winds. A ship from France named *La Sensible* had just dropped anchor. John Adams and Conrad Gérard, the first French ambassador to the United States, had arrived, but Adams had already gone ashore. Adams had known Elkanah's father for years. Abigail Adams, Major General James Warren and his wife, and Robert Paine provided Elkanah with letters of introduction that he originally expected to present to Adams in France. But, hearing that Adams had already arrived in Boston, Elkanah left the letters with General Warren to be given in his absence, with the hope that he could pursue the contact at some later occasion. The *Mercury*'s passengers went across to meet Gérard and hear the most recent news from France. A year later, Elkanah wrote to Adams (who had returned to France) and recalled this near encounter when asking for a letter of introduction that might help him establish business contacts.[2]

Boston's steeples, Dorchester's hills, Hull's beaches, and the little islands of Boston's wide harbor receded as the ship got under way the next morning, coasting south to within view of Plymouth before veering out to open sea.

"I'm out at sea! No harbour can Espy!
T'is all a boundless scene of sea & sky!"

Elkanah found himself "not only launched upon the wide Atlantic, ploughing through foamed green waves, but into the wide world ploughing through the vicissitudes of life, without any idea of returning to my wretched country till a happy peace there restores harmony, concord, & felicity."[3]

He felt sick from the rocking motion even in fairly calm seas, yet cheered by rapid progress under full sail. Hump-back whales and porpoises played all around. Two days sailing slowly along the south edge of the cod-fishing banks included views of distant fishing boats, nearly stationary with sails flapping. The Gulf Stream moved Captain Sampson's ship forward.

Four days out, the *Mercury* hoisted all sails to escape a British frigate that suddenly came up. The Britons signaled friendship. Distrusting, the Americans fled in a chase that lasted hours. Finally the warship fell behind and out of sight. Sunset was sublime. "The utmost art of the skillfullest painters in existence cannot imitate the variegated appearance of the sky at the close of the day, nothing could be more beautiful. The wind lulled into a perfect dead calm, and the moon

Out at sea (engraving and etching by Reinier Vinkeles after Jacobus Buys).

soon after illuminates our horizon shedding its quivering light upon the surface of the dimpled sea." With a strong breeze in the moonlight, flying fish jumped over the bows to land unexpectedly on the deck. Pigs penned at the front of the ship squealed as they tried to catch the slippery prey.

The next day spouting whales swam before the ship, while porpoises and dolphins emerged from under her stern. "Nothing can exceed the beauty of their fanciful and changeable colors, when the bright sunbeams play upon them in the water." Near the western isles off southern England, another British warship gave chase. Full sail again saved the *Mercury*. Then came a gale, Elkanah's first real storm at sea. Past discomfort could not compare with this seasickness. Terrible mountains of water might overwhelm the ship at any moment. But at least the crashing, slapping crests cleaned off the decks where passengers had vomited.

The next morning, land birds flying above the sails and grapevines floating in the waves signaled the approach of land. On the third of September a lookout in the crows' nest called out, "Land!" The passengers rushed on deck. Then he called again, "A fleet ahead!" They resigned themselves to capture as prisoners-of-war. A little later, the lookout called once more, "A city ahead, with steeples, and no fleet!"

The fortifications of St. Martin on the Isle de Rhé dominated the central Atlantic coast of France. A pilot boat brought the American consul to greet Captain Sampson and Major William Knox (General Henry Knox's brother and one of the passengers). The two officers wore full rebel uniforms. The new American flag flying from the ship attracted a crowd on the quay. The small boat brought the travelers to the landing by the ramparts. Gawkers had gathered to see the North American savages. (Most of the French assumed that everyone living in America was an uncouth yet noble savage, living in a society presided over by philosophers like Benjamin Franklin.) The island's governor received them in his impressive residence and "introduced us to several swarthy, black-eyed French ladies, with richly painted faces." Their charms were lost on Elkanah, however, who was still getting used to being on land. "For several hours, I could scarcely walk, awkwardly lifting up one foot, and waiting for the motion of the vessel; and, when seated at the Governor's, it appeared as if the house was at sea."

An excursion through the town confronted Elkanah with novelty: "The clacking of sabots or wooden shoes upon the pavements,—Jack-asses—a young Lady cantering through the streets a-stride, and a thousand miserable devils demanding *la charité*." (No one begged on the streets of Plymouth.) Everywhere people came out to stare at the "Bostones"—the Bostonians—as many Frenchmen called all Americans. The revolution, they knew, had started at Boston. A small ferry carried them to La Rochelle, where tall stone gables nearly met four or five stories above narrow alleys and streets. In his hotel, Elkanah marveled at the duvets, forming an "immense profusion of feathers, bed accumulated on bed." The next morning, September 6, Watson and Knox took their places in a heavy, two-wheeled cart, similar to a sulky, but drawn by three horses side by side. The driver was mounted on a small seat above and behind. He wore his hair "powdered and frizzed, with a long queue," topped with an old three-cornered hat decorated with tawdry lace. A short coat and "monstrous boots hooped with iron" served as a kind of uniform. Nantes was a hundred and five miles away; they changed horses nine times. Hills and valleys alternated, sometimes interrupted by marshland. The bridges were badly maintained. The driver sped, and at the bottom of a steep hill a horse fell, overturning the wagon. They ended up walking further, accompanied by birdsong from shady branches overhead.

At the next village inn they were tricked out of their accommodations by some French officers who pulled rank to demand their rooms in the name of a non-existent nobleman.

Later Elkanah's grasp of French proved just sufficient when he heard their boasts about having fooled the American savages.

Stone bridges across the Loire brought them into Nantes. Elkanah engaged an interpreter and made arrangements to travel by coach to Paris the next day.[4]

Along the Loire

A road along the Loire River made pleasant travel to Angers upstream, where they arrived the next day. They had been advised to pack their own food and wine, avoiding inns along the way. Neither the fortress nor the cathedral at Angers caught Elkanah's attention, even though they were much taller and more massively complex than any building he could have seen in America. Turning away from the river and striking over hills in a direct line to Paris, Elkanah paused at the town of La Flèche to visit a Jesuit college.[5]

Elkanah considered the college church "a fine large building, where there is on one side an excellent library, and the other a *magnific* parlour, where is deposited the hearts of Henry IV and his wife Marie de Médicis. The gallery is also *remplie* of excellent paintings, representing the principal actions of that Prince." That "*magnific*" (magnificent) and "*remplie*" (filled) in the diary are among several indications that Elkanah intended to use the French he had learned in Charleston.

The cathedral at Le Mans might just as well have been hidden in clouds for all the attention Elkanah gave it. Agriculture and population he did note: grapes, wheat, and pastureland covered the hills; sixty thousand people lived in Angers, six thousand in La Flèche, but the soil there he thought "sterile." In the village of St. Cosme, Elkanah looked around, standing "as erect as a statue in the middle of the street, gazing." Within a minute or two, a beggar accosted him. "I determined to wish him to the devil; but the next glance, reproached the idea;—I observed a tear trickling down his wrinkled cheek, whether natural or artificial I know not, but it had the intended effect. It melted my compassion, & I gave him a few sous that may prove a temporary relief. He crossed himself and recommended me to the protection of the Bon-Dieu—what gratitude!— … in two minutes, half the village who had stood watching my motions hurried out and surrounded me upon every side; the lame, blind, deaf, dumb, deformed, young and old;—hilter, skilter, crowded on with their ragged hats held out for 'la charity.' After a circle of at least 30 had surrounded and hemmed me in upon every quarter, I looked around myself with pleasure at the novelty of my situation. I compared it with that of Gulliver's amongst the Lilliprussians, for in truth in the collection of weather-beaten dried dwarfs there was not one whose head reached above the surface of my shoulders. And as they gazed on me with amazement they undoubtedly imagined me a giant." Elkanah and Major Knox escaped to the carriage and left town, the mass of beggars receding as they gained speed.

Out in the country the scene repeated itself. A few children and an old woman emerged from behind a hedge and followed the coach for a couple of miles, begging for "la charité."

> 'La Charité, la Charité,' that's the cry through the country. What a pity that such a fine country as this should be rendered disagreeable to all strangers by the innumerable swarms of these vermin. Indeed there seems to be no step taken to check their increase.

The vermin were kept out at Versailles. In fog Elkanah rode past the royal palace and through town gates into the city's great square. A servant had ridden on ahead to make arrangements for a team of fresh horses for their carriage, as was the custom. The horses were exchanged rapidly, leaving no time for sight-seeing before the last stage to Paris. They even had a change of driver. The quality of their coachman, or at least his attire, improved so much on this part of the trip—known as the post-royal—that the passengers had to pay twice the normal fare. The coachman was "dressed like a gentleman, with an uncommonly long queue, and his hair frizzed and powdered, nay, perfumed."

Paris with Benjamin Franklin

Halted for customs inspection on the edge of Paris, they resumed their ride into the city center but stopped again, this time to admire a life-size equestrian statue of Louis XIV. Nothing of the sort could be seen in America: a monarch astride a grandly rearing horse, raised up in the act of springing forward. Clever placement of bronze foliage below the horse hid a support beneath the center of the statue, but the bronze horse seemed to leap up in a defiance of gravity. Elkanah confessed himself amazed. Haste required that they immediately visit the "first Ambasador that ever represented the United States of America in Europe in that quality—viz. His Excellency Benjamin Franklin Esquire who from his profound wisdom and long Experience seems not only respected but revered by mankind in general."

Then in his seventies, Franklin represented the embodiment of experience and wisdom, a luminary with whom it was Elkanah's great privilege to have contact. He was in awe of the philosopher, just as he had been under the spell of the great leader Washington whom he had met in 1776 during the siege of Boston. Both times he knew himself to be a very young man with much to learn. Elkanah was not alone in his respect. Franklin's esteem among the French reached extraordinary heights. Portrait busts of the American displayed in progressive houses attested to enlightened opinions. Common people followed Franklin's carriage just to see the famous new-world philosopher. Elkanah learned that Franklin's attractive qualities and air of wisdom had given him a secure place in the sentiments of the Queen. "The exercise of that influence, adroitly directed by Franklin, tended to produce the acknowledgment of our Independence, and the subsequent efficient measures pursued by France in its support." Franklin's household at the rural riverside village of Passy south of Paris was "neither extravagant, nor

Benjamin Franklin in a bearskin hat (engraving and etching by Auguste de St. Aubin after Cochin; artist's proof).

contracted, but consistent with an invariable rule that servants of Republics are bound to adhere to, viz. decent Oeconomy." Franklin emphasized his new-world plainness by ignoring the cut of French clothing, the perfume of periwigs, and the fatuity of flowery phrases. But he was shrewd, and, although direct, knew how to express the necessary nuance to the correct courtier at the right moment to gain increased support for America.

Elkanah delivered a packet to Franklin from Congress, together with his own letters of recommendation. Some messages to the French Foreign Minister, the Compte de Vergennes, also needed to be presented. Franklin suggested that Elkanah deliver them in person at Versailles, with a letter of introduction from him. "As my American clothes & capers were not calculated for that meridian, I declined the offer, though not without much reluctance."

Invited to have dinner with Franklin the next day, Watson and Knox returned to Paris. Elkanah had taken a dislike to his traveling companion (although he does not say why), so he went off on his own to several coffee houses looking for someone else "with whom I could speak my native language." Falling into conversation with a Mr. Ross, he arranged to take over the lease of a pair of "elegantly furnished chambers" in the Hotel de York in the Faubourg de St. Germain from this fellow American, who was departing for Holland. Elkanah even managed to take over the employment of Ross's servant at forty S. (sous) per day. The rooms cost a guinea a week, dinner was forty S. per day, breakfast seven, and the use of "an elegant hackney" was fifteen L. (livres?) per day. Supper was forty and wine thirty per day. Those arrangements having been made, Mr. Ross took Elkanah to the Hotel de Rome and introduced him to "Samuel Wharton, Esq. & son," potentially good business contacts.

Crossing the Pont Royal, they joined more than ten thousand other people strolling through the Tuileries Gardens next to the Louvre Palace—an "ethereal retreat," surpassed by none in Europe. The splendid walks between carefully designed and arranged parks of raised flower beds, the three grand fountains or water spouts, and the marble statues of classical gods and heroes could not have been farther in conception from the flower and vegetable gardens of Plymouth. Town Brook and the Jones River were not allegorized in sculpture. In Paris one could see carved representations of the Seine, the Loire, the Tiber, and the Nile, "copied at Rome from the antiquities of that city." And at the farthest extent of the garden stood "two figures a horse-back of an extraordinary size." Size could be recorded to convey something of the sensations inspired by the vistas: the middle lane—nine hundred ninety feet long and ninety-six wide, with smaller parallel paths where "is always seen a vast concourse of the best company." Elkanah ran out of words and pasted two engravings in his diary, the first provided "a good idea of the flower garden and Louvre which faces it." The second gave "a general idea of the whole garden." In addition he made his own sketch of the garden design.

But best of all was the tree-lined "grand terrace-walk" along the Seine, 1,716 feet in length and with a width of eighty-four, raised twelve to fourteen feet above the gardens so that promenading visitors could look out over all the flowers and beyond to the grand scene of the city. "On one side the most elegant buildings of Paris present, and the other the rich dome of the Hospital des Invalides, the Seine gliding along close by us, with its borders lined with many seats [country mansions], and at last an extensive country sown with villages, hills & dales which finally terminates by the mountains of Moudon & St. Cloud."

The next morning several unexpected visitors stood in Elkanah's reception room in the hotel. He assumed they were police but could not guess why they had come. "A portly gentleman advanced, and drawing a tailor's measure from his pocket, unravelled the mystery."

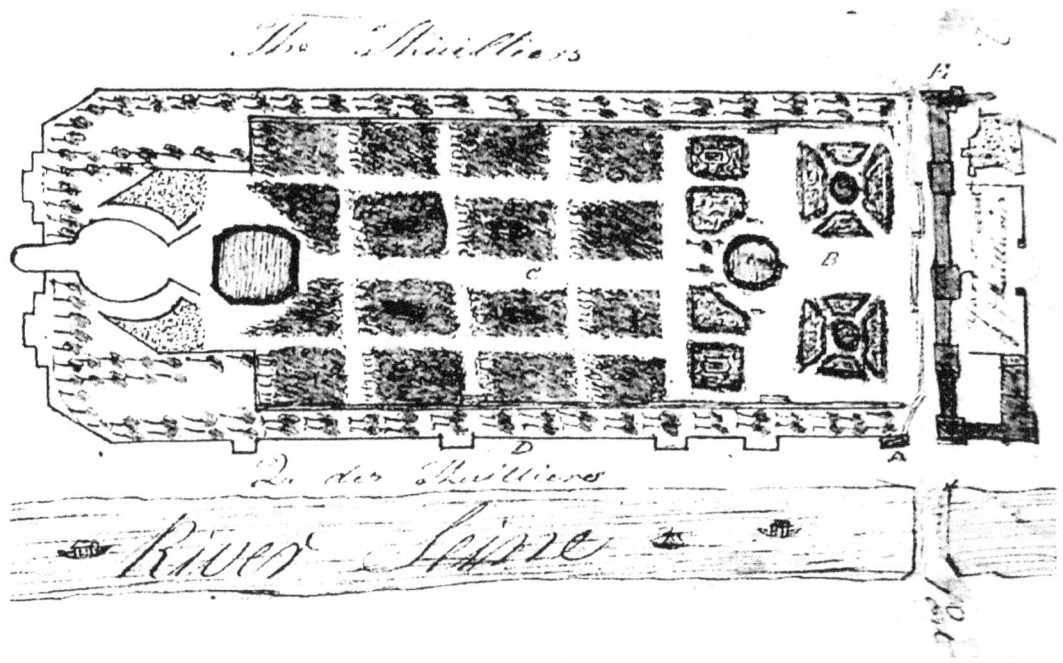

Elkanah's sketch of the Tuileries Garden plan (from the Elkanah Watson Papers, courtesy New York State Library).

Monsieur Blanchard, the servant he had acquired from Mr. Ross, had assessed the inadequacy of Elkanah's American clothing and arranged for a rapid replacement.

More presentably attired with a fashionable scarlet coat, an embroidered silk waistcoat, a gold-headed cane, and his hair tied with a double bow, Elkanah agreed to Franklin's request that he personally hand over the messages directed to the Compte de Vergennes at Versailles.[6] The prime minister received him with notable civility.

After a quick survey of the gardens, Elkanah asked the count's secretary if there were any possibility of seeing the royal family. The de Bourbon family were about to attend mass. With his guide, Elkanah entered the royal chapel. The church was "middle-sized, but most magnificent." Louis XVI and Marie Antoinette came in to the accompaniment of music, taking their seats under a canopy at the front. "The King was somewhat robust, with a full face, Roman nose, and placid countenance. The Queen had an elegant person, a fine figure, an imposing aspect, and florid complexion, with bright grey eyes, full of expression."

Elkanah's visit to Paris lasted two weeks, and in that time he collected general information about the city as well as what he learned by experience. "The city is built of hewn stone and it contained about twenty-six thousand houses, from four to seven stories high, and eight hundred thousand inhabitants." The police were famous for their ability to recover stolen property. Robert Livingston once told him that a watch stolen from him in Paris was returned eight months later, having been traced to Rome and recovered, then sent back to be restored to him. Paris achieved fame also with its tapestries from the Gobelins factory, besides other types of cloth—"satins, velvets, ribbons, etc."

Elkanah attended the wedding of the American consul at Nantes, Jonathan Williams, Jr., with Dr. Franklin, who was the groom's uncle. The ceremony took place at St. Germain, followed by the wedding banquet there at the home of the bride's family. The father of the bride, William Alexander, had been a prominent Scottish banker and was now a friend of Franklin's, although Elkanah heard that he was suspected of being a "secret emissary of the British government." The guests also visited the Madrid Palace, where the exiled King James II of England had lived and, before him, Cardinal Mazarin.[7] People praised the view from the terrace overlooking the Seine as the "noblest promenade in Europe." In the palace chapel, Elkanah paid attention to a painting of the Last Supper by Poussin and a representation of the Trinity by Vouet. Usually, however, he did not record the artist's name when mentioning an impressive painting.

Elkanah made comparisons: if the college building at Providence, four stories high, was the largest building in American, what could he see in Paris? The Louvre, said to be the "largest building (all in all) in the universe," and Europe's most impressive palace, held more paintings, which Elkanah decided to list in his diary. "But it will fill up my Journal to put it all down." He pasted an engraving of the building in his notebook. Besides a *Combat between Love and Chastity*, no doubt represented by allegorical figures, the paintings he chose to list were mostly illustrations of classical myths or history: *Hercules and Omphale, Marcellus and Hannibal*, but also biblical stories, such as *Sarah—Abraham's Wife, Magdelan in Penitence at Jesus' Feet* by Van Loo, and some fashionably sentimental pictures like *The Abandoned Lover, Promise of Being Faithful*, and *The Lovers United by Hymen and Crowned by Amour*. By far the most pleasing paintings, however, were the portraits of *Louis XVI and his Queen with Doctor Franklin upon their Left*. Elkanah heard that the two pictures had been hung together by royal command.

Parisian sightseeing included a visit to a charity hospital—"one long room containing 200 beds, many of which are crowded with miserable patients." Elkanah muttered to his diary, "two disagreeable hours." The church and convent next door were the Abbaye Royale du Val-de-Grace. Another engraving entered the diary. Ninety-five feet high, with a design based on the altar canopy of St. Peter's in Rome, the interior included an oval altar surrounded by six "grand twisted marble columns," each two feet in diameter.

Tired from visiting museums and churches, Mr. Wharton and Elkanah returned to their hotels at dusk, where Elkanah wrote his day's entry in the diary. Later, they took a hackney together and with their servants attended a play in a theater at the boulevards. First, however, they stopped to see a waxworks, where their entry was obstructed by a surly sentry. He refused to budge, being himself a sculpture. The real doorman called it a Bostonian. Of the wax images, "the most striking was that of the celebrated Voltaire, who is closely engaged with a table full of books, papers, &c.before him; and his countenance expressed every sensation of a philosopher." Later, Elkanah exploited the waxwork deception to fool people into thinking they could meet Benjamin Franklin.

At the theater their front-box seat tickets placed them

> where was several young ladies whose delicious perfumes, exclusive of faces as blooming as the rising sun, was surely enough of itself to turn my ideas from the tract of the exhibitions upon the stage. Even if I understood the language perfectly, much more, as I don't understand a word—what a disagreeable situation. The first scene was an —— [sic]. All is dead to me. Everybody is amused and laughing while I am sitting as grave and as solemn as a Quaker, as I have nothing to laugh at, without I laugh because others do. If I do, I must reproach myself with being very foolish. As perhaps I am the only one in this predicament, of the hundreds who are now sheltered

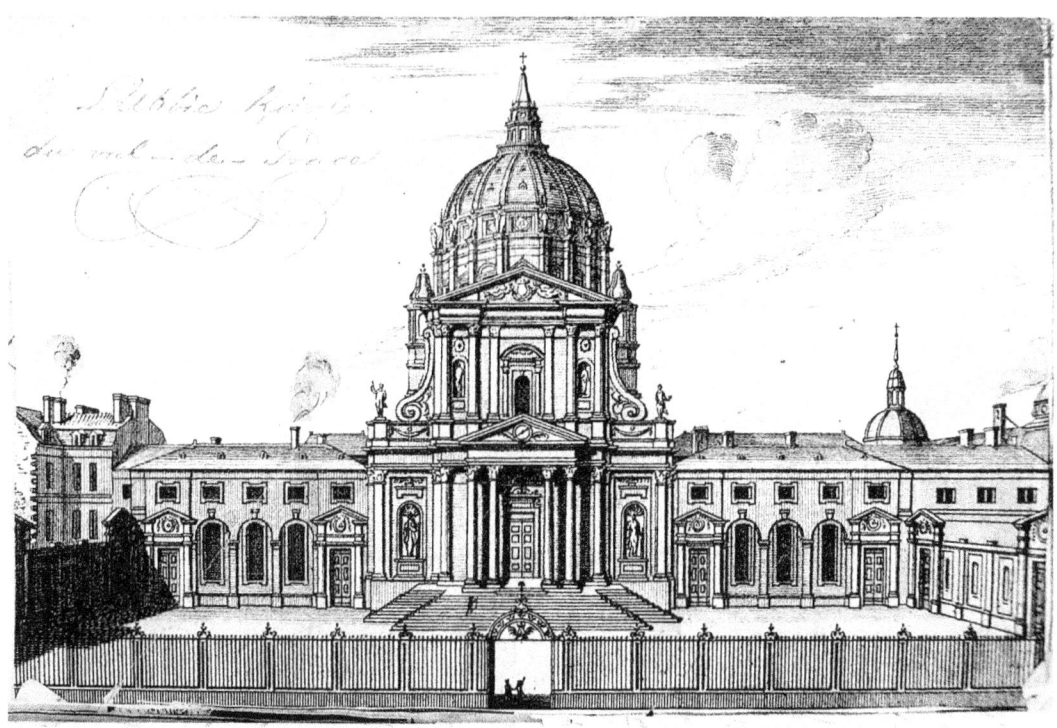

Elkanah's souvenir engraving of the Val de Grace Chapel, Paris (from the Elkanah Watson Papers, courtesy New York State Library).

under the roof of the play-house, the only compensation I could have recourse to, was in feasting my eyes upon the fragrant roses, in full bloom each side of me.

The first scene is over—the curtain falls—a general buzz ensued—these Jolie demoiselles [pretty misses] at each elbow—possibly mistaking me for a former acquaintance—wriggled themselves from their last attitude, flirted their heads around to see who their neighbours were & one of them attacked me prattling about what I know not, as I could make no reply, she probably imagined me deaf or dumb, or perhaps both.

Mortified in this cruel situation, I began to grow fatigued, and after seeing a number of little boys & girls prop upon the stage, dancing with surprising dexterity, and a mountebank—exhibiting what excited my astonishment even to fear, upon a rope elevated about 50 foot from the stage he mounted it by a ladder, where for a half an hour he danced a variety of dances & jumped 5 feet above the rope over a ribbon &c.&c. We descended into the street, where two young ladies genteelly dressed was interceding our coachman to drive them into a particular part of the city. At this moment we came up. Mr. Wharton, stimulated merely by politeness, offered the service of our coach; they accepted—consequently we mounted to conduct them.

Having arrived after a long circuit viz-a-viz leur maison—they pressed us to descend and enter. We declined but their importunities could not be resisted. They conducted us from one story to another, till at length my suspicions were excited, and at first entrance into a spacious chamber they were confirmed by their indecency, and ordering at our expense, supper, wine &c. Being particularly cautioned against dangers of this kind, which frequently proves fatal to inexperienced strangers, I motioned a sudden retreat, Wharton seconded the motion, we left 3 L upon the table, & precipitated ourselves down stairs; from the commotions in an adjoining room, we had every reason to imagine ourselves decoyed into a cage, where we should most certainly have been stripped of our money, watches, &c. if not murdered for better security. We retired to our lodgings & there ends the varieties of this day.

The "commotions in an adjoining room" called up recollections of "The history of Miss Williams" told by Tobias Smollett in the novel Elkanah thought foreshadowed his own experiences as a young man far from home—*The Adventures of Roderick Random*.[8] When he left home for France, his father may have warned him to avoid prostitutes; but it was literature that had prepared him see beautiful and fascinating girls as potentially dangerous whores.

Wharton and Watson visited the Cathedral of Notre Dame the next morning, much impressed by the size. They were told "though in Gothic architecture," the church was considered the best of its sort in all of France. In America the steeple of the Baptist Church of Providence had been considered, "the most perfect piece of architecture in America." Notre Dame displayed gothic imperfection. A vocabulary for understanding the style was not among Elkanah's possessions. He termed pinnacles on the façade obelisks, noticing that they were "richly ornamented with flowers &c.," and that the carving required unending patience. But, "entering the doors of the Church a vast number of images sunk into the front of the building presents before us representing saints, angels, &c.—badly executed." The stained-glass of the rose windows won his approval. He counted 108 columns, all hewn from single stones. Most impressive of all was the high altar and the statues, paintings, "and curiosities" surrounding it. In the center an "excellent group of marbles" displayed "the dead body of Jesus Christ, in the lap of his mother, the Virgin Mary, at the foot of the cross." To the right he saw "the figure of Louis XIII in marble clothed in his robes, upon his knees, and offering his crown & scepter to the Virgin Mary. Louis XIV in the same attitude is represented also upon the left, both upon marble pedestals, the fronts of which are ornaments with divers sculptures of metal, gilted. After this comes 6 Angels, upon pedestals ornamented with flowers, three upon each side, holding in their hands tokens of the love of our Saviour for us grovelling mortals." Mobs destroyed these artworks during the French Revolution.

Elkanah held New England Protestant views of Catholic piety. He was struck by the "number of ignorant bigoted mortals upon their knees idolizing some stature or piece of painting in the aisles." And confessionals inspired him to remark that, "prejudice aside, I consider this part of their superstition as really necessary for the common people; but sifted at bottom, independent of this advantage, very ridiculous." From his enlightened education and experience he felt capable of laying prejudice aside. He says so. Climbing to the top of the church tower gave a commanding view of the entire city, worthy of his sense of superiority.

The American war intruded in the gothic splendor: the British flags taken when the French navy under Admiral d'Estaing captured the Caribbean island of Grenada in July, 1779, had recently arrived in Paris and were hung in the church to commemorate French triumph. Although Americans had expressed dismay when d'Estaing had sailed away from Boston to fight the British in the West Indies, to the French that was all part of the same military action against England. And French victory deserved celebration.

Another church, the Sorbonne, formed the goal the following afternoon. First, however, Elkanah had his coachman drive him out to Passy, where he called on Benjamin Franklin. The philosopher introduced Elkanah to his assistant, the "celebrated Doctor (Edward) Bancroft." Despite their suspicions directed toward Mr. Alexander at St. Germain, neither Watson nor Franklin apparently suspected that Bancroft was the spy who kept England thoroughly informed of what the Americans were accomplishing with their new allies, the French.[9] Earlier, Bancroft had supplied Franklin with secret information about the English government's dealings with America, when both of them had lived in London. Franklin did not imagine he could in turn be spying for the English.

Mid-day dinner with Wharton at a "grand Hotel" back in town would go well with a bowl of punch, they thought. They managed to get all the needed ingredients (sugar, lemons or limes, and wine), but a punch bowl could not be located. Eventually a servant brought "an earthen something that has more resemblance to a pot de chamber than a punch-bowl." They made do.

Esteemed as one of Paris's finest buildings, the church of the Sorbonne inspired Elkanah to write a studied impression of its architectural details. "The different proportions of this edifice are so just that they seem made one for the other," he mused, indicating an appreciation for order that could not be pleased by the ongoing accumulation of parts characteristic of most gothic cathedrals. He thought the Sorbonne dome was rather like that of the Val de Grace, while "the portal is advantageously disposed with columns in the Corinthian and composite orders." The cornices were grand and "of an excellent proportion." The altar "is a very fine ordinance; the principal ornaments of which consist in six marble pillars in the Corinthian order, the bases and tops of which are brass, gilted." Besides a fine painting under the vault, by le Brun, "Our savior J.C. is also represented upon a marble cross of 7 feet in a very natural attitude." Elkanah the connoisseur of natural attitudes pasted an engraving of the Sorbonne in his diary.

The funerary monument of Cardinal Richelieu was the chapel's greatest treasure, carved from a single block of black marble, with life-size figures of mourners, one at each end of the

Elkanah's souvenir engraving of Notre Dame, Paris (from the Elkanah Watson Papers, courtesy New York State Library).

reclining figure of the statesman-priest. Elkanah found the style "exquisite" and commemorated it with another engraving added to his book.

Rain and more rain dampened his enthusiasm for searching out further landmarks the next morning, but he had another invitation to lunch with Franklin out at Passy. The afternoon passed indoors, filled with Elkanah's reports of his experiences and the current circumstances of the war in America. Edward Bancroft thus came to learn anything Elkanah had to say that might be interesting to the English. Franklin warned against relying too much on the import-export firm of Pliarne and Penet, whom he had come to distrust. They had insinuated themselves into the American arms trade without really having the high government connections they had claimed on being introduced to George Washington during the siege of Boston.

After dinner back in town, Elkanah returned to the Tuileries gardens and strolled the paths. "These gardens are frequented in the evenings by people of various professions, and as the boughs of the trees from their close connection occasions a total darkness, it affords a retreat for obscenities of almost every species. Being fully convinced of this truth by two hours' roving, I seated under a tree by myself." This proved dangerous. "In less than six minutes I was attacked by four demoisselles, whose dress at least entitles them to be duchesses. Their operations were so well planned that I found no other sure resource to avoid being reduced to a capitulation, but by a precipitate retreat across the garden." Attempting nonchalance, he approached a pretty chamber maid and tried in "miserable half French" to ask her to change a crown so he could buy some fruit. The girl's employer came up to them and interpreted his actions as an attempt at seduction. She could have been right. (Elkanah might have avoided this confusion if he had asked for change from some passing gentleman, although perhaps thereby inspiring alternative misunderstandings.) The girl's mistress "attacked me with much warmth, which soon collected a crowd ... I pocketed my crown and made a hasty retreat. 'Prenez garde, Monsieur Anglois,' says the good lady, as I turned my back to the mob." Finding safety by mingling again in the crowd, he worked his way back to the security of his hotel to clear his mind by editing his "reflections upon the occurencies of the day."

Another day, Elkanah visited the Hospital of the Invalides. Three thousand two hundred invalid soldiers lived their last days there. Viewing the paintings recalling French wars took all morning.

Art turned carnage into visions of glory, contradicting the memories of the maimed. Proceeding to Franklin's house for dinner, he was once again impressed by the splendid views of the city, of the countryside with its rural mansions, forests, towns, and palaces, and of the Seine River enlivened by sailboats. To Elkanah's surprise, Franklin indicated that dinner would be at the home of a friend. Franklin accompanied him through a garden of several acres to the mansion of Monsieur Le Ray de Chaumont. "This was the first occasion of my dining in a private circle in Europe; and, being still in my American style of dress, and ignorant of the French language, and prepared for extreme ceremony, I felt exceedingly embarrassed." On their entry to the house, "several well-dressed persons (to my unsophisticated American eyes, gentlemen) bowed to us profoundly. These were the servants." In the next room, beyond folding doors, a "brilliant assembly" greeted Franklin, "the wise old man." Elkanah, said Franklin, was "a young American, just arrived." His simple clothing quaintly reinforced the idea that Americans were noble savages.

Elkanah found the table manners informal and attractive, with everyone at ease. Some played instruments, some sang, some danced, others conversed in small groups. At the dinner

The Hospital of the Invalides (engraving by Stankowski after E.W., in Leo de Colange, ed., *Voyages and Travels,* 1887, I, p. 90).

table, men and women sat together, mixed, not separated. The hostess participated as an equal, rather than withdrawn as a superintendent of the dinner's progress. "No gentleman," he was told, "would be tolerated in France, in monopolizing the conversation of the table, with discussions of politics or religion, as is frequently the case in America." Dinner concluded with coffee.

On Sunday, September 20, he visited the gardens and cascades at the royal palace at

Franklin and Elkanah in society (engraving by Thwaites after Lossing, in *Men and Times of the Revolution*, 1861, p. 79).

Marly. An aqueduct of thirty-nine arches extended seven hundred feet to supply the water rolling in one place like "a brook tumbling down a mountain." In a forest another stream cascaded thunderously over marble stairs, "resembling sheets of silver." Sculptured animals spouted streams of water into ponds, surprising the visitor who wandered through labyrinths and gardens. The public could enjoy a "retreat calculated for the amusement of princes."

Innocent pastimes after dinner inspired reflections on Sunday customs in New England. Elkanah hoped to see the end of "the extreme constricted ideas of almost obliging people to hold their breaths on this day." He wished "that mankind may be left at liberty to think and act for themselves within the limits, and agreeable to the dictates, of pure reason, independent of the influence and prejudices of bigoted, contracted, superstitious priests."

A week earlier Elkanah had passed the Elysian Fields. After attending mass, hundreds of people "devoted the rest of the day to the theatre, ball, and every other species of amusement." Many could be seen dancing in the park accompanied by strolling violinists. Relaxation might lift the soul, but ingenious engineering excited the mind. People esteemed the machine at Marly as probably "finest piece of mechanism the world ever produced." Lacking "mechanical terms and head," he thought he should not attempt a detailed description, merely remarking that "it is composed of 14 large wheels stretching across the river. By these wheels 25 pumps are played which throws the water at every turn about 500 feet high." He had read that the water was brought up 3660 feet from the river surface "by conduits of iron which join the pumps. The water is conducted through a steep hill 140 feet perpendicular above the river & 600 feet more to the reservoir from whence it is raised by means of 75 other pumps, through leaden pipes to a tower on a hill, which is situated a considerable distance from the reservoir. From this tower it is conveyed through a high spacious stone aqueduct to the water works at Marly from whence to the reservoir at Lucieno, Versailles, Chanais, Roquencourt, Cheveloup, & Trianon, making in all about six miles." The system provided those towns with a "full supply of water which purifies in its course, & furnishes the inhabitants with water superior to the water used in Paris." Annual repairs cost around twenty thousand guineas and kept around fifty workmen employed.

Waiting for dispatches from Versailles to take back to Nantes to be sent further on the return voyage of the *Mercury*, Elkanah had time to philosophize about life. He could also visit the theater. With a former acquaintance from Providence, Mr. Herry, he got tickets for a performance in the theater at the boulevards. Relieved it would be a pantomime and no "dry comedy," but instead something capable of being understood by the eye alone, the two young men went out for some fun. But Elkanah thought about the evening first in generalizing terms:"As the enjoyment of the society of the fair is the first blessing that we male mortals can possess,—particularly when every internal sensations beats & breathes nothing but love, animated & cherished by either enchanting music, or some celestial situation, & fully persuaded that it is not good that man should be alone, we determined to intersperse ourselves ça à la parmi [here and there among] the crowd. As I am rather difficult in deciding my choice in matters of this importance; I reconnoiterd a while the phizes [physiognomies, faces] that graced the several boxes. At length I was gratified to a fraction, in finding one that contained four or five as I thought young goddesses without a single gallant, with a vacancy in the middle. Just the thing!—I never wished more to have the assurance of a Frenchman then now—I certainly would have dodged into the happy spot sans ceremonie—mais helas! [without ceremony, but, alack!] Suppose I should affect the intrepidity of one I shall most assuredly look & feel worse than a stuck pig. To be stuck between GOD knows who, without being able to open my mouth—the idea had almost proved fatal to my project. However, I began afresh to plead in favour of the propriety of my object; & while gradually advancing & debating the point a young French officer slipped by me, & effectually confuted my manoeuvre, by imping into the identical spot that I had been eagerly eyeing several minutes. The first minute removed all barriers to intimacy between the young officer & lady. And as my suspended doubts were relieved, I concluded to content myself de boute. But madamoiselle, seeing my distress, took a second survey—& then kindly—by dint of squeezing, pressed out a berth which I immediately filled—between two. Having recovered my surprise, I gradually (first one side, & then the other) began to examine my neighbours with close inspection. The one upon my right who I had imagined before to be a blooming lass, perhaps could not be much short of 50, but probably 4 or 5 years beyond the mark, though as bloomy as a rose. Yet age unkindly ploughed the wrinkles of her face too deep to be with convenience brought upon a level with the rest. The counterfeit was too obvious not to be detected by half an eye. Art had undoubtedly exhausted itself in the attempt—but in vain. Years in spite of us will roll on, & entail with them what the old woman seems with all her skill to resist. To see an old potato face converted to the purpose of a linen shop board is no laughable matter! But let's see, who have I got upon my left, dieu remercie, [thank God] an entire contrast—youth, vivacity, & a lovely countenance was obvious from the first glance. Every passion seemed to be summoned to plead in her favour, especially as she had so feelingly felt my distress, and opened a berth to relieve me. Thus supremely happily fixed, I began to attend to the pantomime, but more to Madamoiselle."

Elkanah's dithering diffidence in making an approach to introduce himself to beautiful French girls, a shyness that the young French officer did not share, recalls, as it must have for Elkanah, the hesitation Laurence Sterne described in the person of his hero Yorick trying to open a conversation with a beautiful young woman in Calais, only to be thrust aside by an unabashed French captain.[10]

> Such wanton indecencies were exhibited upon the stage, that I began to suspect that no delicate lady could suffer their modesty thus to be put to the test. Of consequence I concluded that they must be all whores. Indeed a minute afterwards confirmed my suspicions that some of them were, at least. The dear goddess that had began to foment my very soul vanished in an instant, & left me alone to enjoy a dry contemplation. A young petit maitre tipped her a wink; she took the hint, & fled. At this instant a glittering from the floor attracted my eyes. It was a rich pearl, dropped whether accidentally or designedly I know not. I took it in possession, but at loss how to act: keep it I certainly would not, the owner was fled. What then was to be done? In the middle of this controversy she returned—at least 10 percent depreciated in my opinion. The claim was laid and the pearl restored. Gratitude, that noble passion, seemed to excite a wish in her to make me compensation—how, I know not, but it's evident from blinks & squints that something was in agitation. I pleaded ignorance & continued quickly by side of the old counterfeit who was as incapable of exciting the least pleasing sensation as a statue of marble or wax. Consequently being left to myself, as it were, nothing further obstructed my attention to the farce.

Another evening and another play: this time Elkanah visited a playhouse in the midst of a fair consisting of many little shops that were more amusing than the play itself. Young and old together crowded the tables in a coffee house, with "young lads and lasses partaking their collations of wine and desserts as happy as princes." At the far end of the room they saw "a young woman singing most delightfully in consort with other music to attract the byepassers." Again, Elkanah needed to comment on the contrast with New England. "To see a number of fine young ladies drink with gentlemen in a coffee house is what is not seen every day in America—no, no, I hope it never will. Perhaps prejudice sets me in opposition to the custom. Be it so; but I am sure it must tend gradually to eradicate the beauties that grace the delicacy of the sex, and finally, if not checked, presumption will lead on from step to step till a fatal check entails contested hours not worth possessing. From this, & other similar courses must be attributed the general contrast of modest diffidence & forward boldness, between French & English ladies." Young New England's manhood with the innocent virtue of beautiful young women at heart: Beware the coffee house!

Dispatches from the court at Versailles were finally received by the end of the week, September 25, although departure was delayed by a bad storm until the Saturday morning. Dinner with Mr. Wharton and other gentlemen at l'Hôtel de Rome the night before had continued with parting drinks at Ekanah's chamber. "Adieu Paris at least for a while."

From Paris to Nantes

At Benjamin Franklin's suggestion, Elkanah took a different route back to Nantes—first south overland through vineyard country to Orléans. No fences prevented travelers from helping themselves to grapes along the tree-lined road, thus, in Elkanah's opinion, protecting the interior of the plantings from further theft. Perhaps American farmers should plant fruit trees around their crops instead of expending effort on fencing! Contemplating the landless peasantry from his passing coach, Elkanah found them scarcely above the level of serfs. "They live on 'soup maigre' [thin soup], coarse black bread, and a small wine, about equal to cider. Yet they are always cheerful; and they sing and dance over the cares and troubles of life, with light hearts and half-filled stomachs." They, in turn, happily saw a rude but noble American savage drive by.

The forests of Orléans provided fuel for the region and profit for the duke, although no doubt it was peasants who cut the wood, peasants who transported it to market, and peasants who themselves were grateful to get some cuttings of vines to burn when they were trimmed at the end of harvest. At Pont Morant near the city, the Seine-Loire canal built in 1675 began its thirty-mile course to Montgarnis on the Seine. Boat traffic from Nantes could proceed on this canal to Paris. Franklin had called Elkanah's attention to canal construction. Besides this northern canal, the economic benefits from connecting the Bay of Biscay in the southwest with the Mediterranean Sea had proven so great that the government intended to build more soon. Franklin and Watson imagined possibilities for canals in America.

Awaking refreshed in his hotel at Orléans, "early in the morning I descended into the court in search of a convenient retreat—in vain. A young woman decently dressed, seeing my distress and guessing my wish, ran out into the court and opened the door de leur commodité [of their convenience (toilet)]—at the same time calling out to me, with much indifference 'voila monsieur ce que vous cherché' [here, sir, is what you're looking for]. I almost doubted my own eyes & ears but was still more surprised when she continued holding the door open & repeating—entré monsieur, entré donc [enter, sir, get on with it] with as much ceremony and as little embarrassment as though she was conducting me into a parlour. Whatever sensations she might have had upon the occasion, I am sure my modesty never was yet put more to the test, & I am firmly persuaded that I should have stood there & hazarded all consequences till the time if she had not quitted her station, that is, sooner than to have passed the ceremony. But however, as I grow older, & more acquainted with the customs of France it's probable I shall grow more hardy."

Orléans served as a grand warehouse of East and West Indian imports, as well as French inland products, all destined for Paris. The city itself produced silk and wool cloth, besides leather. Silk was also manufactured at Blois, downstream from Orléans, in addition to wines and brandies sent farther downriver to Nantes. With a merchant's estimating eye, Elkanah took notes on production costs and profit margin. The people of Blois celebrated the news of d'Estaing's victory against the British at Grenada with illuminations—torches and bonfires that lit up the streets and the massive chateau rising above the town. As a visiting Bostonian, Elkanah attracted an interested crowd, cheerful about any revolt against the English. Baskets of fruit were presented to him in a glow of enthusiasm. A full moon enabled the coach to resume its way and travel through the night along the elevated, stone-paved roadway constructed fifteen to thirty feet higher than the surrounding river and countryside. Two carriages could pass side by side the entire length of one hundred fifty miles along the Loire. Wheat, vineyards, flax, hemp, and pastureland presented themselves in the quiet of the night, a stillness broken abruptly by the clatter of the horses and the carriage. Mist along the river lifted from time to time to show boats laden with merchandise on its way to Paris.

Some miles before the city of Tours, Elkanah noticed smoke emerging from rocky bluffs along the river. Inquiry brought him to the caves where homes for troglodytes had been hollowed out, even a church. Thought to be the work of the Romans, they were similar to catacombs he had visited in Paris. Some of the apartments, he thought, were "handsomely furnished." Changing horses at Tours, Elkanah and his translator, who had accompanied him the whole trip, hastened on toward Angers and finally to Nantes. "Fortresses, ancient towns, and noblemen's seats" were viewed from the coach, which possessed a "large glass in front" and two on the sides, providing "every convenience for observation."

Leaving Ancenis on the morning of September 28, the coach crossed a high bridge to begin the route to Nantes. At four o'clock the journey ended. Elkanah met old companions and gave his dispatches to Captain Sampson of the *Mercury*, who had been waiting for them in order to depart again for America.

The city had become a major port for Atlantic trade. Ocean-going ships could sail the thirty miles up the river to dock along the quays of Nantes unloading exotic imports and taking away the products of all of France. The slave trade carried out unseen between Africa and the Caribbean had enriched the city. Captains from Nantes knew the routes. Investors here took the profits. Impressive fine houses of smoothly cut white stone looked out on the river and on new public squares. Several convents and an "Institution where husbands have the power of confining wives guilty of infidelity" expressed traditional values in the midst of "ill-paved streets, dark, muddy, and damp." Dominating the city an incomplete cathedral's very tall gothic nave—120 feet high—contrasted with the low remains of the church's Romanesque choir. While Elkanah was there the city council's concept of architectural progress took the form of blowing up an ancient tower that was part of the cathedral. Elkanah

The Quai at Nantes (steel engraving and etching after W. H. Bartlett).

was impressed by the strength of the centuries-old cement. Fissures caused by the explosion of gun powder in the demolition project often went through solid stone instead of the mortar.

Elkanah now had to settle down to the job of establishing a commercial venture in a new town, without much ability in the French language. Uncertain of his future, he wrote to himself, "God only knows, how I am to accomplish this great work, in a foreign country, under every disadvantage, without a letter of recommendation, deprived of a knowledge of their language and trade, and what is still worse a sufficient capital to back me. But here I am in the wide world upon my own bottom; and it is to the supreme being I commit myself, knowing the rectitude of my intentions, I shall exert every laudable effort in my power, & under him wait patiently the event." ("Bottom" in this sentiment refers to being the master of his own ship.)

He remembered later that he had "invested the funds which had been entrusted to me, in goods, and purchased an equal amount on my own credit, and was fortunate." He also sent announcements to his contacts in all the seaports he had visited in America. "Thus commenced my commercial career, which, in three years, enabled me to rear up an establishment, equal to any in the city, for respectability, and known throughout America and Europe on account of the extent of our operations."

The Firm of Watson and Cossoul

During October, 1779, Elkanah invested his funds in goods whose eventual sale would produce profits. He also became deathly ill. A gathering of all the town's doctors produced a cure: Elkanah was drained of 25 ounces of blood. Kept indoors for forty days, he decided that the best way to use the winter lull in the import and export shipping business would be to find a place where he could study French. He moved to the college at Ancenis, twenty-four miles upstream from Nantes. Elkanah wrote to his sister that he hoped "to attain the lingo, shrugs, etc." He intended to study music, dancing, and geography, as well.[11] Two French friends showed the way. They arrived late in the evening on December tenth and were taken to their rooms without meeting school officials. In the early morning, French students who thought Elkanah was still asleep, crept into his room and peeked behind the bed curtains to catch their first glimpse of the new student. All Americans, they'd heard, were wild Indians.

The first day at the school began more officially when a professor visited his apartment to bring him to the dining hall for a breakfast of bread and butter, meat, onions, and white wine. Elkanah's failure to cross himself at prayers before the meal marked him as a "forlorn heretic." Room, board, tuition, and the washing of his clothes were covered by an annual fee of a hundred and fifty dollars. In a letter to his father, December 20, he admitted that he was "very unhappy in not knowing scarcely a word in their language and feel very awkward stuck up like a pig in company with my mouth half open without being able to articulate a single word."[12]

His long illness caused his hair to fall out. He had not wanted a cap or a wig, but his hairdresser started measuring his skull anyway. The remaining hairs had to be shaved and a proper wig acquired.[13] Elkanah would sound French and look French if this education and false hair succeeded. To his sister he wrote in January that he was beginning to understand the language. Sometimes he even caught what was said about himself by people who thought he couldn't follow their conversations. "But," he wrote, "I am almost stunned by the low class of people & students who are eternally hammering new words in my head. If I don't immediately understand them, they often seize me by the hand, & bawl in my ears as if I was totally deaf and dumb. To indulge my own humour I seldom attempt to undeceive them. I am determined to let them go on bawling till spring, as I find it impresses words upon my mind."

His view overlooking the college garden out to open country beyond and to the Loire river all iced over delighted him. Elkanah studied as required, distracted continually, however, by thoughts of his destiny in "the imaginary, busy, clattering, confused scene of commerce." The future would be prosperous, he was sure. "Many of my countrymen dread the magnitude of the debt, the price of our independence," he wrote in his diary. "When, however, we cast our eyes upon the vast regions of the exuberant interior, that debt will dwindle into a shadow, compared with the avails of the millions of fertile acres, which have never yet been disturbed by the plough."

In February he wrote to Dr. François Cossoul, whom he had met at Nantes but who was then staying in Quimper in Brittany. Elkanah proposed that Cossoul come to Nantes so they could enter into a business partnership.[14] "I think we may put our heads together and make a little penny on shore this winter, as well as shipping goods." Elkanah had hired a servant he called by the name "La Fleur" in imitation of Laurence Sterne's humorously nicknamed servant in *A Sentimental Journey*, the Flower of Humanity. Like the almost fictional character in Sterne's book, Elkanah's friendly young man lacked any previous training but demonstrated an eagerness to learn. Elkanah taught him to assist in the practical tasks of the Atlantic shipping brokerage as well as to be his valet and fetch-all.

Elkanah had moved out of the college into the home of a "venerable old priest by the name of Falagan, who lives with his sister and niece." Father Falagan invited Elkanah to attend a peasant wedding party. The "wooden-shoe gentry" of the village gathered in a cottage in the evening, "merrily dancing and singing as a substitute for the violin, with light hearts and heavy heels." Everyone danced, including the Abbé and Elkanah. "Madame bride, in her sabots, or wooden shoes, was only distinguished by a bouquet, which her swain, in great gallantry placed over her heart. Their manner of dancing is much like that of the Indians of America," recorded Elkanah, "but much more animated. We stamped around, hand-in-hand, all singing a dancing tune, advancing and retiring, and, at the close of every cadence, giving a general yell, their wooden shoes clattering the while in concert." Their jolliness made Elkanah wonder if these peasants should not rather be envied than pitied. "If happiness depends upon freedom from care and buoyancy of heart, the French peasantry have the advantage of every other race. Ambition they have none; they aspire to nothing but what they possess: their cottage, their wives, and children, black bread, and the 'petit vin du pays.'" But this simple happiness relieved "ignorance and degradation" that was "the worst political feature of the institutions of France," where the peasants were "deprived of the rights of freehold property, shut out from rank in the army and navy, living on the coarsest fare, and [were] the mere slaves of a proud noblesse and corrupt clergy." Nonetheless, Elkanah persisted in reporting only "content and happiness" when describing the diet and circumstances of French peasants. Revolution? Not yet.

To please the priest where they were lodging, Elkanah and another American student named Wanton Casey went weekly to mass.[15] They were, wrote Elkanah, "often witnesses of the nonsense, superstition, and ceremony in the church, crossing themselves with ashes, kissing the floor, each others feet, etc. etc." He also took long walks in the hills, accompanied by priests ("the black-gowned gentry") who hoped to convert him.[16]

Before lent, there seemed to be competition among the villagers in who could be happiest. During lent, "all is melancholy and devotion, and we are obliged to submit to roots, eggs, and fish. In this we are good catholics par force." Casey and he once escaped to Nantes where they could get something better to eat. But to his Protestant sensibilities, the disappearance of a twelve-year-old girl into a convent where she would eventually become a nun represented the worst effects of superstition. He also saw two sisters, one taking vows to be a nun for life, the other beginning a probationary year. "My God! Is it possible! The unnatural approbation of a father and mother, to the burial of two charming daughters, in this gloomy retreat, is a violation of the laws of God and nature."

Elkanah continued to develop contacts that might help his business ventures. Through Jonathan Williams, the American consul, he could participate in every shipment for the revolutionary cause. To expand his contacts, he took the liberty of writing to John Adams, who had returned to France.[17] Introducing himself as just beginning his commercial activities, Elkanah reminded John Adams of his past friendship with Elkanah's father and of Adams' acquaintance with the respectable position of the Watson family. A letter from Adams could help. He mentioned his trip in 1777–1778, "a complete tour of the 13 American states, where I established such a general chain of connections with the most respectable houses as I think will eventually secure me the most brilliant success in this quarter." His motives were not merely mercenary, he assured Adams. His greater goal was to act so as "to have it amply in my power to stretch out a benevolent hand to the relief of my distressed countrymen and friends."

John Adams responded in April with recognition (although he did not recall their having met on ships passing in Boston harbor). He gave free avuncular advice.[18]

Paris, Hotel de Valois, Rue de Richelieu April 30, 1780
Sir,

Your letter of the 10th March I rec'd but yesterday, I recollect that Genl. Warren mentioned to me his having given you letters to me, but I cannot recollect seeing those letters; I am obligd to you for writing to me, & if it should be in my power to be of any service to you it will give me pleasure to do it although I have not the satisfaction to know you personally I have been so long from home & so much longer from Plymouth, that it is impossible for me to say any thing of your character, but this that I doubt not it is good, having no cause to suspect otherwise. Your family I know very well to be one of the most respectable in the county of Plymouth.

Your Father I had the honor to know very well & I know that he was in those days universally respected to have an independent hereditary fortune, which I have no doubt he still possesses undiminish'd, very probably with large additions to it by the profits of business, I know too that in ancient times (for I must talk to you like an old man) when the friends to the American cause were not so numerous, nor so determin'd as they are now, we always, found your father firm & consistent as a friend to his country. This I know for more than 10 Years before the commencement of the war, & therefore have no difficulty in believing that he has been since that period uniformly strenuous in support of Independence.

You tell me Sir you wish to cultivate your manners before you begin your travels, & since you have had so much confidence in me, as to write to me upon this occasion permit me to take the liberty of advising you to cultivate the manners of your own country not those of Europe; I don't mean by this, that you should put on a long face, never dance with the ladies, go to a play, or take a game of cards.

But you may depend upon this, that the more decisively you adhere to a manly simplicity, in your dress, equipage, & behaviour, the more you devote yourself to business & study, & the less to dissipation & pleasure, the more you will recommend yourself to every man & woman in this country whose friendship & acquaintance is worth your having or wishing. There is an Urbanity without ostentation, or extravagance which will succeed every where & at all times. You will excuse this freedom on account of my friendship for your father & consequently for you, & because I know that some young Gentlemen have come to Europe with different sentiments, & have consequently injur'd the character of their country, as well as their own, both here & at Home. All Europe knows that is [sic] was American manners that have produc'd such great effects from that young & tender country. I should be glad to hear from you as often as you please & to receive from you any intelligence from America or elsewhere & to meet you in Paris.

I am with much respect
Sir your most obedient & hble St.
Mr Elk.h Watson
At Nantes
                John Adams

Their contact would continue for decades. Within a few years it would be John Adams who guided Elkanah around Holland.

That winter Elkanah also met Louis Littlepage, who had stopped at Nantes in February, 1780. He was en route from America to Madrid, where he was to work for John Jay, America's emissary to the Spanish court. Littlepage was considered a youthful genius. He eventually became secretary in the cabinet of the king of Poland, functioning as prime minister.

Watson also corresponded with his sisters in America and with acquaintances who had moved away. Dr. Casey, with whom he had studied French and who had become ill, left for Angers, where he hoped to regain his health. Elkanah wrote to him about mutual friends.[19] "You remember the old officer, our neighbour Bouchez, was upon the point of leaving us for his country place?" Elkanah had received an invitation to spend a few days there, "in company with an elder lady and her niece, a genteel accomplished young demoiselle about 18." The trip downstream along the Loire had just begun when a gust of wind and a cloudburst drenched them. "The old lady fell upon her knees and implored the protection of heaven, and then in an instant made an attempt to huddle herself into a little cabin just calculated for one person." But she got stuck in the doorway, having given no thought to her own bulk. "Indeed my dear Casey, I wish you could have been with me. You know the French young are exceeding coy before marriage. Had it not been for the gust, it would have taken me an eternity to have made the same advances I did. We had no alternative but to weather out the storm in the open boat; it was the most fortunate circumstance in the world, I brought my scarlet cloak with me, which in this situation served more than one purpose, good heavens! Nothing could have produced a more happy effect—politeness, civility, and in short every impulse obliged me to offer all my cloak to a delicate young lady, who stood shivering and wet before my eyes. I importuned. 'Ma foi, Monsieur!' No she was not cold, and could dry herself when we arrived. After a long preamble with my cloak in my hand, doing nothing when it might have saved us both dry skins, the preliminaries were thus settled, that the cloak should be to our mutual advantage. Agreed!—but as our situation justified making the most of it, and as there was no stipulation to the contrary, I arranged the part appertaining to Madamoiselle by extending my arm in a circumference round her shoulders, the other being sheltered under the cloak with hers. By close manoeuvering, after several repulses and sallies, I succeeded to link our fingers together. Thus supremely happy, we dropped down the Loire and arrived at Champtoceaux just at dark."

After dinner at the home of the young lady's uncle, the two of them "carelessly strolled in a fine spacious garden behind the house. Unperceived and undesigned, we tacked from alley to alley till we found ourselves in the grove at the foot of the garden, from whence by a winding path we were imperceptibly led into a little arbour upon the summit of a mountain, which precipitated itself almost perpendicular into the Loire. From this elevation we commanded the richest view I ever yet beheld." Nantes was one direction, Angers another, with the Loire and "cities, towns, seats, islands, plains, meadows, fields, vineyards, & forests within our view." But Elkanah's thoughts were elsewhere, "when I recollected the golden moments chance had put in my power—We remained in this celestial situation about half an hour, & then hurried back.... But there was a hue and cry out after us from every quarter. I know my good friend your amorous constitution will lead you to suggest a thousand unfair conclusions, by the time you get through this letter, but be merciful and charitable. Appearances, I confess, are unfavourable but "—"—"—"— [sic]."

Watson, Tom Paine and American Sculptor Patience Lovell Wright

Elkanah spent the summer doing nothing, or so he said in a brief letter to his friend Casey.[20] Elkanah told a different story to his sister Priscilla. He'd been earnestly comforting the young French widow of an American buried at sea. The future, he hoped, would reward his business endeavors sufficiently for him to "marry the object of [his] bonheur" (felicity), travel with her throughout Europe, and eventually return in wealth to a peaceful America. Somehow this dream that excited his sisters with expectations of a refined French sister-in-law disintegrated—leaving the girls with sympathy for their unlucky brother, who had already been disappointed when a Plymouth woman he had hoped would await his eventual return fell in love and married someone else.[21]

In September, 1780, Captain Sampson arrived with the ship *Mars* from America. He asked Elkanah to go with him to Paris for reasons of "material importance."[22] What that business was is unrecorded; it could have marked the beginning of Elkanah's involvement in political action in France and England—his involvement in negotiating the release of Americans imprisoned in England, for example, or his role in communicating America's vision for peace to England's prime minister in the deliberations that finally produced an end to the war. The visit was only six days; they were back in Nantes on September 27.[23]

Priscilla had asked her brother to have a miniature portrait "taken." He wrote to her in October, "whether my phiz is any degree metamorphosed since leaving America, you'll be able to decide when I assure you that you see me exactly as I appear every day in Nantes streets.... Every one pronounces the portrait well finish'd & a perfect resemblance—a circumstance yesterday confirm'd this general assertion to me beyond a doubt—It was shewn to 2 little children who had seen me before, & who at ye 1st glance said it was Monsieur le Bostonian." He sent Priscilla the portrait, along with ten yards of callico and three "beautiful Itallian aprons."[24]

At the end of the year, Elkanah decided to spend the winter at Rennes. John Brown had cautioned him to stick to reality and not build "imaginary castles in a wavering cloud." In a letter to his former master he assured him that by "adhering uniformly to the three grand pillars of Virtue, Justice, and Decent Oeconomy" he felt certain of "accumulating a fortune in the course of a few years."[25] Taking a long view, he thought he should devote the next thirty years to business and then have twenty more "to devote to my independence and ease." His ambitions seem inspired by those of the young Benjamin Franklin, who retired from business at the age of forty-two to devote his life to science and public utility.[26] In any case, Elkanah hoped to be financially secure and independent by age thirty. In the meantime, he'd study French some more and come back to Nantes in the spring when trade again increased. He promised his sister Patty that he'd write more frequently during the winter.[27] He praised her imaginativeness. "I have a thousand times thought it a pity that you should not cultivate your natural genius," he complained, before expansively judging it "unpardonable in our New England parents, the neglect of the ladies' educations. Few of them to my certain knowledge have the least comprehension of the geographical situation of any other country under the canopy of heaven than the country they inhabit, and perhaps even that not beyond their horizon.... When a latent genius is smothered in obscurity and struggles in spite of itself to shoot forth, nothing but poverty can justify their guardians in the eyes of heaven."[28]

Rennes, the capital of Brittany, had a reputation for the purity of the French spoken there. Elkanah hoped to gain polish in his language, if not in his manners. French ease and elegance he thought required habit and training from childhood onward. The friendliness that marked relations between the generations of families struck him as notably preferable to the stiff austerity and reserve of New England custom. "I have, more than once, seen grandmothers dancing in the same circles as grandchildren," he commented with approval. But the society in town, while well mannered, was insanely given to gambling, and the newest card game was called "Boston." As the first American ever to visit the city, he attracted plenty of attention and was invited out as a curiosity. Surely he'd be good at a game called Boston. One beautiful young gambler demanded that Elkanah be her partner, assuming that his protestations of inexperience marked the modesty of a skilled sophisticate. On perceiving his true incompetence and suffering the real loss of bets, she was happy to release him from the table.

The death of Empress Maria Theresia, Queen of Hungary, Archduchess of Austria, was marked in Rennes with the expectation that all gentlemen would wear mourning attire. Elkanah bought what was needed and complied. Formal condolences were expressed at official receptions. No one questioned whether these gestures in Rennes bore any effective relation to circumstances outside the town of Rennes, including political changes in Vienna. No one asked anyone else about the intensity of personal sense of loss at the passing away of that distant political presence among the Hapsburgs, even though she had been the mother of Queen Marie Antoinette. Custom dictated action. A French colonel brought Elkanah to present his sentiments of respect to the governor of the province. Admitted to a palace, Elkanah found himself in the company of "an extensive circle of dukes, governors, bishops, officers, etc." One of them was Admiral Toussaint-Guillaume Piquet de la Motte, who had recently distinguished himself in America at the battle of Grenada under d'Estaing. The French view of the war against Britain encompassed not only the mainland colonies but also the islands in the Caribbean as well. Elkanah, the only American most people there had seen, was presented to the Duchess of Brittany. "The etiquette was, to advance a few steps, with chapeay-bras under the left arm, and make a profound bow. A long sword at the side was an indispensable article of dress in fashionable society." Elkanah had prepared himself properly. Progressing through a sequence of public rooms, where the ladies amusingly had to shift their enormous bustles sideways to pass through the doors, the guests reached a dining hall, "cheered by an elegant Italian band of music." Elkanah was seated at the head of the table next to the three officials, the Marshal, the Governor of Belle Ile, and the Governor of Rennes. Around forty people were served a dinner with, he thought, at least forty different courses, presented in dishes of solid silver. A centerpiece on the table formed a miniature flower garden, "with Liliputian statues, flowers, grottos, artificial cascades, etc."

Coffee after dinner was served in another room, again with musical accompaniment. This hall opened out to the garden, where guests could stroll. The Duchess paid special attention to the American and saw to it that he was presented with "delicious dishes, by the hands of a little pet black boy, always at her elbow." An aviary filled with songbirds captured the charms of nature's music. Without formality, people returned to the hall "and such as were disposed took themselves off [without saying goodbye], or, in other words, took 'French leave.'" Again Elkanah had discovered a custom whose introduction in the New World he thought would only serve to improve American manners.

He returned to Nantes with great improvement to his French—enough to serve as an interpreter. Elkanah's skills were put to the test when the frigate *Alliance* arrived at the port of l'Orient (a hundred miles northwest from Nantes) in March, 1781. The ship brought Colonel John Laurens, sent by Congress to try to arrange for more financial aid from the French government, and, with him, Tom Paine, who was to serve as his secretary. Laurens proceeded directly to Paris, but, on the advice of Elkanah's friend the consul Jonathan Williams, Paine came to Nantes and moved into the same boarding house as Watson.

Famous he was—internationally famous for his tract *Common Sense* that came out in 1776 and helped focus ideas in favor of revolt. *Le Sens Commun*, a French translation, had appeared the same year, published in Rotterdam but distributed throughout Europe. Nonetheless, in person, Paine "was coarse and uncouth in his manners, loathsome in his appearance, and a disgusting egotist; rejoicing most in talking of himself, and reading the effusions of his own mind."[29] The Mayor of Nantes and other leading citizens came to visit as soon as they heard that the great thinker had come to their town. What these French-speakers made of Paine's reading in English remains a riddle.

Elkanah served as Paine's interpreter, although "humbled and mortified" at his filthy appearance and awkward address. "Besides," remarked the prim New Englander, "as he had been roasted alive at L'Orient," when he arrived in port, "for the, ... and well basted with brimstone, he was absolutely offensive and perfumed the whole apartment."[30] Brimstone was another name for sulfur dioxide, used in this particular medical treatment for syphilis—what could be more effective than the smell of rotten eggs and pervasive farts? The visitors soon departed, "with marks of astonishment and disgust."

Paine resolutely refused Elkanah's pleas that he take a hot bath until Elkanah hit on the idea of withholding English-language newspapers from his visitor until after he'd been cleaned up. He could have the newspapers once he was seated in the tub! In French, which Paine couldn't follow, Watson instructed the bath-keeper to raise the temperature of the bath gradually until "le Monsieur serait bien bouilli" (the gentleman would be well boiled). Catching up on the news while sitting in the bath, Paine "became so much absorbed in his reading that he was nearly par-boiled before leaving the bath, much to his improvement." Now, then, a

An American privateer capturing a British packet boat (etching by S. Fokke after H. Kobell, 1777).

change of clothes would help—if Paine must wear the badges of lost innocence, they should at least smell clean.

Tom Paine's pithy pronouncements in *Common Sense* had startled Europe. "There is something exceedingly ridiculous in the composition of Monarchy." "It is the pride of kings which throws mankind into confusion. Holland, without a king hath enjoyed more peace for this last century than any of the monarchical governments in Europe." "For all men being originally equals, no one by birth could have a right to set up his own family in perpetual preference to all others for ever." "One of the strongest natural proofs of the folly of hereditary right in Kings, is that nature disapproves it, otherwise she would not so frequently turn it into ridicule, by giving mankind an ASS FOR A LION." "Of more worth is one honest man to society, and in the sight of God, than all the crowned ruffians that ever lived." "As to religion, I hold it to be the indispensable duty of government to protect all conscientious professors thereof, and I know of no other business which government hath to do therewith.... For myself, I fully and conscientiously believe that it is the will of the Almighty that there should be a diversity of religious opinions among us. It affords a larger field for our Christian kindness; were we all of one way of thinking, our religious dispositions would want matter for probation; and on this liberal principle I look on the various denominations among us to be like children of the same family, differing only in what is called their Christian names."

Elkanah remembered how the publication of Paine's pamphlet had catalyzed opinion in Providence in 1776, giving coherence and strength to Whig arguments that before had been met with abhorrence. Elkanah even credited Paine's publication with having "aroused a determined spirit, which resulted in the Declaration of Independence upon the 4th of July ensuing." Now he was encouraged and inspired again by his conversations with the great revolutionary. And it got him into trouble.

The French decided to send Admiral François Joseph de Grasse and his fleet to help the Americans against the British. De Grasse's presence would play a major role in the defeat of Cornwallis at Yorktown in October later in the year. The Minister of the French Navy, the Marshal de Castries, passed through Nantes in March, 1781, on his way to the coast to bid farewell to de Grasse and the fleet. Elkanah joined the crowds who filled the streets to see the high officials go by in their elaborate coaches with liveried drivers and servants. Unrelated to the public festivity, but just as the procession was about to pass by, a door opened in a church across the road. A priest emerged from shadows, bearing a monstrance displaying a consecrated communion wafer, or Host. A little boy came first, ringing a bell; then, under a canopy held up by four men, the priest walked holding up the sacrament; "forty or fifty stupid peasants, in wooden shoes, followed." They were on their way across the street to visit someone who was dying and about to receive last rites. By tradition, everyone present was expected to kneel as the wafer passed by, but because of deep mud, most merely leaned on canes, took off their hats, and bowed their heads. The couriers and coaches for the visiting dignitaries came to a halt to allow the priest and his procession to cross the road. The priest directed his steps to come stop right in front of Elkanah: the infidel had been recognized! "Pointing directly at me with his finger, he exclaimed, 'Aux genoux' (upon your knees)." Elkanah excused himself; there was so much mud, and no one else was kneeling. The priest insisted, "in a voice of thunder, 'Aux genoux.'" The irritated Yankee replied in French, "No, Sir, I will not." The crowd pressed in, threatening violence, enraged at Elkanah's insult to their sacrament. A nearby friend of Elkanah's urged him, "For God's sake, drop in an instant." Aware of his sudden, real danger, he wrote later in his diary that he had "reluctantly settled my knees into a mud-puddle." Polite people, both Catholic and Protestant, "condemned the rash and inexcusable conduct of the priest." Here was none of the denominational variety and tolerance praised by Paine.

The next day, still enraged, Elkanah located the priest's home and forced his way into the man's study. Claiming diplomatic protection as a friend of Benjamin Franklin's, Elkanah commanded the priest to apologize to him in the same position—on his knees. Threatening further legal action through the American consulate and a formal complaint to the bishop, Elkanah without delay reported the event to Colonel Williams, the consul whose wedding he had attended at St. Germain. Both Williams and Tom Paine insisted that Elkanah change his address, to avoid reprisals from angry priests and their ignorant followers. At their urging he kept indoors for a couple of weeks and let the matter rest without further action. Enlightenment had not yet reached the folk of Nantes, and the number of people who had read *Le Sens Commun* was small.

Tom Paine moved on to Paris at this time, involved in negotiations for French aid to America. Elkanah may have served as his interpreter in Paris, as he had in Nantes, although John Laurens might have put himself forward for the task. Laurens had just enough French to make diplomatic mistakes that came across as unprecedented impertinence—even haranguing the king himself. Benjamin Franklin kept busy calming offended Frenchmen, while supervising Paine's work at composing convincing pleas for support against England. However the negotiation was accomplished, whoever accomplished what, whether Franklin, Laurens, or Paine, by summer the French had granted six million livres as a gift in honor of Franklin's efforts, and they offered to guarantee ten million as a loan, if the Americans could obtain that amount borrowing from Dutch sources. This came in addition to the assistance of the fleet under Admiral de Grasse. But it was not the amount Congress had sent Laurens to obtain, and the Dutch loan had not yet been arranged when Laurens returned to America.[31]

Some of the gift consisted in equipment and uniforms for thousands of soldiers. Elkanah helped arrange the shipping, and for that he needed to travel back and forth between the capital and the coast. In Paris, Paine probably accompanied Elkanah to Masonic meetings, at least those generally open to the public. Paine was at least sympathetic to the Masons, although whether he joined remains unknown. Of course, as a Brother, Elkanah did not divulge what went on in the meetings. Benjamin Franklin and Elkanah Watson, and probably Tom Paine, must in any case have heard the music of the Paris Masonic orchestra led by the composer, Joseph Bologne, the Chavalier de St. George. Renowned for the Mozartian quality of his music, as well as famous as the greatest living fencer, the Chevalier de St. George glittered in Parisian society. He was also one of two classical composers at the time whose great accomplishments and (half) African ancestry contradicted European expectations of racial inferiority. (The other was Ignatius Sancho, a composer living in London whose widow Elkanah later met.) Racist antagonism to this master violinist, composer, and swordsman was off-set by the generous welcome by Masons who prided themselves on their clear-sighted rejection of superstition and irrationality. (Paine later ridiculed absurd claims of Masonic antiquity that contrasted mightily with Masons' self-satisfied claims to be guided by Reason.)

The Chevalier de St. George's Olympic Lodge Orchestra—sixty to seventy musicians, all Masons—performed in the Palais Royal: not only his own music but also new pieces by Haydn and other composers, probably including Mozart.

Watson had seen the Palais Royal during his earlier visit to Paris. He bought an engraving depicting the building, but he was more pleased by the gardens than by the building and its art collections. Yet the gardens shocked him. "The 'Palais Royal,' belonging to the Duc de Chartres, of the Royal family," he wrote in his diary, "was but a mass of moral corruption." More than a hundred shops had been set up in the arcaded walkway around the public gardens, and people came there not only to buy books or silk ribbons but also to choose prostitutes who invitingly leaned against the balustrades and vacantly winked from the shaded archways.

A woman to whom Elkanah could legitimately pay attention was Patience Lovell Wright, America's first professional sculptor. "Her complexion was somewhat sallow; her cheekbones, high; her face, furrowed; and her olive eyes keen, piercing, and expressive. Her sharp glance was appalling; it had almost the wildness of a maniac's." Her "features, walk, and manner were half Indian." Born in New Jersey, she achieved fame for her sculptured portraits in wax. Elkanah had been calling down from his hotel balcony to give orders to his English servant in August, 1781, when he heard a voice from a balcony in the attic story above. "Who are you?

An American?" On hearing that he was, indeed, Mrs. Wright came downstairs and introduced herself "with the familiarity of an old acquaintance." She knew everyone, all the Americans in Paris at any rate; and she visited Benjamin Franklin almost daily. With highly original opinions, she spoke vigorously and rapidly, uttering "language, in her incessant volubility, as if unconscious to whom directed, often putting young men to the blush."

She had met Franklin in London around the year 1767. Her studio in Pall Mall had become a fashionable lounging-place for her sitters and their friends, "the nobility and distinguished men of England." Superficially an uncomplicated, forthright woman, "her deep penetration and sagacity, cloaked by her apparent simplicity of purpose, enabled her to gather many facts and secrets important to 'dear America,'" as she always called her native country. Mrs. Wright produced several of the royal portraits among the waxworks displayed at Westminster Abbey, although only hers of William Pitt the Elder survives. The king and queen, according to Watson, "often visited her rooms; they would induce her to work upon her heads, regardless of their presence. She would often, as if forgetting herself, address them as George and Charlotte." She mentioned that circumstance to Elkanah more than once, evidently quite pleased with this display of Whiggish egalitarianism. She left London when the Revolutionary war started, having until then provided information about cabinet secrets and other political gossip to Benjamin Franklin for the American government, a dangerous life "by which she was placed in positions of extreme hazard."

Elkanah and Mrs. Wright exchanged tales of Benjamin Franklin's notorious sexual liaisons. But when Elkanah later began to write down what he himself had seen of Franklin's Paris affairs, he started bravely, allowed himself to be distracted by reminiscences of Mrs. Wright, then changed his mind and decided, after all, not to provide salacious details of Franklin's experiments in natural philosophy.[32]

Mrs. Wright asked Elkanah to act as her interpreter when she learned that an "eminent female chemist of Paris" who spoke no English (as she herself spoke no French) intended to call on her at noon the next day. With her "sharp nose, and with broad patches of vermillion daubed over the deep furrows of her cheeks," the visitor was "an old weathered dry'd up hag." Elkanah sat between the two ladies, each talking at a quick rate, but had no chance of translating or coordinating an orderly conversation. Suddenly he ordered "silence for a moment!" He asked each woman if she had understood what had been said. "Not a word," was Mrs. Wright's response; the French woman had also comprehended nothing. She got up, curtseyed, and left. "What an old monkey!" exclaimed Mrs. Wright. Clearly the visit served some concept of formal politeness but had nothing to do with any exchange of opinions or ideas.

Elkanah commissioned Mrs. Wright to make a portrait head of Benjamin Franklin, a process that included several sittings at Franklin's house in Passy. At a late stage in the modeling, she took the head wrapped in a napkin out to Passy for comparison with the great man she was attempting to portray. In the evening, returning to the city, she was stopped by customs officers who wanted to search for tax evasion on imports. She became infuriated, not comprehending why she should be stopped. She was sure she carried nothing dutiable. But she spoke no French. She had to give in; the officers unwrapped the wax head and, searching by lamplight, thought they found the severed head of a man just murdered. They'd stumbled on a dangerous lunatic escaped from some asylum, probably. They decided to lock her up for the night. Somehow she indicated that she should be brought to the Hotel de York. Aroused by the noise of her unorthodox return, Elkanah interrupted his journal writing and intervened, eventually re-establishing peace. Everyone else was amused, but not Mrs. Wright.

Soon after, the portrait sculpture being completed, the two of them took it to Passy where they had been invited for dinner. Holding the bust next to Franklin himself, she proclaimed, "There are twin brothers!" Mrs. Wright had the idea that the effect of the sculpture would be improved if clothed in something appropriate. Elkanah approached William Temple Franklin (who acted as an aide to his grandfather Benjamin) with a request for "a suit of your Grandfather's Old Cloaths, that never can be of any service to him, or any Body else—to be plain—Madam Wright, has fabricated (I think) a most striking Likeness of him in Wax in my Possession—which I wish to sitt up in my Study—dressed in his own Cloaths."[33] Benjamin Franklin, evidently amused, sent Elkanah "a suit of silk clothes which he wore in 1778."[34]

When he returned to Nantes, Elkanah took Franklin's clothing and the bust with him. Thinking of the effects of the Parisian waxworks portrayal of Voltaire, he set up the clothed sculpture of Franklin in the corner of his sitting room, next to a closet from which wires were arranged so that someone in hiding could move the arms of the model. He laid out an open atlas, some compasses, and mathematical instruments on the table. "Thus arranged, some ladies and gentlemen were invited to pay their respects to Dr. Franklin, by candle-light." Everyone

Elkanah introducing the French to Wax Franklin (engraving by Barritt after Lossing, in *Men and Times of the Revolution*, 1861, p. 116).

bowed or curtsied in formal greeting on entering to make a visit to the famous American. The figure, moved by wires, bowed in return. But the sculpture's silence gave the joke away. The first group to be fooled, however, found it amusing enough to inform the mayor, so that he could come present himself to the visiting great man. He arrived "in full dress, to call on the renowned philosopher." Elkanah's partner Cossoul knew the mayor, and they could laugh together. People who had been fooled brought in their friends for the same experience. Later Elkanah successfully tried the same trick in London. He even contrived to connect the figure with some electrical apparatus, as if Franklin continued to experiment on his famous discoveries.[35]

Watson returned to Paris for a couple of months in the summer and autumn of 1781. On the way he spent a night at La Flèche, where the parish priest offered hospitality. He was a former soldier who had become ordained in later life. A supporter of the American cause, to him, Elkanah was "a Bostone, and an ally." He wanted to hear everything he could about George Washington, "Le grand Vas-sang-ton." In the morning, with no success, the priest attempted to convert Elkanah from his Protestant views to those of Rome, all most cordially and without any demand that he kneel in the muck.

An alternate road brought Elkanah the opportunity to visit the monastery at La Trappe for yet another view of Catholicism. The coach looped north from Le Mans to the monastery and then down again to Dreux, to continue on the more familiar road. At the Trappist monastery, Elkanah was given breakfast—a small amount of "meat, roots, bread, and cider." The monks "drink no wine, and abstain even from eggs and fish." Their diet consisted of cider, black bread, roots without butter or olive oil, "occasionally, beans or light soup, with a dessert of two apples." Such austerity, he thought, "would be insupportable by the human frame, unless sustained by their extravagant fanaticism, or, possibly, earnest devotion." The complete silence of the Trappist rule was considered most extraordinary. Elkanah was so disconcerted by the strangeness of this existence that he had no taste for sightseeing for the rest of the journey to Paris. What had these men found so far from rationality? They weren't saying.

The Austrian emperor Joseph II of Hapsburg-Lothringen visited Paris incognito at this time, calling himself the Count of Lille. The deception was moderate at best. Elkanah saw him in Paris, perhaps at some Masonic occasion. He admired the emperor marred by "extravagant and eccentric peculiarities." Elkanah had heard of the emperor's governmental reforms and especially praised his having "suppressed several orders of monks, as so many nuisances to society, a loathsome fungus hanging on the body politic, mere drones in the hive." Such measures gave hope to Elkanah that the American Revolution's influence for good would help enflame "this dawn of light which is evidently kindling up in the European hemisphere."

In Nantes and in Paris, the business of importing and exporting kept him busy, although much of the work could be carried on by letter. A variety of freight included tobacco from America and clothing from France for American soldiers, shipped in quantities in the thousands.[36] Brandy exported by Watson and Cossoul found buyers in England and America. The transactions also allowed him the liberty to give free passage on one of his ships to America to Joseph Wright, the son of Patience Wright. Joseph, eventually known for his portraits of George Washington, was an artist who, like his mother, had worked in London.

As early as October, 1780, Elkanah carried on business correspondence with John de Neufville in Amsterdam, who conveyed Elkanah's greetings to John Adams, America's agent in Holland.[37] De Neufville had the reputation of being Amsterdam's richest merchant. In earlier generations, his family's business activities had extended from St. Petersburg to the Mediterranean. John de Neufville provided mortgages for slave plantations in Suriname, besides carrying out business in various European and American ports. He had been the main effective force in bringing about the initial secret agreement by which Amsterdam and Holland chose to support the American Revolution. Documents about this had been in Henry Laurens' possession when the British captured him. De Neufville financed John Paul Jones's stay in Amsterdam in 1779. He also kept Benjamin Franklin informed of Jones's Amsterdam activities while in port to refit for more raiding on ships around the British Isles. De Neufville hoped to be the principal Dutch financial agent for America, and he drew up proposals by which the interest on Dutch loans could be paid by the shipment to Holland of American products. De Neufville became one of the principal bankers who put together the loans negotiated by Adams to finance the American cause, although he remained independent of the firm created to take care of the later developments, moving to Bonn in 1783 (leaving his son Leendert to run the business in Amsterdam). In 1785 de Neufville moved to Boston, then to Albany.

Much of Elkanah's correspondence pursued various bank drafts and checks from or to Americans. In November, 1780, for example, Watson asked de Neufville to forward an enclosed letter to an American, Mr. Joseph Gridley, and to take care of a bill for him, either accepting it, negotiating it, or passing it on to Elkanah's company. Gridley, as Elkanah informed de Neufville, was "a gentleman of a good family in Boston and a particular acquaintance of mine. Any civilities you may show him will be gratefully acknowledged by me."[38] The transfer of large amounts of money, as well as the payment for negotiated cargo, and the cashing of checks involved many brief letters sent all over Europe. On March 28, 1781, Watson wrote to Franklin asking him to take care of payment for a small check, dated December 28 the previous year, that had been forwarded but was considered lost. On May 20, the company of Watson and Cossoul wrote again to inform Franklin that the bank had subsequently found the missing check.[39]

As the firm's prosperity increased, Elkanah could give financial aid to people he knew in America where actions of war had reduced friends to poverty or distress. He also contributed funds to relieve captured American military officers jailed in Mill Prison near Plymouth in England. In his memoires Elkanah mentioned having helped in the prison escape of Colonel Silas Talbot and Captain Smeadley. In fact, the "escape" from prison was accomplished by a negotiated exchange of prisoners. Talbot was released and arrived in Cherbourg. From there he came up to Paris, no doubt visiting Watson again on the way. Talbot had been the captain of one of John Brown's ships, the privateer *George Washington*. She had harried English warships along the American coast. Watson kept a letter written from prison by Talbot in August, 1781, thanking him for sending twenty-five guineas, as well as for writing to Mrs. Talbot to let her know her husband's situation.[40]

The correspondence could mix commercial interests with more personal. In March, 1781, Elkanah wrote to his relative Winslow Warren, then at Amsterdam. Winslow had just written to him a week and a half earlier. Elkanah let him know that until recently he'd had a packet of letters for him from Winslow's father, General James Warren, the Plymouth revolutionary and husband of the historian Mercy Otis Warren (Winslow's mother). Captain Sampson had taken the letters from Elkanah to deliver them back in America, because, until Winslow's letter had arrived in Nantes, no one knew he was in Europe. Elkanah told Winslow that if he came to Nantes, he'd meet some of his countrymen, including Samuel Bradford, who sent his greetings. Elkanah offered to be Winslow Warren's agent if he should want to invest in anything to be sent back to America for a profit. The firm of Watson and Cossoul employed four French clerks and three from London, with ten ships nearly loaded and ready to sail from the Loire. "I am now shipped very largely upon every bottom abound for the several parts of the Continent," Watson commented with undisguised pride.[41]

Letters also communicated the latest news of the progress of the war. On March 5, 1781, two days after he'd written to Winslow Warren, Elkanah sent a letter to John de Neufville & Son in Amsterdam. He reported that the story that mutiny had broken out among the Pennsylvania revolutionary soldiers, said to be dissatisfied about lack of pay or "some grievance," proved to be an inaccurate rumor. True, they had decided to demand their due, but they'd done so in an orderly way, calmed by the Marquis de Lafayette and the president of Pennsylvania, Joseph Reed. Two soldiers had indeed argued for joining the British if the Americans wouldn't pay, "but the idea was so repugnant to the body, that they hung the proposers upon the first tree, a startling proof of virtue even by the injured as any heaven can accord it." Elkanah complimented the Dutch for their support of American independence. He was looking forward to "a firm and solid peace founded upon the basis of Liberty and Independence—and an unlimited trade with the universe." And, by the way, he added, "Pray make my compliments to Mr. Warren."[42]

With expansive ideas of universal improvement, and imagining himself a leader in the march toward enlightenment, Elkanah wrote down some of his observations of the contrasts between France and America and sent them off to be printed and distributed among his countrymen.[43] Some customs were reasonable, he said; others were not, being purely arbitrary fashions. "Those who have only vegetated beneath the smoke of their native land seldom discover any improprieties or imperfections in customs become familiar by habit. But an observing traveler, who posts through other regions, emancipated from the shackles of his youth, with a mind open to conviction, discovers at once the absurdities of his own country, as well as those he traverses."

Now that he had reached the age of twenty-three and had through his extensive travels acquired wisdom as well as experience, Elkanah was ready to dispense advice. Contrary to the prejudices taught him in his youth, he had discovered the French were not bone-sucking frogs whose manners consisted of the gestures of face-pulling apes. The French knew the secret of good living. They had dispensed with "the ridiculous habit of drinking healths at table." Only the lower classes still did that sort of thing. An acknowledgement to the hostess was sufficient without glass after glass raised to honor ever more far-fetched topics or persons. The French custom of leaving social gatherings without making a fuss was preferable, too, he thought, to whatever passed for politeness in Providence. Most uncivilized, however, was the common American habit for young fellows to demonstrate their good nature by getting drunk. "In France, no gentleman gets drunk; he would be debarred, and forever discarded from the society of virtuous females. None but the dregs of community are thus degraded." Perhaps Elkanah imagined he was following in the footsteps of Poor Richard. No doubt his sage advice, if indeed anyone published it in 1781, could have contributed to an improvement of manners in the encampments of the revolutionary army.

Presiding over all the business deals, the composition of platitudes, and the letter writing was the portrait that Patience Wright had modeled of Benjamin Franklin. Attired in the clothes that the diplomat and philosopher had discarded for the fun of it, Franklin's inspirational presence united the commerce, the politics, and the sentiments of America and Europe.

Three

Belgium and England

Belgium, Canals and the Masonic Apron for George Washington

Business slowed in the autumn of 1781. Elkanah decided to explore northern France and the southern Low Countries with his servant La Fleur. His route was somewhat undecided—might even cross the English Channel. Starting from Paris on October 27, the first place a tourist should stop was the abbey church of St. Denis, with France's royal tombs. The innovative gothic architecture must have seemed as "badly executed" as Elkanah had found the grand arches of the cathedral of Notre Dame in Paris. Perhaps he had been more pleased by the cathedral at Rennes, rising in layers of proper columns and capitals—Doric, Ionic, Corinthian, Composite, and something else whose name he'd forgotten, disappearing in indistinctness at the top of the towers as high as any building he'd ever seen.

The chateau at Chantilly, considered "one of the most magnificent palaces" in all Europe, sat surrounded by a decorative moat. Immense stables housed three hundred English race horses. Columns and sculpture also decorated these comfortable dwellings for horses, whose windows had silk curtains. Paintings in the chateau glorified battles—the heroics of the Princes de Condé. Afternoon hours passed by in the contemplation of "marble statues, jets d'eau, cascades, labyrinths, grottos, artificial ponds and islands, canals with pleasure boats, and a thousand other pleasing and enchanting evidences of taste and affluence." Along the ornamental canal, Elkanah "observed ladies seated upon cushions, on the bank, calling the carp up, and feeding them with crumbs of bread."

After spending the night in an inn, Elkanah and La Fleur rode through the prince's forest. Twelve miles of trees hid deer, wild boars, and other animals for the royal family to hunt, forbidden to anyone but nobility. Crossing the Nonette River brought them to Senlis, whose cathedral steeple could be seen for thirty miles. People said that none higher could be found in France. Thick towers of ancient town fortifications contrasted with the stylish garlands and balustrades of Chantilly.

The road north continued through Compiègne and St. Quentin.[1] Town hall tower and massive medieval church could be seen far in the distance over the empty wheat fields. These gothic remnants belonged to a shaded past rejected and ignored in the ongoing construction of the king's simple chateau at Compiègne. Smooth walls, Doric columns and capitals, hardly any sculpture—the severity contrasted not only with gothic architecture but also with the gaiety of Versailles and Chantilly. The romantic conceit that simple, bulky forms expressed virtuously strong simplicity of character marked a revolutionary rejection of the formerly fashionable frills of the rococo style's straggling, broken curves. Whoever lived in such severity must exemplify moral virtue or perhaps military heroism; such, in any case, was the apparent implication, although perhaps this king was not an actor worthy of his stage. In America, republican virtue would speak to itself in newly constructed surroundings that appropriately echoed Greek architectural probity (although perhaps clad in clapboard). The new republic dressed up in the imagined clothing of the ancient democracy.

The massive walls of the ancient fortress of Peronne, too, had nothing to do with modern clarity or elegance. Arriving at night, Elkanah had some difficulty gaining entrance to the city through a series of dark and forbidding defensive gates constructed to withstand assaults by arrows, lances, and catapults.

Leaving the Somme valley the next day, Elkanah moved on toward Cambrai. He stopped at farms or hamlets to feed and water the horses and grease the axles. Wealthier peasants had decorated the archways over wagon entrances to their farmyards with flat pilasters and Doric capitals—a long way from the palace at Chantilly, but distantly related by this gesture of style. With a house to one side and barns around a courtyard, whoever lived in such solid comfort could expect deference, at least in the neighborhood. Many more peasants, however, lived in one-room hovels without courtyards, without arched entrances. Chickens and a pig provided company enough—with luck, also a cow. Hamlets of a cottage or two formed at crossroads. Little more than such isolated settlements could be found for long distances of dusty roads. Village church bells ringing far off might mean funerals, but not of anyone he knew. Horseshoes thudded on the earth of farmland or clicked on stone as the way turned along outcroppings or crossed an arched bridge. Birds flew over fields, greedy for grain still secret under stubble. Trees by streams' last leaves descended, or held on twisting against the sky. Yellow and brown withered pale beneath branches bare for snow.

The countryside ended at the Porte de Paris, an ancient gate in Cambrai's thick stone walls. Smoke rising from brick chimneys conjured up memories of hearths at home. Wealthy abbeys and a mighty cathedral collected their tithes and filled vast barns, waiting for tenants to bring their expected dues. The "cathedral and La Maison de Ville [town hall] are interesting objects," he thought, without describing them further. More attention went to the house of "the great and good Fénelon, the immortal author of *Telemachus*." That novel instructing its hero and its readers in the universal brotherhood of man and the necessity of humanitarian service was a book everyone knew—no need to explain it to Elkanah's friends. Taking the form of an addition to the heroic story of the Iliad, Fénelon's criticism of the autocratic rule of King Louis XIV enjoyed great popularity throughout Europe. Americans unhappy with another king discovered in Fénelon quasi-antique justification for their fine feelings of frustration with British tyranny.

Further north, Douai's monasteries, university, and theological colleges formed a bulwark of dogmatism inimical to Elkanah's self-image of illumination. This was not a place to stay, unless he managed to meet members of the Masonic lodge founded just four years earlier. As if to defend the opinions of earlier generations, the town was strongly walled. The spacious squares of Arras felt more congenial. Public design focused on commerce. The civic steeple's cheerful peal pleased the ears far more than did the chants of monks. America's town greens could learn from the arcaded architecture all around the marketplaces here, sheltering anyone with a mind for trade.

Just before Lens on the road to Lille, they crossed a bridge over a canal. Their road continued near the canal and the Deule canal it joined. Tow-path horses pulled loaded barges to or from Lille. Elkanah imagined how America *c*ould be improved by similar canals—America, "a land or real liberty, and an asylum for all the oppressed nations of Europe." America might be new, but "canals will at some future period be found more useful in that country than in any other, by connecting our extensive inland seas, the most extensive on this globe, with the Atlantic." Elkanah could see himself discovering personally profitable ways to contribute to

Pulling a canal barge (etching by Ch. Jaque).

America's increasing prosperity and international strength. He would pay careful attention to the technical details of canal and lock design and construction in France, England, and Holland.

Lille's bastions and moats formed a complexity of fortified strength admired throughout Europe. Cannon portals and guards' turrets dominated the steeply slanted walls that resolved themselves into thrusting star formations. The town displayed its wealth in the fronts of fine houses, where brick was ornamented with classical decorations of carved stone. Great squares were faced by the finest mansions. Crowded alleys connected curving streets. Solid stone houses were uncommon; most were half-timbered buildings with brick between the posts and braces, like many houses in Flanders. The same mixture affected spoken sounds. "I could with difficulty comprehend the jargon of the common people, who speak an infamous 'patois,' compounded of vulgar French and Flemish."[2]

Impressed by the canals connecting trade routes along rivers, Elkanah decided to take passage on canal boats. He arranged to leave his carriage and horse at Lille, to be called for on the return trip. A crowded stage coach brought him first to the market town of Tourcoing then to a border town, where he could enter what he called the "German dominions" of the Emperor Joseph II, now known as Belgium.

That Joseph II had made a start to abolishing monasteries cheered Elkanah. He had passed through many miles of French farmland where peasants labored to support a clergy he considered parasites. That sense of social improvement could account for his finding the flat landscape not so much boring as pleasantly bucolic. Farmers grew good grain and mediocre tobacco.

From Menin on, Elkanah shared a one-horse cabriolet with a cloth merchant and drove straight and level roads forty miles to Ostende.[3]

Joseph II had recently declared the town a free city. For that reason he had ordered the demolition of Ostende's defense works. The harbor was relatively shallow but broad enough for the five hundred ships Elkanah estimated he saw. Many ships had passed through locks to enter the great dry-dock. Others were moored along each side of the mile-long quay, all the way out to the harbor entrance. Barrels and boxes rose in stacks beside ships that had brought them in or were going to take them away. Ships' spars and booms could be swung around for loading or unloading with a system of block and tackle. "The confusion of tongues among the merchants and sailors of almost every maritime nation assailed my ears." He thought of home. Could Plymouth ever match this?

Here was the point to venture over to England. Should he dare to cast himself "upon an uncertain destiny in an enemy's country—although the country of [his] ancestors?" The danger matched what he'd felt when traveling south from Providence with John Brown's money sewn into his coat. Rather than risk imprisonment as a rebel spy, he turned eastward. Elkanah wrote that he and his servant "crossed the Grand Bruges Canal near the harbor and walked on with several passengers on the edge of this noble canal, the finest perhaps in the world, to a sluice or lock at which we entered and proceeded on our way to Bruges with about fifty passengers."

Two-hundred-ton boats could sail from the sea all the way to Bruges on the broad canal from Ostende, dug about twelve feet deep six hundred years before. Their own boat could carry a hundred passengers, divided by prevalent social distinctions.

> The after-room of the boat was reserved for the nobility, and those who could afford to pay for the luxury.... It was an elegant parlor ... with gilded ceiling, silk velvet cushions, and silk curtains."

The middle-class compartment provided quite decent comfort on a much larger scale. "The residue of the boat was cut up into a kitchen, and subdivisions for the inferior classes of passengers.

We paid the very moderate price of 1 shilling 3 for our passage to Bruges & a small extra for the use of the gilt parlor.

Rows of poplars and pollarded willows shaded the tow-path, where a pair of horses pulled the boat along at around three miles an hour. Built-up banks raised the canal, giving a view out over cultivated fields. Elkanah considered "this novel mode of traveling exceedingly amusing and agreeable." Beggars along the tow path cried out, "Charité, charité," while performing "many dexterous feats of tumbling, rolling upon the ground, and casting their feet against trees, with their heads down, often in the most indecent and disgusting attitudes."

Sailors out at sea beyond Ostende used Bruges' cathedral tower to determine their position along the coast. The spire grew larger and more distinct as Elkanah's canal boat slowly approached from the west. The cathedral tower was "loaded with bells, producing a harmonious musical chime, said to be the finest in Europe." Inside the churches he was shown paintings

A passenger boat at the gates of Bruges (engraving from *Scenery of the Rhine, Belgium and Holland from Drawings by Capt. Batty,* **1826**).

"by the Van Dykes and other eminent Flemish artists," whose landscapes and night scenes he admired for their "deep transparent shade contrasted with strong reflection from firelight or moonlight."[4] Did Elkanah see Michaelangelo's sculpture of the Madonna and Child in Bruges' Church of Our Lady? Or did he see only what caught his eye in Paris—"ignorant bigoted mortals upon their knees idolizing some statue"?

Bruges' civic belfry and cloth market testified to centuries past when wool had enriched the city and brought cloth merchants from all over Europe. Now Elkanah found that linen was the chief cloth product of the town's thirty thousand inhabitants.

The confluence of canals and rivers at Bruges brought "animation and vigor into its commerce and manufactures." One of the canals took Elkanah twenty-four miles farther past meadows and fields to Ghent. Once again, "the children of the happy peasantry were dancing in groups, or skipping along the embankments of the canal. I was charmed and delighted in the contemplation of this noble country, and its animating and lovely scenes." What could be more elegant and comfortable than travel by canal boat?

The agricultural prosperity of the region could be attributed to the discovery centuries earlier of the benefits of crop rotation. Red clover was grown in fallow years to provide fertilizer. The Flemings kept this a secret for centuries, but eventually "about the time of the settlement of New England," the method was figured out by the English. "A new era in the agriculture of England" began.

At Ghent, the canal met the Scheldt and Lys Rivers. Additional small canals gave rise to countless bridges to connect the town's twenty-four islands. Many houses in Ghent had small walled gardens, so the city felt far less densely populated than Paris. Weavers in Ghent produced cheap linens and ticking, besides the production of lace and thread. The town's main export, Elkanah heard, was the wheat grown in the flat expanses around the town. The cathedral displayed "rare architecture and contained many fine paintings." He doesn't mention Jan van Eyck's *Lamb of God* altarpiece, whose nude panels depicting Adam and Eve were to be considered indecent when Emperor Joseph II looked at them. Presumably Elkanah would have agreed, considering his shocked reaction to children turning cartwheels without the refinement of underwear. What did strike him about Ghent was that the city "was inundated with monks. The Roman Catholic religion predominated; but the recent edict of the sagacious Joseph, will, I trust, create a new epoch, and remove from the people the thralldom of a mercenary priesthood."

A crowded public coach carried Elkanah and La Fleur to Brussels. The passengers included priests and noblemen as well as more common folk. Elkanah could afford to sit with the notables inside the carriage and thus did not have to climb up to the more precarious perches available on the roof. The road was surprisingly level and paved all the way from Ghent to Brussels, contrasting greatly with the roads Elkanah had traveled in America. The main meal that day was taken in the company of English, American, and French travelers. Including the wine, the meal that he found "sumptuous" cost only twenty-seven French sous.

Brussels, a city of seventy thousand surrounded by a brick defensive wall, offered numerous works of art, both in the cathedral and in the town hall. The only paintings Elkanah recorded, however, were an anti–Jewish picture of someone stealing the communion bread (or "host"—the theft a medieval legend) and a portrait of Joseph II displayed in Brussels' impressive gothic city hall. What Ekanah saw may have been the new series of Gobelins tapestries in the great church of Saints Michael and Gudule, showing the legend that Jews in the

The public coach at Ghent (steel engraving and etching by J. Rogers after W. H. Bartlett).

fourteenth century had stolen a communion wafer from a Catholic altar and had stabbed it. People who believed in transubstantiation were capable of imagining that the host reacted with pain and bleeding. Rationalists who belonged to the Masons did not take this seriously. Elkanah's admiration went instead to the enlightened emperor: "His wise and liberal measures of free trade, toleration, and other analogous acts, allured to this growing city vast emigration and wealth." To these wise policies Elkanah credited "the expansion of the city, the erection of elegant buildings, and the formation of new and spacious squares." Canals, dry docks, paved highways, free trade, toleration—these were what a young America could use.

Elkanah returned to Paris via Douai, Cambrai, and Senlis, but before turning south he re-visited Ghent to look in on Silas Deane. Deane had been America's first diplomat, sent secretly to France in 1776; and with Arthur Lee he remained as an assistant in Paris to Benjamin Franklin. Discredited because of diplomatic errors, he had first returned to America to defend himself against charges of embezzlement, then he had gone back to France before settling in exile at Ghent.[5] He had promised high rank and pay to French military officers who, on the strength of this, went out to help the Americans only to discover that Deane's promises, grandly given with spurious assurances of authority, were not going to be honored by Congress. Deane next offended French officials when his private opinion that they might not be trustworthy allies was revealed in illicitly published correspondence. Hearing of American defeats, he suggested appointing a foreign prince to replace George Washington as head of the army. A little later, with more bad news about American losses, he wrote to several people that it might be a good idea to negotiate a rapprochement with England. Elkanah described him as "misanthropic ... intent on getting money, and deadly hostile to his native land." Watson warned Franklin that Deane should be considered an enemy. Franklin was not entirely convinced, and later, in 1823, Watson relaxed his censures by adding a comment that his friend John Trumbull excused Deane's bitterness. Mercy Otis Warren, however, spared no mercy for Deane. In her view, "Mr. Deane had nothing to recommend him to such a distinguished and important appointment, except a degree of mercantile experience, combined with a certain secrecy or cunning that wore the appearance of knowing things much beyond his ability, and the art of imposing a temporary belief of a penetration far beyond his capacity. His weakness and ostentation, his duplicity, extravagance, and total want of principle, were soon discovered."[6]

From Senlis, Elkanah diverged a little southeast to pay his respects at the tomb of Jean Jacques Rousseau at the chateau of Ermenonville. Poplars grew around the monument on an island in the middle of a lake, a place where the philosopher had formerly come to meditate. "Here lies the Man of Nature and of Truth. Vitam impendere vero—To devote one's life to truth." Those words were inscribed in stone. Rousseau had died here at the house of a friend a little over two years ago.

Elkanah reached Paris again in mid-November. At Passy for dinner, he came upon Benjamin Franklin, who sat at a table reading, the earpieces of his bifocals disappearing behind the sides of his wig. His left arm rested on the table, with "his chin supported by the thumb of his right hand," just as in a painting by Robert Martin from 1767.[7]

On the table in front of him lay a musical score. Franklin, although accustomed to the respect and admiration of the highest reaches of French society, put his young visitor at ease. "Did you know that I am a musician?" he asked. Franklin led Watson over to an instrument he had invented and called "the Armonica." In Franklin's glass harmonica, hemispheres like glass bowls arranged on a rod are tuned to the pitches of an ordinary scale, so that by touching them with moist fingers tunes and chords can be played. Franklin had improved the concept of using wine glasses filled to different heights to tune them. Instead, round goblet bowls, nesting in each other without any one contacting another, formed a series graduated from large to small, from lower notes to higher notes. Pitches could be identified by the specific colors on the rims. The sound has no parallel in other instruments. Franklin played a Scottish tune. Elkanah found it "striking and interesting to contemplate an eminent statesman in his seventy-sixth year, and the most distinguished philosopher of the age, performing a simple pastorale on an instrument of his own construction." Elkanah's enjoyment was increased by contemplating the fact that Franklin had risen to such heights of intellectual prominence, "an object of veneration in the metropolis of Europe" and "influencing the destiny of nations," from a beginning as "an untutored printer's boy in America."

Almost no news had reached Elkanah during his three weeks' tour, other than the bitter tales recounted by Silas Deane, which he thought Franklin needed to hear. But he was hoping to be brought up to date on events in America. Franklin, however, had received no clear indication of how the forces of France and America had met those of Britain. Admiral de Grasse had arrived at the Chesapeake. General Washington and General Rochambeau had come together, while Admiral de Barras was bringing seven warships from Rhode Island down to augment de Grasse's fleet. Thousands of British soldiers had sailed south from New York to help General Cornwallis, who was expecting reinforcements on their way from England. Franklin and Watson spent the evening examining maps and imagining tactical possibilities. If the British did this, then the French would not be able to do that, and Washington would be exposed in some particularly dangerous way. On the other hand, if de Grasse deployed his fleet in this way, rather than that, and the British failed to break up the fleet de Barras was bringing south, then the reinforcements by sea from England would not be able to reach Cornwallis. On the whole, the Americans' prospects looked bleak. Elkanah wrote in his diary, "I left him at night, in the company of Dr. Bancroft, an American residing in London, but an ardent Whig. And I returned to Paris in deep despondency, sighing over the miseries of our bleeding country."

Early the next morning Elkanah was roused from his sleep by a loud banging on his door. Franklin had sent a messenger with a circular Franklin produced on a primitive copying machine.

> Copy of a note from Count de Vergennes to Dr. Franklin, dated Versailles, 19th Nov., 1781, 11 o'clock at night.
>
> Sir: I cannot better express my gratitude to you, for the news you often communicate to me, than by informing you that the Duc de Lausan arrived this evening, with the agreeable news, that the combined armies of France and America have forced Cornwallis to capitulate. The English garrison came out of Yorktown the 19th of October, with honors of war, and laid down their arms as prisoners. About six thousand troops, eighteen hundred sailors, twenty-two stand of colors, and one hundred and seventy pieces of cannon—seventy-five of which are brass—are the trophies which signalize this victory; besides, a ship of fifty guns was burnt, also a frigate, and a great number of transports.
>
> I have the honor, sir,
> De Vergennes
> To his Excellency, Dr. Franklin.

An eyewitness on board one of the French ships reported with the detail that Franklin and Elkanah had wanted when they were imagining possible troop and ship movements.[8] Admiral de Grasse had arrived at the mouth of Virginia's James River at the beginning of September, bringing reinforcements for the American army under Generals Washington, Rochambeau and LaFayette. Led by the Marquis de St. Simon, 3,600 soldiers began landing on September 2, a process that would take several days. This addition brought the numbers in the American army to two and a half times the strength of the English under Lord Cornwallis. The ships from which they were disembarking had not yet rejoined the main fleet when, on September 5, an English fleet of twenty-seven sail appeared, aiming to bring support for Cornwallis's British troops ensconced in the towns of York and Gloucester. Despite the absence of nearly 2,000 sailors and officers who were still engaged in the transfer of St. Simon's reinforcements for the American army, De Grasse's fleet formed a battle line in forty-five minutes. Battle began at four in the afternoon, although wind conditions limited the number of ships that could engage in the fight. The English under Admiral Graves feared a general battle, as they had fewer ships and were suffering greater losses than the French, even being forced to set fire to their own warship, the *Terrible*, which had become so badly damaged it could not be saved. Night's darkness ended the fight at seven in the evening. The next day, the English kept away, repairing broken masts and patching damaged hulls. The French took advantage of shifting wind to approach the English again on the 7th, but suddenly the wind dropped and the ships stopped, becalmed in sight of each other. On the 8th, the fleets came closer, but for the next few days the shifting winds prevented fighting but enabled changes in position. De Grasse maintained a positional advantage that blocked Graves's ships from providing any aid to Cornwallis on land. On September 11 the French captured two English frigates, the *Richmond* and the *Iris*, near Chesapeake Bay. A squadron of French ships coming with masts and other repair supplies from Rhode Island, as well as thousands more land troops for Washington's army, joined the fleet, bringing its strength to thirty-six ships of the line, plus thirteen other warships, three frigates and numerous smaller boats. On September 18, Generals Washington and Rochambeau came on board Admiral de Grasse's flagship to coordinate plans for the battle on land and sea. The fleet took up a defensive position to negate any English efforts to relieve Yorktown and Gloucester, while at the same time beginning the siege of Yorktown on September 29. Washington surrounded the town with trenches and began attacking on October 7. Cornwallis requested a truce ten days later, surrendering on the 19th. Six thousand English and Hessian soldiers, 1500 sailors, and 2000 American royalists became prisoners of war. Besides one hundred eighty cannon captured on land, the American and French forces had taken forty ships, including one carrying fifty cannons and another of twenty-four. When Admiral Digby arrived at Chesapeake Bay on October 27, with forty-four ships including twenty-six ships of the line, bringing reinforcements for Cornwallis of four thousand soldiers, it was too late. Seeing the French fleet and hearing of Cornwallis's surrender, Digby decided to clear out. He sailed away to the southeast without coming in any closer. News of the victory was sent off to Paris immediately, arriving exactly one month after Cornwallis's capitulation.

All Paris rejoiced! Bonfires and illuminations lasted three days. Franklin was kept busy receiving the congratulations of American and French adherents to the revolutionary cause. Elkanah found him in "an ecstasy of joy." Franklin declared, "There is no parallel, in history, of two entire armies' being captured from the same enemy in any one war." The fireworks at Paris were duplicated and reduplicated in all the cities along the Loire, as Elkanah made his way back to Nantes.

In the winter following this grand news, Elkanah was inspired to express his gratitude to George Washington by commissioning an elaborately embroidered Masonic apron as a gift to the commander.[9] American and French flags are shown crossed over a Masonic pyramid. A tasseled cord tied in knots of friendship surmounts the central ornament and its shining sun's rays of enlightenment created from gold thread. The light of a candle shines above all. Thick golden fringe surrounds the entire apron. Ironically, nuns in Nantes carried out this work, despite the papal decrees of 1738 and 1751 forbidding Catholics to join or give assistance to the Masons on pain of excommunication. Watson and his partner Cossoul sent a letter to accompany the gift:

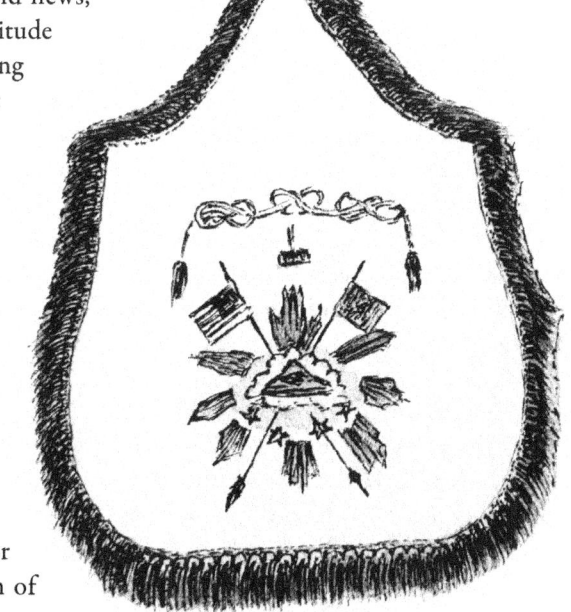

The Watson-Cossoul Masonic apron for George Washington (Alexandria-Washington Lodge No, 22; author's drawing).

To his Excellency, General Washington, America.
Most Illustrious and Respected Brother:
In the moment when all Europe admire and feel the effects of your glorious efforts in support of American liberty, we hasten to offer for your acceptance a small pledge of our homage. Zealous lovers of liberty and its institutions, we have experienced the most refined joy, in seeing our chief and brother stand forth in its defence, and in defence of a new-born nation of Republicans.

Your glorious career will not be confined to the protection of American liberty, but its ultimate effect will extend to the whole human family, since Providence has evidently selected you as an instrument in His hands, to fulfil His eternal decrees.

It is to you, therefore, the glorious orb of America, we presume to offer Masonic ornaments, as an emblem of your virtues. May the grand Architect of the universe be the Guardian of your precious days, for the glory of the Western Hemisphere and the entire universe. Such are the vows of those who have the favor to be, by all the known numbers,

    Your affectionate brothers,
    Watson & Cossoul.
East of Nantes, 23d 1st Month 1782.

For Watson and Cossoul the year 1782 was their most profitable. The business of shipping grew rapidly to the point that seven clerks were employed. Elkanah proudly could announce that they "had a little fleet of six ships and brigs lying at the mouth of the Loire." In the summer, however, an influenza epidemic spread throughout Europe, having appeared in 1781 in North Africa, America, China, Russia, and finally the next year in Europe. The firm was hit hard. "Our family, clerks, servants, officers and sailors in our employment, all were prostrated by it, and our operations were suspended." Weakened, Elkanah could not attend to business affairs for weeks. As his recovery gradually became stronger, he decided to travel to England—partly for his health and partly "to take advantage of any commercial changes which might result from the general peace that now seemed imminent."

Watson's Sentimental Journey

Elkanah's trip to England required that he first go up along the familiar banks of the Loire and then the overland route to Paris.[10] Preparations were made to travel with Henry Laurens, then residing in Nantes. Laurens had been paroled from English imprisonment, after capture at sea and the discovery of his appointment by the rebel government to be American ambassador to The Netherlands. His imprisonment by the British required that someone else serve in The Netherlands—John Adams. After months in jail, Laurens had been allowed to visit family in France. Unable to leave Nantes at that moment, Laurens agreed to meet Elkanah at Paris or London.

Laurens' diplomatic papers had been retrieved when he had thrown them overboard in an attempt to prevent the English from learning about a secret treaty of assistance with the Dutch. The discovery of that treaty resulted in a declaration of war by the British against the Dutch.

On August 31, Elkanah and his servant La Fleur left Nantes in a post-chaise, the French version of the sulky he'd driven in his tour from Providence to Charleston. He'd already traveled this road so many times that people knew him wherever he stopped to refresh his horses or eat a meal—"Voilà encore Monsieur le Bostone." (There's Mr. Bostonian, again!) They reached Paris in three days, arriving on September third. The next morning Elkanah began his round of visits by meeting John Jay, America's ambassador to Spain, who had come up to consult with Benjamin Franklin and America's Consul General, Thomas Barkley. Barkley's job included sorting out the details of financial arrangements involving American merchants like Elkanah who acted in various ways as agents for government acquisition of supplies.

American diplomats converged on Franklin at Passy to coordinate efforts to bring about a peace, now that American military successes left England little imaginable choice. Elkanah conferred with Benjamin Franklin and John Adams. He met the English agent Benjamin Vaughan, thought to have authority to open secret and informal negotiations for England's new pro–American prime minister, Lord Shelburne.

Benjamin Franklin's ill health caused Elkanah to fear that the ambassador might die before the signing of the peace and recognition of American independence.[11] Franklin warned Elkanah that going to England he would run the danger of being suspected of spying, because of his well-known commercial activities that put him in constant contact with American privateers as well as rebel diplomats. He did grant Elkanah a passport for travel in France, however, and provided letters of introduction to several famous people, including "Dr. Priestly of Birmingham, Dr. Price of Hackney, and Mr. Burke" (Joseph Priestly, Richard Price, and Edmund Burke). Vaughn asked him to deliver diplomatic correspondence to Lord Shelburne, which Elkanah promised to do first thing on arrival in London. To do so would place him under the protection of the prime minister.

Before taking off for England, however, Elkanah relaxed, spending Friday "indifferently at the plays."[12] A couple of days later, he was invited to dine with a large group of French and Americans. During the meal, news arrived that one of Britain's largest warships, the *Royal George*, had suddenly sunk while at anchor off the English coast at Spithead just beyond Portsmouth, the Royal Navy's headquarters.[13] Of the twelve hundred on board, around nine hundred perished, including visiting women and children—not in the midst of battle but within sight of shore. An attempt to repair a minor leak had required that the ship be heeled or slanted into the water away from the place that needed patching. A worse leak opened on the side thus placed below water. The ship suddenly filled and sank in a whirlpool of timbers and drowning crew, dragging a smaller ship anchored nearby into the vortex.

When the news reached Paris, horror over the sudden deaths overshadowed attempts to assign blame. Elkanah's perception, curiously, was to notice that the reaction of French women, many of whom wept at the news, demonstrated warmth and tenderness. The women "seemed to be oppressed with the most sincere sorrow and regret." This did not erase his stereotypical expectations, however, either of women or of the French in general. "I am aware," he commented in his journal, "that this deep sympathy was evanescent, for the light-hearted French never dwell upon, or cherish any sorrow, but habitually dance over the ills of life."

On Monday, September 9, Elkanah started off for Calais, passing through St. Denis, Chantilly, Amiens, Abbéville, and Montreuil. Arranging with a fellow passenger to take turns driving and resting, Elkanah reached the coastal port of Calais in two days. "Nothing very material happened on the road," he wrote in his diary, except for their having been accosted in Amiens by a great crowd of ragged beggars. Sunrise when they arrived at Calais revealed a view that included the Channel and the distant English coast, his "first glimpse of the land of my fathers."

Literature met life at Calais. Their carriage clattered into the cobbled hotel courtyard, where Elkanah recognized the innkeeper who came out to greet them, hat under his arm.

Monsieur Dessein, the same, had been Laurence Sterne's host, as described in the beginning of *A Sentimental Journey*. "His manner, the position of the hat, his wig, and polite civilities, all attested the identity of the man; and while I was conversing with him, the scene of Sterne's description seemed to be realized by the approach of a monk, begging for his convent."[14] Sterne's hero, Yorick, had behaved rudely to a monk begging similarly, then had felt chagrin at his own behavior, finally expressing regret and becoming acquainted with the monk, a former soldier who in turn apologized for having imposed by begging. Sterne's characteristic exploration of his hero's own moods and attitudes, his constant analysis of his reactions and preconceptions, carried his story through many pages before finding resolution in an exchange of snuff boxes by Yorick and the monk, to be an eternal reminder of their new-found friendship. The reader could assume from the quasi-autobiographical style that Yorick was the author—a self-consciously refined presentation of Sterne himself; and, in turn, Elkanah could find material for his own journal in a similar observation of people and events, however insignificant, described in a self-conscious anecdotal style based in part on what he had enjoyed in reading Sterne. To live a scene from Sterne's book must have produced an especially exquisite

Elkanah as Yorick, meeting M. Dessein at Calais (engraving by Thwaites after Lossing, in *Men and Times of the Revolution,* 1861, p. 144).

ambiguity. Elkanah asked Dessein if he knew how world-famous he had become by appearing in Sterne's book.

Arriving in London

The Channel crossing could be accomplished in around three hours. They sailed along the white chalk of the Dover cliffs, then anchored in Dover harbor, beneath the walls of the massive castle. Their packet boat was boarded by agents for inns. "Stay here! Gentlemen, you will find excellent accommodation at our inn!" As a gesture of rebellion, Elkanah chose to stay at the King's Head. The inn sign commemorated the beheading of King Charles in 1649. Death to tyrants! His feelings were mixed: "This was the land of our rancorous foe and imperious tyrants. Still, it was the land of our forefathers."

Brick houses in England reminded him of houses at home. France's smooth white stone walls were foreign. The contrast with France did not express itself merely in the architecture. National difference showed also in the people. Englishmen were burly—perhaps from drinking beer all the time. The French were "meagre."

After viewing the castle, they left Dover to go through Ashford and Maidstone to Canterbury. The cathedral, Elkanah noted, was "in the style of the Gothic models of France, and other Roman Catholic countries." Their course took them through Chatham, Rochester, Gravesend, Dartford, Greenwich, and Woolwich. An American tourist on a grand European

Dover (unsigned aquatint, ca. 1790).

tour might have examined the ancient cathedral and Norman castle at Rochester. A spy could have learned much about the British navy by surveying Chatham's docks on the Medway, by interviewing pensioners at Greenwich's naval hospital on the Thames, or by inspecting armament at the Woolwich arsenal. But for the moment Elkanah was simply enjoying a view of the Thames River and the pleasant sails of shipping to and from England's chief city. "The lofty dome of St. Paul's seemed to welcome our approach to London. Now gilded spires began to appear, then vast piles of chimneys, forests of masts, and the confused scenes of a world within a world rapidly opened to our enraptured gaze."

Elkanah stopped first to leave a message where he expected he would rendezvous with Henry Laurens. Then he immediately took the dispatches to Lord Shelburne. The prime minister greeted Elkanah hospitably, freely discussing American affairs and inquiring after the health of Benjamin Franklin. Elkanah next began delivering private letters entrusted to him. The Duke of Manchester impressed him as a quintessential English nobleman. His new mansion Elkanah declared "splendid."[15] His conversation surprised Elkanah in its directness. "I observed by one of the morning papers, that a messenger of peace had arrived the preceding evening. Are you the person, Sir?" "Yes," Elkanah answered. "I brought dispatches to Lord

The lofty dome of St. Paul's Cathedral, London (engraving and etching, ca. 1770).

Shelburne, and trust that this circumstance will ensure me personal safety, and an opportunity of freely traveling in England."

"Undoubtedly, Sir," the duke answered. He attempted to learn from Elkanah just how much knowledge he had of "the fact that the government had just come to a decision to acknowledge our Independence." Elkanah had learned to be circumspect—not to reveal how much or how little he knew about subjects discussed by foreign officials, so now he attempted to converse in phrases that sheltered him in diplomatic ambiguity; but in truth, Elkanah had not been aware of that news. If the duke could tell that he had been ignorant of this, his estimate of Elkanah's importance might diminish. On the other hand, Elkanah's lack of information might merely indicate that America's spies were not as well placed as England's. Whatever his status, or perceived status, now Elkanah could travel without fear of being arrested as a spy or a rebel collaborator.

For about a week after his arrival, Elkanah acquainted himself with London and nearby areas. Soon after his interview with the Duke of Manchester, he explored the park at Blackheath south of the Thames and visited Greenwich Hospital. Five thousand "maimed and worn-down sailors" lived there in comfortable retirement in buildings whose palatial architecture designed by Sir Christopher Wren achieved in English eyes an effect superior to that of Les Invalides, the similar institution in Paris. Elkanah was impressed by the buildings, by the "noble terrace ... the court and colonnades," all of them grand. Tame deer grazed in the grounds as London's citizens relaxed in the park.

Invitations to dine brought him the opportunity to make comparisons between English customs and circumstances and those common in America, as well as with what he had observed in France. At a splendid and magnificent dinner in a mansion at Blackheath, table manners were more like those in America than in France. Women gathered around the hostess, not mixing in the conversation of the men. The "ladies of England and America are cold, distant, and forbidding." French women's behavior, in contrast, was "airy and animated." French women "take the lead ... and talk upon every subject, whether they understand it or not." English servants were skilled and attentive but silent. French servants, like Americans, took part in the table conversation. Elkanah estimated the sort of person who became a servant in England to be "generally an ignorant and servile being, who has no aspiration beyond his present dependent condition." How unlike America! "Our domestic feels the consciousness, that he in turn may become himself a master."

France differed greatly from England in another matter—there, travel by road was safe. In England highwaymen were notoriously common. One of the gentlemen with whom Elkanah dined at Blackheath had that very evening seen the robbery of a coach on the heath. Elkanah was forewarned in case he planned to travel beyond the town.

At Hackney Elkanah took advantage of an opportunity to hear Dr. Richard Price preach. The building was unostentatious, without any emphasis on its function as a church. After the service, Elkanah presented the letter of introduction provided to him by Benjamin Franklin, who had become Price's friend when living in London before 1775. Price invited Elkanah and a friend who was with him to have further conversation for a while in his study, which they entered through a door behind the pulpit. Price was renowned as a Unitarian philosopher and as a financier. His publications in favor of the American revolution earned him the friendship of many American Whigs. Price's *Observations on Civil Liberty, the Principles of Government, and the Justice and Policy of the War with America* came out in 1776.[16] "Our colonies in North America appear to be now determined to do and suffer every thing, under the persuasion, that Great Britain is attempting to rob them, of that Liberty to which every member of society, and all civil communities, have a natural and unalienable right. The question, therefore, whether this is a reasonable persuasion, is highly interesting, and deserves the most careful attention of every Englishman, who values Liberty, and wishes to avoid staining himself with the guilt of invading it." That stirring beginning launched an examination of the meaning of Liberty in general and of Civil Liberty in particular—producing an argument derived from the ideas of John Locke that favored American demands for self-government free from dictatorial control and taxation from England. Elkanah's friend remarked that America was indebted to Price for his supportive publications. Elkanah thought the philosopher's humble response worth noting. Price said that "he had lived long enough to know that he knew nothing."

In following days, Elkanah visited Richmond west of London, where he happened to "walk in the train of the Royal family, and saw the King, for the first time."

Nearby, Elkanah moralized about Osterley House, a mansion and gardens combining the work of architects William Chambers and Robert Adam, modified by the banker Robert Child. Having in Watson's view "squandered" half his wealth on remodeling the seventy-five rooms of the house to represent the architecture and furnishings of many distinct nations, Child died two days after receiving the keys. Elkanah thought that this marked "the reprobation of Heaven upon this absurd prostitution of wealth, which, worthily directed would have carried blessings to thousands." Moreover, his daughter had eloped and "was in the arms of a bankrupt debauchee." Elkanah seems not to have noticed that Robert Child's widow Sarah took his place and became a senior partner in the bank. Nor did he count the blessings the project had brought to hundreds, if not thousands, by employing artists and craftsmen.

No doubt Elkanah toured the historic and otherwise worthy sights of London, but what he chose to write about is a visit to see an Irish giant. For a small fee he could enter a room to see the "monster in human form." This man seemed drunk and ferocious. Elkanah heard that his height was eight feet two inches and that his name was Burns (actually O'Burne). Later, after making small amounts of money by allowing himself to be shown in country fairs, he sold his body "to an association of surgeons, for five hundred guineas."

The news came out that King George would be giving official recognition to America's independence when Parliament reconvened in early December. Elkanah wanted to be there, as he could imagine no greater event. In the meantime, he decided he'd explore the country, "visit their manufacturing districts, ... examine their agriculture, and the general improvements in roads and canals." He hired a post-chaise, much lighter and better designed than the French equivalent which had lumbered along like an ox-cart.

A Tour of England and American Independence

The stone bridge at Maidenhead arched over the Thames and granted a "brilliant view of meadows and valleys richly cultivated." Traveling with his friend La Fleur, whom he had hired in France, Elkanah headed west through Henley and Bray toward Oxford.

Turnpike gates interrupted their passage every ten or fifteen miles, at a cost of fifty cents each time. Elkanah found that an exorbitant charge. Everything could be had for less in France.

Oxford (wood engraving, from *Nederlandsch Magazijn,* Oct. 1835).

Coming down from rolling hills into the low valley of Oxford, they crossed the very long Magdalen Bridge into the university city. Elkanah could spare only a few hours to seeing the city, which he found "highly interesting on account of its twenty colleges and numerous students and professors." But his reaction to the architecture was decidedly not affected by later romantic associations of gothic windows with an idealized medievalism. "There is nothing marked or engaging in the architecture of these colleges," he wrote in his diary, "it being antiquated and inelegant." Their libraries were admittedly rich, their gardens beautifully ornamented and laid out, but this could not be his world.

Blenheim Palace's monumental display of grandiose architectural gesture commemorated the military victory of English forces led by Marlborough against the French in 1704. Had all Oxford looked like this pile of classical columns, carved capitals, and gorgeous garlands, Elkanah would have praised its elegance and modernity.

The carriage took the travelers farther north to reach Stratford upon Avon, ranked high by Elkanah as a place for veneration of Shakespeare, whether or not it was antiquated or inelegant.

The house where Shakespeare was born lay close to the White Lion Inn, their overnight lodging. The inn sign was a portrait of the town's famous son, inscribed with a quotation from John Milton, "Here sweetest Shakspeare, fancy's child/ Warbled his native wood-notes wild." In the house of his birth, Elkanah met an old woman, "who pronounced herself the only surviving descendant of the illustrious poet." She indicated the bard's chair—what was left of it after bits and pieces had been removed by souvenir hunters. The chair could remind Elkanah of his ancestral Plymouth Rock, steadily shrinking as its chips became relics to be carried far away as mementos of historical pilgrimages. The poet's memorial inside the parish church implores the living to leave the bones of the dead undisturbed, famously threatening any who might not. "Blest be the man that spares these stones, And cursed be he who moves these bones."

Elkanah commented that a large charnel house outside the church received the disordered bones of bodies disinterred to make space for new burials within the church. "Shakspeare, doubtless, had, from childhood, watched the operation of this system, and his sensitive mind was agitated and shocked by it."

Elkanah's friend, Joseph Green, brother-in-law of the Earl of Ferrers, welcomed him in Birmingham. Surprisingly, several American Tories had chosen to live in exile in that city, among them Peter Oliver, Chief Justice of Massachusetts and a close friend of the royalist governor Thomas Hutchinson, whose daughter married Oliver's son. One of Hutchinson's sons was in Birmingham, too. Elkanah refers to the exiles as "several of my Tory connections." Evidently, Oliver could be conversationally polite, despite his devastatingly caustic opinion of the self-aggrandizing motives of all rebels.[17] Watson must have met Oliver while growing up in Plymouth, when Oliver had been a local judge beginning his career.

Walking through Birmingham with Elkanah, Oliver pointed out three men also promenading. "They are amongst the most eminent philosophers of Europe," he informed the young New Englander. Judge Oliver introduced Elkanah to them—Dr. Joseph Priestley, James Watt, and Blind Henry Moyes. Benjamin Franklin had given Elkanah a letter to recommend him to Priestley. During the several days of his visit to Birmingham, Elkanah visited Priestley often at his house a mile outside town. "Dr. Priestley was a thin man, with a sharp nose and face, and wore a full bushy wig. He exhibited to me his extensive electrical apparatus, which occupied a room; and his laboratory, which filled another apartment. No man has effected more interesting developments in science." He is now remembered for his publication of his discovery of oxygen, which he called "dephlogisticated air." Priestley led services in a small church, "his tenets being Socinian." Elkanah, a Mason, was in contact with Richard Price and Joseph Priestley, both of them intellectual giants as well as Unitarian (Socinian) ministers. Like Franklin and many of his friends, Elkanah sought rational knowledge and lacked concern for traditional orthodoxies. Theology held at most mild interest for him. He believed, with George Washington, that Providence was guiding and protecting America's quest for independence and political freedom, and that this development was part of an unfolding progress within Nature. Miracles and the internal coherency of the concept of the Trinity do not seem to have bothered his thoughts. Calling himself a skeptic, Elkanah recalled that "at the age of 15 being at Providence I soon noticed a variety of sects, such as Anabaptists, Quakers, Episcopalians, Unitarians, and Universalists. The latter were then forming into a society under the auspices of their founder Murray, who I had often heard preach, & he was countenanced by Mr. Brown. His plan of universal salvation, I confess, cleared me entirely of every remnant of puritan faith which I had inculcated from my youth." Elkanah wished the strident sects could settle on some single, rational piety.[18] He showed no apparent reluctance, however, to attend whatever service was available. The first he attended in Birmingham was that of the Church of England. He sat next to Peter Oliver, who gave him a friendly jab in the ribs when the minister prayed, "O Lord, turn the hearts of our rebellious subjects in America."

James Watt, who developed the steam engine, was Priestley's brother-in-law. The two collaborated on their investigations into steam. Elkanah met Watt regularly when visiting Priestley, and Watt told him in detail about the applications of his invention. Several engines were now being used to improve the tin mines of Cornwall. Watt was paid half the amount saved by the introduction of his machine, which already amounted to five hundred pounds' income a year. More of Watt's machinery had been built at Mathew Boulton's factory at Soho, a neighborhood just outside Birmingham. Watt and Priestley were also involved in the new idea of electroplating copper with silver, which revolutionized the production of fine looking table and ornamental ware. In addition, they were experimenting with a photographic method of reproducing watercolor paintings.

Once during a visit, Priestley read Elkanah a letter he'd received from Benjamin Franklin. The news had arrived that Admiral Rodney had defeated Admiral de Grasse in the battle of the Saintes near Jamaica. Here was English revenge for de Grasse's important part in the battle of Yorktown. An innovative manoeuver had placed some of the English ships behind the French line putting the French where they could be bombarded from both sides. No one was sure whether this tactic had been conceived by some unknown genius or had simply been the chance result of an unexpectedly successful sortie against the enemy line, so that the attackers had sailed through to the other side and could fight from behind. "Franklin imagined himself and Priestley suspended in a cloud, hovering over the scene, and witnessing its dreadful progress."

Birmingham's canals connected the industrial city with Liverpool and Manchester in one direction and with Bristol and Oxford in another. Coal for the factories came by canal boat. Coal smoke fog blanketed the city. Locals not only had become used to it, they enjoyed it, or so they said. Elkanah reported it as "exceedingly offensive to the olfactories of a stranger." Watt explained the construction details of the Birmingham Canal, connecting to the Staffordshire and Worcestershire Canals. Twenty locks, each built at a cost of five hundred pounds, brought the water down a one hundred and thirty-six foot drop. The canal produced dividends for its investors of between twelve and twenty-four percent annually. These new engineering projects could be duplicated. Wealth could be quick if he could construct the best canals in America.

In honor of Elkanah's intended departure the next morning, Mr. Green invited all the Americans in Birmingham to share a supper. Of the twenty-six present, Elkanah was the sole rebel. A polite agreement allowed him to speak his political views freely, as did all the others theirs. "Unconstrained, we passed an amusing evening." Peter Oliver, however, indicated his fear of John Adams, who was, he thought, "the most dangerous man to British domination in America." According to spurious Adams letters published in London newspapers, Adams sought vengeance against Loyalists wherever they had fled.

Surprisingly, when Elkanah asked his friends for advice on the route to follow next and the sights he should see, the best and most accurate information came from Dr. Moyes. Remembering everything he had heard, the blind man could tell Elkanah whatever he wanted to know. Besides being skilled with edge tools to the point of constructing complex machines, Moyes was a gifted lecturer on subjects of chemistry, astronomy, algebra and other aspects of the sciences known as Newtonian philosophy. Elkanah, like many people, admired his efforts to overcome the loss of sight while an infant. "He afforded a wonderful instance of the triumph of genius and energy over the most difficult of human obstacles."[19]

Elkanah's friend accompanied him to the town of Lichfield. Fewer than four thousand people lived there, but the medieval cathedral's three spires gave a sense of grandeur to the little city. Green introduced him to the sister of the famous actor David Garrick with whom they spent an evening in homage to the great Shakespearian, who had died just a couple of years before. "Her eyes were full, penetrating, and jet black, like her brother's," wrote Elkanah. He had never seen Garrick himself but must have heard descriptions of his appearance and his famous style of acting. The cathedral he considered "One of the most magnificent old Gothic churches in England." Awed by its venerable antiquity, Elkanah "spent an hour in a sad sojourn in the church-yard, viewing the cathedral and the tombs around it." The beauty of the cathedral remained, despite war, vandalism, and the deterioration caused by weather and time. "The hands that created it have long since crumbled into dust."

Modern inventions, industry, and commerce were Elkanah's touristical goals, not cathedrals. He moved on toward the port city of Liverpool. Crossing and re-crossing the Trent River and following the Duke of Bridgewater's canal brought Elkanah and his servant through Stafford and Namptwich to Newcastle under Lyme, a little market town with a fine classical town hall presiding over the main square.

"Near Newcastle, we were enraptured with a most gorgeous and lovely view from an eminence, formed of a widely spread plain, diversified with fields and groves and glittering streams, studded with villages and elegant villas, and animated with a thousand herds, lowing along its meads." Sunlight shone on distant trees while closer fields were shaded by the shifting forms of great white clouds.

At Warrington on the Mersey River, Elkanah put his carriage in storage and took his place inside a stage coach for the rest of the trip to Liverpool, accompanied only by La Fleur. The monotony and motion of the ride, with the continual rhythmic clatter of hoofs, lulled Elkanah into sleep. He kept his loaded pistols under the cushion, dozing, then falling asleep with his arms folded, rocking to the movement of the coach as it pitched forever forward. The regular motions fit unpredictable bumps into well-sprung rushing arcs—lurches becoming long curves soft enough for sleep. "Suddenly I was aroused by a check to the full speed of our horses. I rubbed my eyes—heard a confused noise of voices, and, looking out, saw by the light of the full moon that we were surrounded by a band of armed men." A voice called out, "We'll hang him, by God!" In the dark, someone turned the brass handle and pulled open the carriage door. "Come out!" Elkanah saw angry faces and wondered if the news had spread that he, a rebel, dared pass through these hills. Had they come out to avenge the hanging of Major André, the British officer captured as a spy in Benedict Arnold's attempt to betray West Point? Hiding his watch in the upholstery of the carriage, Elkanah cocked his pistols and commanded the mob to stand back. Surprised, they asked, was he not "the commanding officer of the press gang?" When Elkanah convinced them he had nothing to do with the navy or its methods of kidnapping local youths for impressment, they pulled away and permitted the coach to travel on. Sailors who had been oppressed, they wanted revenge. Elkanah had seen the officer they wanted just that evening at Warrington. In his opinion, "the barbarous and demoralizing system of impressment, would disgrace the most despotic government on the earth. And yet, in this country of boasted liberty and laws, it is tolerated by the government, and sanctioned by established custom." Anywhere in the country, young men could be stolen and forced to serve on Navy ships for years, but the danger hit coastal villages hardest, when the Navy suddenly snatched away local fishermen.

The wildness of the hills, the moonlit ride, the attack by the mob—to complete the adventure they were given a "dirty little chamber in the attic" when they arrived in the courtyard of the Golden Lion Inn at Liverpool, late.

In less than a century Liverpool grew from a rural parish of fishermen and became an international port city of forty thousand. Merchants gathered at a new Exchange Building to carry on the business of import and export contracting. Elkanah's father's ships had traded here. Making the most of a tidal rise of thirty feet, Liverpool had dry docks as well as quays along open water. Salt refined here since the late seventeenth century supplied British fisherman working throughout the Atlantic, so that they no longer had to rely on supplies from Portugal or France. Extensive saltworks used sea water brought into the pans by machine to process rock salt dug in the area. Coal for the evaporation fires came to Liverpool by canal boat. Canals had become essential to industrial growth. More were under construction or at least projected.

Elkanah returned to Warrington and picked up his carriage again so that he could travel toward Manchester, where a confluence of canals enabled the movement of American and Egyptian cotton brought from Liverpool to be spun and woven in the city's new mills.

On the way to Manchester, passing through hilly farmland, Elkanah heard violin music coming from a farmhouse. Young men and women were dancing "with all their might and hearts, their four-handed reels." Elkanah joined them, shared a drink, warmed himself by their fire, and then left to continue his journey. Aside from their broad Lancashire accent, Elkanah "could easily have imagined" himself "at a frolic in the bosom of New England. Yet one Yankee, in the same sphere, possesses more mother-wit than half this circle. I believe this remark may be made with justice in reference to a large mass of the rural population of England." Americans might make a success of democracy because they were intrinsically brighter than Europe's peasantry. Elkanah was confident.

Double Locks on an English canal (engraving and etching by W. B. Cooke after S. Owen, 1814).

Manchester's cotton industry had been "wonderfully facilitated" by the introduction of ever more complex machinery. Mechanical inventions "perform ... almost the entire labor, to the exclusion of thousands of famishing poor, who are thus deprived of their ordinary occupation."

Despite this poverty that seemed an inescapable consequence of progress, Elkanah hoped that he "may live to witness in America the application of machinery to these purposes, and the introduction of canals, with all their infinite advantages." Manchester displayed an opulent and elegant surface, with "fine streets and extensive squares." At Worsley Mills, seven miles outside the city, the Duke of Bridgewater's "stupendous works" excited Elkanah with the possibilities of modern engineering. In addition to the duke's canals, which followed hillsides and crossed valleys and even in aqueducts crossed rivers, the duke's engineers had constructed tunnels to reach coal mines deep in a mountain. Elkanah and his servant bought tickets to travel in narrow boats, fifty feet long, that could navigate the tunnels. The tour covered about three miles underground. Arches of brick or stone helped support the tunnel roof, a bit over seven feet high, filled with four feet of water leaving little head-room. "The sensation that one feels is indescribable, in approaching through this gloomy avenue the dark colliers, who were just discernible by the red glare of their lights, in the region of blackness and night." Coal from the pits was loaded into boats and transported through the canals to Manchester and beyond.

From Manchester, they drove over the mountains toward Leeds. Rochdale's hilltop church could be reached from town by a long set of stairs. From this eminence Elkanah viewed the mountains all around the valley. It was October 17. The snow on the peaks was early. Before Halifax, "ascending the fearful mountain at Blackstone-edge, we were assailed, when half-way up, by ... a pitiless storm of hail and wind." Even attempting to stand proved dangerous. But here was an experience romantics sought. "The atmosphere was wild and squally. And whilst this circumstance in some measure obstructed the prospect, it added infinitely to the grandeur and novelty of this wild mountain scene. A snow-storm next attacked us, whilst still ascending; and in a few minutes, the surrounding hills and mountains held up their heads, as if rejoicing in their white mantles."

They continued toward Halifax as night fell. Grouped lights from villages in the valleys and on the hillsides, and single beams of candlelight from scattered farmhouses sparkled in the dusk. The moon came out and edged surrounding clouds with silver. Hill-tops of snow reflected and dispersed the blue cold light of the moon as it sought out the ripples and rapids of a stream flowing along the base of the valley.

Halifax, a town to six thousand people, held a cloth fair every Saturday. The Clothiers Hall was said to "include five hundred rooms." Snow blanketed streets and roofs. From Halifax to Leeds they could follow the banks of the Aire river, passing the ruins of a monastery. Elkanah rejoiced that "popish institutions" were gone from England, but instead, he discovered that "the people of England are ground to the earth by the intolerable abuses of a political national religion. To this establishment every religious sect is made tributary. The poor farmer, no matter to what mode or form of worship his conscience may direct him, is compelled to yield one-tenth of his hard earnings to sustain a host of bishops and priests, a class of whom riot in wealth and luxury."

The Clothiers Hall at Leeds brought together local merchants and weavers from the region. Twice a week deals were closed in whispers. The weavers did not know their competitors' prices and had to negotiate according to what their poverty could allow them to take for their labor. The merchants, able to talk privately to each of the sellers, had a clear advantage.

A river to the east and a canal to the west connected Leeds with both coasts. Elkanah was invited to spend a social evening at the mansion of a gentleman to whom he had brought letters of introduction. The group that gathered expressed pro–American sentiments, to his

Canal Tunnel (engraving and etching by Thomas, ca. 1800).

The Peak District (steel engraving and etching, in *Picturesque Europe*, ed. Bayard Taylor [New York: Appleton, 1876], p. 138).

surprise. He felt himself "in the midst of my rebel friends in America." But as a precaution he usually did not bring up political topics when talking to strangers.

The early onset of bad weather inspired him to drop his plans for a trip to Scotland. Turning south again, at Sheffield he discovered a package of correspondence waiting for him, from friends on both continents. George Washington's eloquent thanks for the gift of the masonic apron came into his hands here.[20]

> State of New York, Aug. 10th, 1782.
>
> Gentlemen—The Masonic ornaments which accompanied your brotherly address of the 23rd of January last, though elegant in themselves, were rendered more valuable by the flattering sentiments and affectionate manner in which they were presented.
>
> If my endeavors to avert the evil with which the country was threatened, by a deliberate plan of tyranny, should be crowned with the success that is wished, the praise is due to the Grand Architect of the universe who did not see fit to suffer his superstructure of justice to be subjected to the ambition of the Princes of this world, or to the rod of oppression, in the hands of any power upon earth.
>
> For your affectionate vows permit me to be grateful, and offer mine for true brothers in all parts of the world, and to assure you of the sincerity with which I am,
>
> Yours,
> George Washington.
> Messrs., Watson & Cossoul, East of Nantes.

Here again letters of introduction allowed him to enter briefly into local entertainments, where Elkanah could display the letter just received from George Washington himself. He was taken to a play, but found "the audience thin, the actors bad." Sheffielders concentrated on their manufacturing industries too much to support what were considered mere amusements. Enveloped in coal dust and with a sky shaded by smoke, Sheffield's factories and water works were worth two days of his time. Always curious for innovations in manufactures and in agriculture, Elkanah wrote down that local farmers used a fertilizer he hadn't heard of—bones and horn pulverized by grinding wheels.

Following the river Derwent, the post-chaise climbed into a mountain range. Wild cliffs, narrow passes, and overhanging crags lit by glimmering moonlight produced an experience of rocks and rapids approaching the sublime. In the remote heights near Matlock they came upon a long building serving as a resort for bathers in the warm springs. The end of the season had come abruptly with the early snows. Climbing the top of the mountain here, Elkanah enjoyed the vista across several counties. Down below, he took the opportunity to enter the tunnel of a lead mine, where, torch-lit five hundred feet below the mountain top, miners "were at work, wearing out a wretched existence." Despite rudimentary air shafts, the mine felt humid and oppressive. In sharp contrast, at the resort, Elkanah experienced the marble-lined baths whose water had "the temperature of new milk." Remnants of the summer's visitors gathered for gaiety in the assembly room—"the sad relics of a brilliant company which had resorted to this celebrated bathing-place and had been dispersed by the frosts of autumn." Mirrors along the wall reflected more the candle flames of emptiness than convivial high spirits.

Descending from the mountains, their route to Derby took them through gentle farmland meadows. A silk factory in the city employed a couple hundred people tending to machines that were driven by a single water-wheel rotating three times a minute. He heard that each time round, the wheel produced seventy thousand yards of silk thread—astonishing, if accurate. Derby porcelain also attracted his notice. He considered it a "very admirable imitation of China porcelain ... executed with exquisite beauty and perfection."

In Birmingham again, he conversed at length with Priestley and Watt, and felt his "mind elevating and expanding." His friend Joseph Green also arranged that they visit the Earl of Ferrers. Once again, the fate of Major André brought emotions of conflict between admiration for his heroic attitude in death and anger or justification for the fact of his hanging. The rules of war could not be relaxed, said rebels. Spies were spies to be hanged. It was revenge for the hanging of Nathan Hale, not principle, said Tories. On that point was no compromise, and Elkanah came no further than to think of him as "poor André." It was at the Earl of Ferrer's house that Elkanah's friend Green had introduced André to Anna Seward. Her tragic poem praising the virtue of his patriotism and the purity of his love thwarted by death had moved hearts throughout England and America when it appeared not long before, in 1781.[21] Angry denunciation of America rarely raged more furiously. "Oh Washington! I tho't thee great and good, Nor knew thy Nero-thirst of guiltless blood! Severe to use the pow'r that fortune gave, Thou cool determin'd Murderer of the Brave!" An attempt to appear politely apolitical could not still the emotions.

On November 10 Elkanah continued his trip back to London, but not directly. First he passed westward through Worcester, Tewkesbury, and Gloucester, each with an imposing medieval church that Elkanah did not have time for. Their dominant presence in each small town increased his awareness of their inspiring antiquity, their power to force upon the present, thoughts of the passage of time, of the insignificance of the mundane. But he was in a hurry. He arrived at Bristol around ten in the evening on the end of a long day. He'd traveled eighty-nine miles over roads sometimes quite rough. The morning of the first day in Bristol, he delivered his letters of introduction, which again gave him the advantage of personal hospitality in an unknown city.

Bristol's broad quay, a mile long, used ingeniously efficient cranes for loading and unloading ships. The dry docks and floating docks two miles downstream could handle a hundred and fifty ships. The city's Atlantic commerce showed itself to Elkanah in twenty "sugar-houses" to process the cane sugar from slave plantations in the Caribbean. Various other factories provided full employment. More factories like these would help in America, he thought, where "a large proportion of the inhabitants eat the bread of idleness from the absence of manufactories." Was he giving any thought to the slavery in sugar production? From a hill above town he had a view of countless ships at anchor, and of the countryside from Bristol to Bath on the one side and across the water to Wales in the other direction. At the foot of the hill were the Brandon hot baths, a summer resort with concerts every morning. Elkanah left Bristol for Bath, where such amusements were emphasized even more.

From a decreasing distance along the river Avon the new and elegant Bath Crescent showed evening lanterns lit in front of the refined facade of curved, pillared residences. Windows shone the light of lamps within. Elkanah chose to stay several days to enjoy the baths, the music, and the ease of promenading among the fashionable and wealthy visitors taking the waters. The new buildings in classical style he judged "truly elegant and imposing." The magnificent fan vaulting of the abbey church might not have existed, as far as Elkanah's taste was concerned. One can only assume he saw it. His admiration went to more recent construction. "At the King's bath, the buildings are constructed on a scale of gorgeous magnificence and splendor. An obelisk, seventy feet high, rises from the centre of the bath, having recesses and seats at the base, to accommodate those who are boiling out their various disorders. Strange to relate, after performing this expurgatory office, the same water is pumped up and drunk by the diseased, in the room which overlooks the baths." Elkanah wasn't ill and didn't want to become so. He looked down from a room above, the Pump Room. A fog hid the faces of people in the bath, "but an occasional puff of wind would present to me a most singular and ludicrous spectacle: old and young, matrons and maidens, beaux and priests, all promiscuously wading and splashing in the bath, a band of music the while playing some solemn march or exhilarating dance."

Back at his lodgings in Bath, Elkanah was surprised to find his friend Henry Laurens, whom he had left at Nantes. The next day while returning the visit at Laurens' apartment, Elkanah witnessed the receipt of news from London. Henry Laurens' son had been killed in military action near Charleston, South Carolina. The father was inconsolable; "his faculties seemed to be crushed and paralyzed, his philsophy forsook him, and he abandoned himself to the agonies of a bereaved father." Some days later, Laurens returned to London, where Elkanah arranged to meet him.

Returning to London through Devizes a local legend commemorated there by a monument revealed something of Elkanah's beliefs, in his response. The story was that a woman who had bought something in the local market had falsely claimed to have paid when the seller demanded his due. According to Elkanah, the woman had called out, "'May God strike me dead, if I have not paid it.' She fell down and immediately expired." Her clenched fist still held the coins she hadn't paid. Writing about this some years afterward, Elkanah mentioned that he had met someone later in America who claimed to have been an eyewitness to this "memorable judgment and remarkable coincidence" in Devizes. Elkanah philosophized without apparent irony, "Let skeptics deny, and philosophers deride; facts like this bear fearful and powerful witness to the interposition of an Omniscient God in the affairs of man."

The town of Marlborough with a population of five hundred had the right to two members of parliament, while cities thousands larger had no representation at all. Nothing justified this. "The Rotten Borough system of England is one of the most corrupt and abhorrent features of their political institutions." Reform sentiment was growing, so Elkanah's opinions could easily find agreement among the people he met. After Marlborough, Elkanah passed through Hungerford, Reading and Henley on the way back to London.

Elkanah rejoined Henry Laurens in the city, relieved to find his friend in the company of supportive and sympathetic friends. Laurens was gaining his freedom in a prisoner exchange by which the Americans released General Cornwallis. Laurens introduced Elkanah to some of London's social leaders, which in turn led to further contacts. He was invited to dinner one evening in the home of Mr. Vaughan, whose son was the diplomat Elkanah had met in France at Benjamin Franklin's place in Passy. Mr. Vaughan seated him next to Thomas Howard, Earl of Effingham, a well-known public friend of the American cause. Effingham had resigned his commission in the British army to protest the war against America. Elkanah noted that Congress had honored him in 1777 by naming a frigate the *Effingham*. Rubbing shoulders with the titled of England, Elkanah was surprised. "I have been astonished to discover so much ignorance and vulgarity in the same class that exhibits so much that is exalted and ennobling in the character of man. With a few notable exceptions, the distinction is vast and obvious, between those noblemen of nature, who, by the force of native energy and greatness, have attained that eminence, and those *creatures of accident*, who are noblemen by inheritance."

One of the chief creatures of accident was the Prince of Wales. Elkanah met him during the interval while attending an opera. Judging the prince "elegant and dignified in his appearance, but debauched and profligate in his private life," Elkanah wondered if the decline of Great Britain from mighty empire to imbecile decay would be hastened by the accession of this man to the throne. As for the opera, that was uncongenial to an Englishman, let alone an American. "To me," he remarked, "an opera is a most insipid jargon of nonsense. The music and singing are unintelligible and an unnatural affectation, a jumble of musical sounds, grating to my American ear." British dancing was lumpish compared with what he had seen in France.

Perhaps the most eminent nobleman by nature, at least the one who most gave that impression, was Edmund Burke. Laurens had introduced Elkanah. At an informal breakfast with Burke, Elkanah felt insignificant in the presence of the man he recognized as an "intellectual giant," a "distinguished author, eloquent orator, and accomplished statesman." He was relieved not to have to say much while Burke held forth. "In my checkered life," he wrote later, "I have often been brought into intimate intercourse with great and accomplished men, and have always found myself at ease and self-possessed. Yet, the glare of this transcendent luminary humbled and embarrassed me. With Dr. Franklin, always kind and familiar, I could hold converse as with a venerated father. But Burke seemed a being of another sphere." Elkanah credited Burke with being the "primary cause of wresting from the reluctant King a decision to recognize our Independence," although that was admittedly in co-operation with Charles James Fox, Richard Brinsley Sheridan, and Henry Seymour Conway.

At Birmingham the Earl of Ferrers had given Elkanah a ticket to admit him to the House of Lords on December 5, 1782, when the king was to deliver his speech recognizing America's independence. The earl met Elkanah at the entrance to parliament and whispered the advice, "Get as near the throne as you can; fear nothing." Elkanah managed to position himself directly in front of the throne. Next to him he recognized Admiral Lord Howe, who had organized the British retreat from Boston in March, 1776. Tapestries around the room depicted the defeat of the Spanish Armada in 1588. Britain had triumphed then, though more the result of storms that seemed providential than a consequence of military might. Dim light came through the leaded lozenges of the gothic windows that served mostly to keep the fog outside. American loyalists present appeared as glum as the weather. Elkanah looked across the crowd and, besides the gathered noblemen, saw John Singleton Copley and Benjamin West, America's leading portrait and history painters.

He had commissioned a portrait of himself from Copley. It was not quite finished. The money for this artwork had come from a bet. Elkanah had won a hundred guineas "at the insurance office" when news arrived that Lord Howe had relieved Gibralter, where the British garrison had not been resupplied for a year. A Spanish fleet had tried to prevent access, but with favorable winds, the British fleet had reached the harbor and the British fortification. At dinner that evening with Copley, the famous painter from Boston, Massachusetts, Elkanah had decided to commission a portrait of himself.

All who had assembled in Parliament expecting the king's proclamation had to wait two hours before a long salute of thundering guns finally announced the arrival of the king. He came into the chamber through a door next to the throne, sat down, and unrolled a scroll he took from his pocket. Then the members of the House of Commons entered the room. The king read his proclamation. Having always attempted to carry out the desires of parliament and people, he said, he had always aimed for "'an entire and cordial reconciliation with the colonies. Finding it indispensible to the attainment of this object, I did not hesitate to go to the full length of the powers vested in me, and offer to declare them.'" (Elkanah inserted, "Here he paused, and was in evident agitation, either embarrassed in reading his speech, by the darkness of the room, or affected by a very *natural emotion*.") The king continued, "'and offer to declare them *free and independent States*. In thus admitting their separation from the crown of these kingdoms, I have sacrificed every consideration of my own, to the wishes and opinions of my people.

Copley's portrait of Elkanah Watson—engraving reversed to show the painting's compositional arrangement (engraving by Rogers after a deguerreo type by Tousley of Copley's painting, in *Men and Times of the Revolution,* 1861, frontispiece).

I make it my humble and ardent prayer to Almighty God, that Great Britain may not feel the evils which might result from so great a dismemberment of the Empire, and that America may be free from the calamities which have formerly proved, in the mother country, how essential monarchy is to the enjoyment of constitutional liberty. Religion, language, interests and affection may, and I hope will, yet prove a bond of permanent union between the two countries.'"[22]

Elkanah was overcome with the memory of suffering and desolation caused by "the stubbornness of this very King." But in words of triumph he summarized the period put to the immediate past. "The great drama was now closed. The battle of Lexington exhibited its first scene. The Declaration of Independence was a lofty and glorious event in its progress. And the ratification of our Independence by the King consummated the spectacle in triumph and exultation. This successful issue of the American Revolution will, in all probability, influence eventually the destinies of the whole human race."

A dinner of celebration was held at Copley's house. But first Elkanah went with the painter to his studio, where his portrait was nearly finished. He could see himself leaning elegantly against the base of a classical pillar, twenty-four years old, proud in a red coat over a grey silk waistcoat, his royal court attire from France.[23] His clear, untroubled gaze might be looking toward the future. He holds correspondence, with more on the table next to him. One letter is addressed to John Brown & Co., Providence. In the left background Copley painted a ship, which Elkanah intended to represent the vessel bringing news to America that the British government had acknowledged America's independence. "A sun was just rising upon the stripes of the union, streaming from her gaff."[24] The painting was completed except for that flag, which Copley had been reluctant to add before the official speech had been given. Returning to the studio after hearing the king's acknowledgement of the fact of independence, "with a bold hand, a master's touch, and I believe an American heart," Elkanah wrote in his diary, John Singleton Copley "attached to the ship the *stars and stripes*. This was, I imagine, *the first American flag hoisted in England*."

On December 6, Elkanah watched a debate in the House of Commons. Not an elaborate and formal display of rhetorical skill, instead, sarcastic repartee countered acrimonious ad hominem attacks. Burke rose to ridicule the King's address given the day before. "It was a farrago of nonsense and hypocrisy," Burke said, fully aware that the king had not in fact spent the last several years always aiming for "an entire and cordial reconciliation with the colonies." Elkanah noticed "young Pitt, the newly-created Chancellor of the Exchequer," who with asperity accused Burke of "buffoonery and levity." General Henry Seymour Conway brought the exchange to a close by stating clearly, "'The recognition of American Independence was explicit and unconditional.'"

As the House adjourned, Elkanah was invited to come down to the floor. Edmund Burke introduced him as a "messenger of peace" to Pitt, Fox, Sheridan, Conway, and other members of parliament. Elkanah felt a sense of honor and privilege to meet them, well aware of their importance in British politics and at the same time modest about his own part in conveying the messages of Franklin and other American diplomats.

Elkanah had a few more days in London before returning to France. During that interval he visited Windsor Castle. Architecturally it couldn't compare in his estimation with what he'd seen in France. Its position on a bluff overlooking the Thames, however, "infinitely surpasses them and indeed is unrivalled." He saw the king and the royal family promenading together with many noblemen and mingling with the people on Sunday afternoon. They had also been in church when Elkanah attended the service in St. George's Chapel. That beautiful gothic building with its varieties of fan vaulting did not inspire admiration. Elkanah thought it "much inferior, in style and compass, to the royal chapel at Versailles."

Paris, Financial Crisis, England Again

Elkanah left London on December 12 and traveled day and night to Paris, arriving three days later in the winter dark, very late. Again he stayed at the Hotel d'York, where he found Henry Laurens, whose room was separated from his own by no more than a folding door. The noise of a heated discussion woke him from exhausted sleep the day after his arrival. English and American diplomats in Laurens' room were trying to work out an acceptable boundary between Canada and the United States. At dinner the following day at John Adams' house, he learned from the commissioners that the boundary disagreements had been resolved. A peace treaty would be signed soon, he was told, although that did not take place until September, the next year. Moreover, the boundary agreed on was not to be respected by English troops in North America until after the War of 1812.

Visiting Franklin as soon as he returned to Paris, Elkanah was relieved to be able to give him a copy of a London newspaper which with circumstantial particulars had announced Franklin's death. Franklin thought this funny and said it was the third time he'd been declared late and lamented.

Besides catching up on news in Paris, Elkanah also received a welcome letter from his father, although he was annoyed that he had to pay postage due. There'd been no word from him for four years, no answer to many reports sent from Europe. "I had every reason to think" he wrote back to his father, "you had either renounced your paternal feelings, that my letters were disagreeable, or that I had inadvertently offended you. If so, you ought at least to have openly accused me that I might vindicate myself. Thus circumstanced I was determined never to have troubled you with another line, till my doubts were either confirmed or relieved."[25] Now that he had received a warm and loving letter from his father, one dated long before its delivery, Elkanah was "overwhelmed with joy" and happy to resume contact as a dutiful son. He informed his father that he "therefore determined to bury in eternal oblivion all past events & look forward with pleasure to pass through life in the utmost harmony with my only parent. My GOD I have always shuddered at the Idea of living upon any other footing & I must add, that the fault never laid with me." His father should be proud of him, he thought, for his accomplishment in having risen "out of Native obscurity by dint of my own Enterprise & Industry."

Elkanah returned to Nantes and resumed the negotiations of his importing and exporting business. He also gave thought to his return to America, confident in his ability to rely on the fortune he had built from investments, many of which were tied up in ongoing shipments. He hoped to buy a farm near Newport, Rhode Island. The system of buying, shipping, selling, and distributing dividends was, however, complex and relied on predictable payment by letters of credit and exchange that were mostly drawn on the National Bank of France.

When in response to the abrupt shift in commerce resulting from the end of the American war, a change that put in doubt the repayment of loans to America, the French Treasury (a forerunner of the French National Bank) by royal fiat stopped all payments for one year, Elkanah's business was so disrupted that it had to close. As he put it, "the army and navy bills on the government had been made payable at this Institution, and the distress and prostration of commercial affairs, which resulted from this measure, were universal and most disastrous." All Americans whose business involved French credit and payment were sucked under by this unexpected bank failure. Watson and Cossoul obtained a legal surcease of payment for one year, announced to their creditors by printed notices in French and English.[26] Elkanah left Nantes at the end of March, 1783, "prostrated and impoverished." The inactive firm remained in Nantes under Cossoul, while Elkanah moved to London to try to recover business momentum.

Elkanah said farewell to his longtime servant and friend, La Fleur. Then with Cossoul he traveled for the last time up to Paris. On the way, they visited the royal palace and gardens at Versailles. They found the "numerous exhibitions of taste, luxury, and magnificence" to be "interesting." The king and queen were just going out hunting, with horsemen and hounds as well as huntsmen to shoo game in the way of the sportsmen so they might have a chance at valiantly killing something. As they continued toward Paris, the noisy and dusty hunting party crossed their path. Etiquette required that they stop, dismount, take off their hats, and look on admiringly. The hunted deer sped toward them on the road, followed by the crowd of riders. "Within twenty feet of us, the deer bounded over a hedge and darted off in a new direction." The king wore a "lace cocked-hat, short coatee, and heavy boots and spurs." He jumped the hedge, followed by the dogs and his noble friends. The chase disappeared, leaving only the sound of hounds and the notes of horns to fade in the forest. Once again, Elkanah had seen a king. As in North Carolina, his sympathy favored the hunted deer.

Business did not return to normal. There was no way around the disaster for private businessmen, although John Adams put together loans in The Netherlands that salvaged the credit of the American government. The government's bills could be redirected to be paid in Amsterdam. Elkanah could do nothing more in France; he would make his elusive fortune in London in the summer, establishing a branch of Watson & Cossoul in Billiter Square.

His former high contacts evaporated in the face of his misfortune, some ignoring him ostentatiously. Few friends remained when he had no ability to live grandly. Nonetheless, through careful buying and selling, Elkanah's profits enabled him to clear his firm's French debts. Cossoul's wife Moriseau wrote him a friendly letter asking about business but also inquiring how his love life was prospering. She let him know that she and her children were well and that little Louis, her son, would some day be able to thank him for his good intention (implying that Elkanah was the child's godfather). Many years later Elkanah added a marginal note: "the busy tattle at Nantes wou'd have it that Louis was my Son—gibble-gabble without Cause, So help me Father Peter."[27] He found comfort in vague religious sentiment. "Leaning upon a *Holier Arm*, we are taught submission and contentment. Adversity tests our virtues, and tries sincerity, above all, teaching us to look deeply into the treacherous volume of the human heart."

In the summer, Elkanah's brother Marston embarked from Newport, Rhode Island, to visit him in London. Their father sent along a kind letter offering help in acquiring a farm for Elkanah if he planned to return to America, not apparently aware of the business failure. Imagining future profits, Elkanah, Sr., planned to move back to Plymouth from Freetown, perhaps to undertake ship building. He wanted to know the current selling price of white oak

Nantes, 1st Mar. 1783.

As the long expected event of Peace has at length taken place, we are apprehensive that England will command the principal bulk of the American trade, in consequence of which, after the most mature deliberation, we have determin'd to divide our house into two branches, the second to be conducted under our Mr. WATSON in London where he proposes establishing himself uuder the firm of WATSON, COSSOUL & C°. & being united to an old experienc'd merchant in that City accustom'd to the American trade.

Mr. WATSON has but just return'd from an extensive tour through the most principal tradeing ports, & manufacturing towns in England, which must in its consequence effectually enable him, to give such dispatch, & to transact business so advantageously, as cannot fail to be both pleasing & satisfactory to his Friends, who honour him with their confidence.

Most of the American commodities will meet a ready sale in England at present, particularly wheat, tobacco, rice, indigo, whale-oil, pott & pearl-ash, &c. as soon as the prices of these articles are fix'd at some peace medium, we shall take care to forward you immediate price currents from London.

We beg leave to observe that our house in Nantes will remain under its present firm & will be conducted by our Mr. COSSOUL who will always have it in his power to add weight, to the confidence we have establish'd upon your side the Atlantic.

We are with respect,

Your most obedient humble servants,

Announcing the move to London—placcard printed by Watson and Cossoul, Nantes, 1783 (from the Elkanah Watson Papers, courtesy New York State Library).

planks in England and France.[28] Marston's visit was short—by the end of August he was returning to America, carrying letters from Elkanah to his sisters.[29]

Despite Elkanah's limited budget, he managed some touring. September, 1783, found him in Margate, a growing seaside resort that profited from expansive vistas of pure sea air. The bathing carts amused him. Making private cabins of canvas, furnished with "chairs, a table, looking glass, and other necessary appliances," horses pulled these down into the waves, where the back door of the cart could be opened. Steps were let down so the bathers could wade or swim from them. As the carts went down to the sea forming a row all along the beach, swimmers sometimes made "ludicrous, if not serious mistakes" in trying to find their own cart again after swimming.

At the public breakfast in Margate's elegant Assembly Rooms, Elkanah acted the role of physiognomist—analyzing character by observing faces ("phizzes") as he had seen Mrs. Wright do in Paris. The gathering comprised ten "disappointed, desperate old maids, seven of whom were as yellow as potatoes, with a slight patch of vermillion daubed on with much care"; twelve "young lasses, seven of whom passed the [looking] glass with such an air of triumph and toss of the head as easily told one who they set themselves down ... for"; eight "worn down libertines, three of whom seem yet to have some hopes of regaining their constitutions, and the others have little to hope"; five "old white wigs, deacons and parsons out of the country, sitting at places and sanctified as in the church"; seven "married couples, although cold and distant to each other," contrasting with two other couples "affectionately strutting around the room, arm-in-arm"; three "Irish fortune hunters laying close siege to a rich old heiress"; two "French polite maitres fresh arrived from Paris"; and one "Modest American Spectator."[30]

A friend invited Elkanah to leave London and tour the Isle of Wight in March, 1784. Coming down from Farnham and Petersham to Portsmouth over snow-covered hills, Elkanah saw warships at anchor in the Royal Navy's main port. He also noted the "top-gallant masts of the 'Royal George' projecting above the water." That was the ship whose sudden capsizing had been reported in Paris. Besides viewing the ships in harbor, Elkanah was allowed to "inspect the extensive naval arsenal." Across the grey sea lay the Isle of Wight. A fortnight there allowed for exploration on horseback despite disagreeable weather. American ships put

Bathing at Margate (engraving by Thwaites or Barritt after Lossing, in Watson, *Men and Times*, 1861, p. 211).

in at Cowes, expecting to pick up instructions on where to take their cargos to obtain the best profit among the different possible port cities in Britain and on the Continent. Elkanah felt pride on seeing the new flag of his country—"destined in the next century," he thought, "to be borne in triumph through the domains of Old Neptune."

An open packet boat sailed through a gale to take them from the Isle of Wight to Southampton. Continuing past the little walled town, by evening they had reached Salisbury. Elkanah's taste was broadening. He spent much of the next day "in exploring a noble cathedral, which is pronounced one of the most perfect and magnificent specimens of Gothic architecture in England." If cathedrals in France had awakened his rationalist revulsion for the incensed fog of what he could only consider Catholic superstition, the medieval buildings of the Church of England provided an acceptable, sanitized alternative. Outside Salisbury the ruins of Old Sarum aroused his ire once more at the unreformed system of parliamentary representation.

This former town, where no one lived, had two members in parliament chosen by few electors, sometimes only by one. Populous new cities existed with no representation at all. Triumphant in the success of the American revolution, Elkanah thought that "if abuses such as these cannot be corrected by pacific means, to purge and purify this noble nation, a temporary sacrifice must be made for the welfare of millions yet unborn"—fine words to justify an imaginary baptism of blood! The reality of the French Revolution would clarify the danger of anarchy within just a few years, but America's new independence could ideally justify the

Salisbury Cathedral (wood engraving from *The Saturday Magazine,* Oct. 25, 1834).

deaths and destruction there for anyone who, like Elkanah, could imagine a future of American triumph. On Salisbury Plain, sheep grazed the grass of Stonehenge uninterested in politics.

From Salisbury, they rode westward through Wilton, Shaftsbury, Sherborn, and Yeovil to Plymouth. Farmland filled with cattle and sheep, fields divided by hedges, estates supporting new mansions witnessed to prosperous agriculture.

But there were no forests, and Elkanah missed the whitewashed cottages of independent peasants he'd seen in other regions. Plymouth's harbor, more exposed than that of Portsmouth, had fortifications with three hundred cannon. Guiding and warning ships at sea, Eddystone lighthouse rose out of the surf, a "wonderful triumph of human art and energy." No such lighthouse had yet been built in America, although Minot Light (Scituate, Massachusetts) would eventually imitate Eddystone. Near Plymouth, Elkanah looked at the walls of Mill Prison, where Americans captured during the war had been imprisoned.

Returning to London by coach, Elkanah listened to two ladies he considered "genteelly dressed, and evidently of a respectable class in society." One told the other, "'I have seen a wonderful sight—a little girl born in a place called Boston in North America. And, what is very astonishing, but I pledge you my word it is true, she speaks English as well as any child in England. And, besides, she is perfectly white!'" Her companion was astonished. "'Is it possible!' she exclaimed in no counterfeit astonishment." Elkanah had learned that "Many of the people of England suppose us to be a nation of Indians, Negroes, or mixed blood."

Back in London, curiosity inspired Elkanah to observe English voting practices when a member of parliament for Westminster was to be chosen at Covent Garden. Voting lasted three days. He went to watch every day. Twenty thousand spectators gathered in front of St. Paul's Church. He was shocked that factions supporting the candidates hired gangs to prevent supporters of their opponents from reaching the polling place. "Here all was confusion and conflict, bloody noses and broken heads, intimidation and corruption."

The candidates were Charles Fox, Lord Hood, and Sir Cecil Wray. Their campaigning inspired satirical prints by several artists including Thomas Rowlandson (who produced at least five separate images on the topic). Sailors for Hood bludgeoned Irishmen for Fox. The crowd took up the fight, and first one gang and then the other chased their opponents out of the square only to see them return from some other street or alley and fight some more. A Frenchman commented to the American, "'If this is liberty, Heaven deliver my country from it.'"

Curiosity also brought Elkanah in contact with Thomas Wildman, who lived near him in Highgate. Appropriately named, this man had achieved fame as a bee-keeper and tamer. He supplied bees to gardens throughout London. Elkanah observed his control of whole swarms which he could lead to perform amazing groupings and movements before returning on command to their hives at his house. His trick was the discovery that, by gently holding the queen bee and placing her wherever he wanted the swarm to move, the rest of the bees would come to the new location to re-establish community. He had published a book, *A Treatise on the Management of Bees*, in 1768.

Finding himself free of obligations for several weeks, Elkanah made arrangements to cross the Channel and tour Holland. Business might be dormant, but he could at least improve the time. He left the King's Arms Inn in London at five o'clock in the morning on May 25, 1784, on his way to the port of Harwich where he could cross to the Netherlands.[31] His chance companions in the public coach looked pleasant enough, so he hoped the trip would not be disappointing. Eight or nine miles beyond Colchester, their road followed the banks of the tidal waters of the River Stour to Manningtree, where he could see the new mansion of Richard Rigby, who had grown immensely rich from the bribery involved in his job as paymaster for the army. Off to the left, in the water, a seventy-four-gun warship was being repaired. Over the next hill, the view expanded to the sky above the German Ocean (as the North Sea was sometimes called). The traveling was "exceedingly romantic and agreeable till we reached Harwich." That town, however, was "a villainous dirty little hole." The packet boat "being ready to weigh anchor, we were speedily relieved from the impositions to which strangers are ever subject in such places." By that, Elkanah meant tipping various people who arrived out of nowhere to give help where none had been asked. And, above all, he had been annoyed by grasping customs officers. "I must vent my malice," he wrote, "against the villainous search officers at Harwich who extorted 3/6 [three shillings six pence] from each of us for doing what they are paid for. I contended in vain to oppose their injustice but was reluctantly forced to bend to the rod, or submit to delay and inconvenience." On to Holland, then!

Four

The Netherlands

Holland—Delfshaven and Rotterdam

Captain Hearn of the *Prince of Wales* ordered his sailors to hoist the anchor for departure from Harwich at seven in the evening.[1] Their baggage stowed below, passengers on deck watched the moving coast while keeping alert to the work of the sailors. The ship hugged the coast of Suffolk then turned to cross toward Holland. Wild squalls forced Elkanah and other passengers to seek shelter below. He had never seen such an elegant packet boat, small yet feeling spacious. Through the rough rocking of a thunderous storm he managed to sleep until four in the morning, surprised on waking by smooth sailing before a light breeze.

Mist obscured the low Dutch coast. No hills guided shippers like in England where maps included silhouettes of the landscape as seen from the sea. Only "light houses, windmills, rows of trees, and distant spires" punctuated Holland's horizon.

Rising wind pushed them to the flanking piers of Hellevoetsluis harbor. An idle, pipe-smoking Dutchman symbolized the entire nation. "In this moment I felt such a spirit of universal Philanthropy possess my soul, that I could most cordially have given him a friendly shake of brotherly love, which convinced me how much our happiness in this world depends on those social bonds which ought to link us altogether."

Bricks set on end paved the quay and streets. Ships at anchor contrasted with wrecks supposed to be the hulks of the fleet that Admiral Tromp had commanded against the English in the seventeenth century. Hellevoetsluis was strongly defended and dazzlingly tidy. Nothing contradicted the expected stereotype. "In truth, the houses, dress, and everything around us wore the face of neatness so peculiar to this singular nation and country."

So different was Holland from any place he'd seen before that he felt himself observing from a great distance—"let off in an air balloon, and lost in the moon or some other region totally new or strange." Narrow houses with tall pointed gables presented a design he decided was "the old Spanish manner." The people were unlike the English and French, but not unlike what he'd heard about the Dutch. "The men and women in the vulgar class are quite boorish and inanimate, and appear characteristic with their ships, heavy and square." The women dressed oddly and were all the same height. All wore tight caps with "very vulgar brass ear rings of an enormous size, and as a proof of their taste, what should you think of black beauty spots over their temples as big as a crown and as ragged as if torn from the silk?"

Departure for Den Briel by coach the next morning was supposed to be at seven o'clock. A typically Dutch dispute delayed them. The coach driver refused to bring his wagon to the door of the hotel. Local porters had to be paid to carry the baggage from the hotel to the coach, just half a dozen houses away—at six stuivers a trunk. The two carriages, one with baggage, the other with passengers, trundled heavily along muddy roads across the island of Voorne to the town of Den Briel.

Nothing notable could be seen in the flat fields. The cows' horns were shorter than those in England and the sheep had none at all. Every church tower was crowned with a stork's nest. Even the church in the middle of Den Briel, whose blocky tower served sailors at sea as a landmark, had a stork's nest on top.

Den Briel had seen the beginning of military action in the Netherlands' revolt against Spanish tyranny in 1572. As Elkanah conceived it, fighting started with the use of privateers, just like those from New England that first sailed out against the Royal Navy. Dutch history could thus serve as a parallel with American history, placing the more recent events in a context of well-known Dutch heroism.

The walled town's canals divided tree-shaded streets. Sash windows' spotless large panes reflected the green leaves. Real little mirrors could be seen everywhere, too. Elkanah "thought it very droll to see reflecting glasses [spy mirrors] hitched upon the outside of the most genteel windows, so that Madam Mevrou can sit unobserved by her window and reconnoiter every object moving up and down the streets."

At the far end of town, the travelers again met an unfamiliar Dutch custom. Instead of haggling with the skippers for a price on the ferry ride to Rotterdam, the choice of skipper was being settled for them among the boatmen themselves, by throwing dice. The ferry from Den Briel to Rotterdam along the Maas River cost 9/6 (stuivers and duits, not shillings and pence).

A brisk northwest gale blew them straight ahead toward Rotterdam. Along the river were groves of trees, villages, and rows of poplars. The son of the Pilgrims felt that Delfshaven, two miles before Rotterdam, "will be ever dear and memorable to the heart of an American as the point of embarkation of our Puritan forefathers." His own ancestors, the Pilgrims who left Leiden in 1620, should be eternally commemorated, an opinion shared by other descendants.

Dams protected Delfshaven against flooding, with fortifications to guard against attack. Three men-of-war lay at anchor before the town. Riverside mansions appeared to Elkanah as the "most magnificent houses I can recollect to have seen anywhere."

Rotterdam was a confusion of fine houses and jostling masts, of church spires and trees, of waterways and bridges all mixed together. Ships of up to three hundred tons burden could be unloaded from broad canals in front of the warehouses of the merchants who owned them or their cargo. Most ships, however, were moored along the quay called the Boompjes (little trees). Beyond them the river traffic sailed past in both directions. "Imagine yourself every other moment upon a snug little draw bridge leading over a canal running through spacious streets, with a continual commotion of boats and barges upon each side of you, a clean paved wide street before you, and beautiful houses, with trees bordering the canals. Hold fast to these grand outlines and you can easily traverse by your fire side most of the towns in the Seven Provinces [of The Netherlands]." Elkanah thus provided a general framework that could be modified, city by city, with local details, such as the statue of Erasmus he saw in Rotterdam.

Having climbed to the top of the tower of the church of St. Laurens, he enjoyed the vista. "The City of Rotterdam appeared like a high finished curious picture below us, and the country beyond a delightful background cultivated like a continued garden all the way to our horizon. I have not yet in any instance experienced a more happy hour than we spent in contemplating this wonderful country, which seems like an enchanted fairy land. In ranging our eyes over this extended prospect, we encompassed within our view through spy glasses Delft, Dort, Hague, den Briel, Utrecht, & Amsterdam which in fact included the best part of Holland. I thought it beyond the power of conception to imagine a more lovely sight, but I found the picture much improved by reducing it to miniature in a concave mirror which we had with us."

Bells rang out with a power that shook the bones of anyone climbing down the tower. The music from these numerous tuned bells had a sound Elkanah had never heard before, stopping him in the street to demand he listen to the melodies sent out over all the roofs. Inside the church, an old sexton was packing old bones in boxes to be re-buried to make space for new burials. This was the custom in Holland.

An impressive epitaph in the church was translated from Latin for him by a young Oxford graduate who was a fellow-passenger and tourist. In memory of Johan van Brakel, the inscription declared, "The terror of the sea, To whom/ Fire, earth, and water submitted,/ Is covered with this stone,/ His spirit even now,/ Seems ready to burst into flame/ And to break from its earthly/ Habitation/ As he broke the chains of Iron." According to Elkanah's researches in the *History of the United Provinces,* the Dutch admiral Brakel had achieved fame by sawing through chains that blocked the navy of Crusaders when they invaded Egypt in the thirteenth century, using huge iron blades attached to the stems of three boats. The city of Damiate was conquered. Elkanah's recording of this anecdote reveals that translation was not as easy as he

Rotterdam (steel engraving and etching by A. H. Payne after W. H. Bartlett).

had thought. The monument at Rotterdam commemorates Johan van Brakel, a Dutch admiral of the seventeenth century, who was credited with having broken through a chain. But this chain had no connection with the medieval Crusader legend; it had blocked the Medway River during the Second Anglo-Dutch War in 1667.

Outside the city gates, he saw wealthy Rotterdammers riding out to country estates in "clumsy carriages" pulled by good-looking black horses. The Dutch rarely rode horseback, he was told.

English-speakers were hard to find, but there was no trouble using French when approaching anyone who looked well-bred. The assumption that anyone polite could speak French implied "that it is almost vulgar for a man to speak his native tongue." As regards Dutch, Elkanah came to the defense of the language. "Everyone knows it is in truth vulgar and harsh but perhaps there are no two languages which bear a greater affinity to each other than the Dutch and English." French was a language that Elkanah couldn't grasp for several weeks even though he had studied it in America. Embedded in the Dutch he heard in Holland, he thought he discerned complete phrases in English, or Dutch phrases that had become current in colloquial English. "It is well known that the Dutch is an original language, and the English on the contrary a compounded one, much of which they owe to the Dutch." He even felt he could fully understand the meaning of a letter he'd seen that was written in Dutch, because of a large number of English words and phrases in it.

Elkanah proclaimed that it was time to compare the world with America, whose young flag of thirteen stripes now flew in Rotterdam's harbor. The streamers of Europe had begun to fade from tired old age. "But the stripes shine with the luster of a rainbow after a thunderstorm—which happily for mankind is blown over—and left the world in a calm." The inspiring flag fluttered on the *Speedy*, which was unloading rice, tobacco, and turpentine from America.[2]

Besides the American ships, several Dutch vessels attracted his notice. They intended to carry a thousand immigrants bound for America. The idea filled Elkanah with pride. "What a feast for the soul, when we reflect that the present age in America have by a virtuous and arduous struggle opened an asylum for the oppressed nations of the earth! This consideration alone (when we reflect on its extended effects & probable duration) is worth all the dangers and toils we have endured in the conflict. Since the world first existed no people ever had a more solemn and important charge committed to their hands. The welfare of millions for ages to come depends on the persevering virtue of the present generation. America stands comparatively like the dazzling sun in the heaven, center of light and the wonder of the admiring world who feel the influence of its rays. The persecuted will find ease and rest, and tortured virtue and exiled worth will penetrate among us from East, West, North and South. Mild laws executed with energy will secure us happiness, and bid astonished probity defy its tyrant." Modesty offered no hindrance to the enjoyment of these visions.

Delft, William of Orange and George Washington

Elkanah jumped onto a horse-drawn canal boat whose route to Delft started from a mooring beside Rotterdam's new Delftse Poort (Delft Gate). He took passage in the cabin at the stern, where eight to ten people could reserve comfortable places at an additional fee.

(The basic rate was about one English penny per mile. Elkanah found no cheaper transportation anywhere.) Twenty-eight more passengers were seated on hard wooden benches along the inside of the hull, covered by a platform that served as a promenade, being paved with shells set in tar. The first-class cabin roof served as a platform, also. Elkanah and the others "paraded upon the top of the house, with a crowded room under our feet, and clouds of tobacco smoke issuing out from little windows on each side."

From the deck he had a view through rows of trees to roads outside the city where again he saw the ornate carriages of the wealthy. Similarly decorated little boats carried passengers on their way out of town to country houses. Freight came and went in horse-drawn barges or smaller sail boats. Gliding under drawbridge after drawbridge, boats heading one direction dropped their draw lines while others coming the other way passed, in a system that smoothly coordinated the traffic with no interruption or delay. Fields and houses by the canal showed the lives of dairy farmers. Mansions set back in their gardens exhibited the tastes of the wealthy at a proper distance. Each one had a little tea house at canal's edge, some of them square, others octagonal. They seemed to be all windows. Many were decorated in Chinese style. "We have a full peep into them, where we see the gentle people regaling themselves in parties—drinking tea, smoking, playing cards, music, or reading." Life in a Dutch country mansion could inspire dreams. As the boat continued toward Delft, Elkanah had to break off writing a letter about this because two old Dutchmen had sat down on either side of him, puffing at their pipes. Combined with the slight instability of the boat's forward motion, the smoke was beginning to make him queasy.

He descended into the boat's common quarters where he found an opportunity to sit down next to a beautiful woman from Brussels, dressed entirely in French fashion. Her husband sat next to her on the other side. Greeting her with a pleasantry, Elkanah boldly asked her

Gazebo by the canal (steel engraving by John Andrew, in Jacob Abott, *Rollo in Holland*, Boston, 1857, p. 193).

where she came from; and "if the gentleman by her side was her husband, gallant, or brother?" She answered him readily. Her husband, busy reading, seemed to have no difficulty with his wife's engaging this stranger in conversation. After half an hour, Elkanah imagined that he "felt the same friendship and tenderness for her, as if our acquaintance had been of several years' standing." Communication, of course, used French, and in that language, according to Elkanah, custom had "established a certain innocent Ladies' language, which would in England be construed into a decided intrigue."

The passengers disembarked at Delft, not far from the arsenal. The woman's husband walked ahead as Elkanah linked arms with the woman and strolled "over the pavements as lightly as a young couple upon a full march to the shrine of hymen. Every moment interested us mutually in each other's welfare." While they walked through Delft toward her house, she passed Elkanah a paper with her Rotterdam address written on it. He promised to visit her on return later from Amsterdam. Elkanah took leave of this surprising and unexpected acquaintance at the entrance to her house, where she rejoined her husband and went indoors. Somewhat confused and not a little excited by this encounter, Elkanah returned to his other friends from the journey, who joined him in some sightseeing.

Elkanah never had the chance to look her up in Rotterdam, but he kept her note giving her name and address: Mrs. Valton, living at Rotterdam in a corner house on the Wijnhaven.

In contrast with Rotterdam, Delft had elegantly clean streets unencumbered by the packages, sacks, and barrels that came with trade. Many of the residents of houses on the major canals and public squares had become wealthy through investments elsewhere and had retired to live from the income of their fortunes. Their servants could polish the glass on their windows and scrub the thin brick paving in front of their fine stone steps. Around five thousand other houses in back streets and alleys held poor laborers unseen by the tourists.

Delft had been known for its earthenware and what Elkanah called a "fine imitation of porcelain." Now, however, the English produced more and better earthenware, while French porcelain had overtaken Dutch production. The antiquated city's walls had defended it from enemies in the past but not from commercial competition.

Elkanah wrote that the city hall was "a handsome old gothic structure." Among the many paintings displayed, the most worth seeing, he thought, was a representation of the assassination in Delft of Prince William of Orange—"tragic and divinely executed." The assassin Balthasar Gerards fired his pistol at the Prince, father of the country, in a papist plot in 1584. The dramatic painting showed the assassin clutching a letter from King Philip II of Spain that promised a grant of nobility to anyone who succeeded in killing Prince William.

Elkanah and his friends next visited the Princenhof, the palace where the murder had taken place. "They showed us the spot where he fell at the foot of the stairs, and two holes the balls made in the wall." Elkanah wrote about the murderer's punishment. Immediately captured, Balthasar Gerards was "rolled naked in a cask drove full of sharp nails till he expired." Delft's town hall, however, is not gothic. Its Renaissance design and detail date from 1618 to 1620. All the details are classical in a manneristic style with which Elkanah must have been unfamiliar. Evidently the effect was just as strange to him as medieval gothic architecture. Obelisks were indistinguishable from gothic pinnacles.

Even odder is Elkanah's confusion about the punishment of Balthasar Gerards. The murderer was tortured in 1584 with red-hot iron instruments, then cut in quarters and his heart torn out while still beating, after which his head was cut off. Death by being rolled in a barrel in which nails had been driven, on the other hand, was the legendary method of execution of Gerard van Velsen, the assassin of Count Floris V of Holland in the thirteenth century. History's parallels confused him again.

Delft's Old and New Churches were "capital buildings, each adorned with lofty steeples and uncommon harmonious chimes." Monuments of note in the Old Church were those to Admirals Piet Hein and Maerten Harpertsz. Tromp, as well as the memorial to Anthony van Leeuwenhoek, who developed the first high-powered microscope. Piet Hein's figure lay beneath a classical temple-like canopy, while Tromp's sculpture included a low-relief depiction of warships engaged in one of his victorious battles, with trophies of war along the sides. Carillon music sounded as they entered the immense New Church to see the magnificent tomb of Prince William of Orange. The prince's long and difficult struggles against the Duke of Alva in the Dutch war for independence brought emotional thoughts of George Washington to Elkanah's mind. "Recapitulating in my mind the variety of [William of Orange's] conflicts—his fatal end—and the similarity of his and our Great Washington's characters, my enthusiasm betrayed me into an involuntary sigh of homage, accompanied by a tear which I detected stealing slyly down my cheek. Indeed, their fame and the importance of their achievements are such in the scale of human events that their names deserve to be writ by the sun's fingered rays on the surface of the heavens." Many Americans felt the parallel of Dutch and American resistance to tyranny. As Elkanah put it, "The struggle of Holland for freedom, so fraught with blood and suffering, seemed a type of our own."

The murdered prince's favorite dog was depicted at his feet in the marble sculpture of his body atop the tomb. According to tradition, the dog had died of grief soon after his master. Fame's trumpet, represented allegorically above a sculptured representation of his body, proclaimed the glory of the prince's deeds. Another statue in bronze showed him in armor, seated in a commanding pose looking out at the world. Twenty-two marble columns accompanied many carved ornaments in brass and marble.

Near the grave of the prince they saw that of the "famous and wise [Hugo] Grotius." Grotius was esteemed in America as the founder of international maritime law and as an eloquent contributor to the rise of religious toleration. "This unfortunate man fell a victim to the rash resentment of Prince Maurice successor to his father William I."

Watson and John Adams in The Hague

The bells of seven o'clock called them back to their canal-boat, rushing through the streets "upon a full canter." They had the roof of the cabin all to themselves, giving an evening view of the countryside from Delft through the village of Rijswijk to The Hague. The weather continued to be clear and serene, "but the thick exhalations prevented the moon from showing us the country.... However, the lights from the summer houses compensated in some degree. The dampness of the evening air, so pernicious in Holland, obliged us to box up in our cabin." The cabin windows showed only the banks of the canal, with little drawbridges over smaller connecting waterways. Ducks slept in the grass on the banks. "The stench from the canals was intolerable as we approached The Hague, which not a little surprised us." Sewers emptied into the rivers and canals in any city.

Arriving in The Hague late, they had difficulty finding their intended hotel. A lounger offered his assistance, for a fee, whose amount was undefined and likely to increase. Elkanah's companions, "who were greens in the ways of the world," agreed to accept his aid. But Elkanah intervened and broke off the contact as soon as they located the street where the hotel could be found. "With the best grace I was capable of, [Elkanah] wished him a decided good night." The staff at the Hotel English Parliament could speak both French and English (besides Dutch). The service was "capital."

Elkanah wrote down general information about the town—its location just a couple of miles inland and nine miles away from Leiden. It would be called a city except that it had no town walls and no city charter. Nonetheless, The Hague's beautiful, rich mansions caused Lord Chesterfield to call it "the most elegant city in the world." Forty-five thousand people lived in six thousand houses, enclosed by a tree-lined canal. Spacious shady streets led from square to square. The town was "the seat of this government and the residence of all foreign ministers." People who lived in the town worked for or provided supplies for these officials. The town was healthy, "being something elevated, and in the heart of a fruitful country surrounded everywhere by fine cities, villages, beautiful country houses, magnificent gardens and charming meadows."

The date was June 2, 1784. "It was Sunday so I took care to put on my best duds, especially as my first step was to pay my respects to the American Ambassador, John Adams, Esq."[3] Adams, however, wasn't home, so Elkanah decided to look in the Dutch church services. Dutch churches had been cleared of "those gaudy ornaments so common in France and other Catholic countries." The effect was not, however, whitewashed emptiness, but one of "a certain melancholy gloom, owing to the walls' being covered with the arms of the principal families, which are all worked upon black velvet. It gives the appearance, or at least an idea, of the inside of a large tomb." The ministers were "thumping the cushions" to full congregations, most of whom stood without removing their hats. There were no pews in the center of the church. Some women sat on folding chairs brought along from home. The floors were paved with grave slabs; benches would get in the way if this or that grave had to be opened to deposit another coffin in the vault.

After church, Elkanah joined a large crowd of nobility and burghers at the Grand Parade—the Lange Voorhout. In this broad boulevard lined with beautiful mansions, the Prince of Orange, together with two young princes, was reviewing the troops from the garrison of The Hague. Elkanah managed to stand close to the prince. He was "of a middling stature, effeminate, with a disagreeable stooping gait. Add to this a stupid, inanimate countenace." All five of the tourists who were sightseeing together agreed that the Prince of Orange looked quite a lot like his uncle, the King of England. King George II's daughter Ann was the mother of the Prince of Orange.

For some time after leaving the military exercises, Elkanah and his friends walked the town, strolling past the mansions. Across the little lake from the old castle of the counts of Holland that had become the Dutch parliament he found a street of the finest houses, "superbly built, many of hewn stone ... like so many palaces." The Dutch who lived in The Hague were, he discovered, a "model of the Parisians, very polite and entirely frenchified." The Dutch language had been replaced by French in polite society. He liked the way the women looked. "The genteel ladies are in general very handsome." The Dutch, however, were "much addicted to gaming."

At two o'clock Elkanah again presented himself at the official residence of John Adams. This grand mansion now belonged to the "13 United States of America." Adams intended it

The town hall of The Hague (steel engraving and etching by A. H. Payne after W. H. Bartlett).

to be the home of future ambassadors. He had furnished it decently "with Republican simplicity," providing an extensive library. As with most large houses in The Hague, there was a small formal garden behind it, but no garden area on the street side. Elkanah was greeted cordially and asked to midday dinner.

Afterward, in the ambassador's carriage, Adams and he toured the finer parts of the town, then proceeded along a tree-lined avenue northwards to the fishing town of Scheveningen (which Elkanah wrote as "Schevling"). Many people were walking or riding along the two-mile route to enjoy the breezes and sands of the beach. "The novelty, and the roaring of the uncouth cookmaids with which the wagons were crowded exceedingly pleased me. But their singing—rather, yelling—was comparatively like the squalling of as many cats roasting over a roaring fire." There seemed to be a contest for loudest and least harmonious. Their peculiar costumes and their distended faces presented a comical display.

John Adams, America's ambassador to The Netherlands (engraving and etching by R. Vinkeles).

The colors of the ambassador's livery matched those of the American military uniform. Everyone recognized the carriage and its occupants as Americans. Elkanah was compelled to tip his hat so frequently he thought that "a few more jaunts to Schevling would have put me under the necessity of buying a new hat." The village church spire marked the end of the road shaded by the leafy arches of the double line of trees. At the avenue's terminus, the view displayed the wide horizon of the North Sea, breakers rushing onto the beach at the foot of the coastal dunes. The grass-covered dunes effectively kept out the sea along parts of the coast, but dykes and embankments provided the main security.

Many people came out here in the summer from The Hague to bathe. Someone told Elkanah that fishermen's daughters served as outdoor cloakroom attendants, guarding clothing removed by people swimming. Not only that, but the girls "wipe them dry with towels as they leave the water," without batting an eyelash. One can get used to anything, he thought, willing to try. He didn't see the fishermen's daughters, but he could believe the story. What he saw were a few fishing boats far out to sea.

On one side of the long shady roadway an elaborate gate proclaimed the entrance to the renowned formal gardens of Count Bentinck. His family had become earls of Portland in thanks for their support of William III, when he and his wife Mary Stuart took the throne of England as William and Mary. Elkanah was told how fine the gardens were, how superior to every other garden in the province. "Style, simplicity, and picturesque views" could be enjoyed by the public. John Adams and he admired the parks of flowers and hedges that bordered paths leading to a "fine orangery, a grotto, water spouts, a forest, terrace, walks, hills, flower gardens, a lake, and a menagerie." The nearby dunes provided the height for cisterns to supply the fountains with gravity flow. For those with time for a promenade, here were varieties of rare delights.

On driving back into town, their carriage halted as the Prince of Orange returned to his palace on foot, accompanied by many liveried servants and soldiers. John Adams invited Elkanah to take dinner at the embassy and meet Adams' friend and associate, Monsieur Charles Dumas. Dumas had been helpful to America's interests in France, besides arranging for Adams to meet people of importance in The Netherlands. "With two such enlightened heads, and deep erudition, it would have been my own fault," Elkanah wrote, "not to have sifted every information I was so greedy to get in possession relative to the present convulsed state of this complicated government." He took notes.

The next day, after breakfasting together at the embassy, John Adams took Elkanah to see the Huis ten Bosch—the House in the Woods. A mile outside the old town of The Hague, the woods were said to be the largest natural forest in Holland. The palace had been built in 1645 originally as a hunting lodge for Princess Amalia. Widowed, she turned it into memorial to her husband, Prince Frederick Hendrick of Orange—a house of mourning. Hidden in the middle of the forest, the elegant building appeared to Elkanah to be withdrawn from the possibility of gaiety. Fine paths led away into the somber trees, which drew back to reveal a French formal garden behind the house. A long avenue led to the gates surmounted with the coat-of-arms of Oranje-Nassau. Broad stairs led up to a grand entrance in a wall of carved stone pilasters, contrasting with the flanking wings of the house built of brick. A large cupola rose above and behind this formal front. The Grand Salon surmounted by the dome contained paintings depicting the triumphs of Prince Frederick Hendrick. Elkanah thought they were "the productions of the famous Rubens and Van der Werff." In fact, these paintings were by Jacob Jordaens, Rubens' less widely known pupil.

London's Banqueting Hall had paintings by Rubens installed in 1636 that might have inspired this quasi-monarchical imitation. Both panegyrics proclaimed the glory of leaders whose deeds brought peace to their countries. Here, Frederick Hendrick received honor with his father, Prince William the Silent, and his brother, Prince Maurits. Seated on an imaginary triumphal chariot, Frederick Hendrick's glory was expressed by the four proud horses bearing him forward to lasting fame. Princess Amalia, Prince Frederick Hendrick's widow, was portrayed in the center of the cupola vaulting, above the gallery "where the musicians formerly played to sooth her melancholy." Elkanah claimed to have been born "with a tincture of a painter's soul." He "found in the salon a luxurious feast for the eyes."

A depiction of Vulcan in his forge, near the fireplace, was esteemed the high point of the collection. What Elkanah liked best, however, were the standing portraits of the princes William of Orange and his son Maurice. Luxury was evident throughout—carpets of high quality covered the black walnut floors. But the display made a restrained impression compared

Huis ten Bosch—the House in the Woods at The Hague (anonymous etching published by Carel or Abraham Allard, ca. 1700).

with Versailles. Elaborately sculptured plaster ceilings may have cost a fortune, yet their white forms seemed almost prim without French gilding. The bed of the Princess of Orange was enclosed by a railing consisting of expensive Japanese lacquer panels. The bed itself glittered with mother of pearl. The price was said to have been 28,000 guilders, although Elkanah had no clear idea what prices in Holland might be for something more ordinary. A floral still-life painting by a Flemish painter was pointed out for its monetary value, around 15,000 guilders. Elkanah wrote that he "was so delighted with the paintings that [he] left them, after a full hour's eager examination, with regret."

John Adams dismissed the carriage. They spent a couple of hours in conversation while walking in the forest. The tall oak trees reminded Elkanah of wilder, rural groves in America. Birds unfamiliar at home showed their beautiful colors while singing foreign tunes. The blue and grey Flemish Jay was new to Elkanah, but he looked in vain for the scarlet American Cardinal. And no wild turkeys disturbed the grazing deer. Instead, grey herons calmly waited for fish beside ponds and ditches. Storks built nests on wagon wheels set high on poles in meadows not far from the house, folding their black and white wings to settle down.

The midday meal at the "American hotel" (as Elkanah called the embassy building) preceded another sightseeing trip. South of The Hague, just two miles through farmland set off by lines of trees, the village of Rijswijk surrounded a large brick church. The town's fame derived from the Peace of Rijswijk, signed in the palace here in 1697. France had found the alliance against it of Spain, England, and The Netherlands too strong to justify continuing a war going nowhere. The treaty agreed to recognize the Dutchman Willem III as King William III of England. For Protestants, an alliance of The Netherlands and England, symbolized so solidly by the marriage of William and Mary, could not have been more fortunate.

The Palace at Rijswijk, one of Europe's many smaller architectural gestures of homage to the splendor displayed at Versailles, lay about a quarter of a mile from the village center. A carefully tended artificial forest separated the palace from the public road. Elkanah passed beneath arched entries and discovered the palace to be "nobly built all with hewn stone, but going fast to ruin." A marble stair and marble floors gave witness to the far-flung trading empire of the Dutch. That marble came by ship from Italy. Other cut stone came from quarries in Belgium or Germany. In the elaborate gardens on the south aspect of the mansion, a connoisseur could find plants brought together from yet more distant lands. An echo effect like that of the whispering gallery in St. Paul's Cathedral in London attracted tourists to the palace's assembly chamber.

Adams and Watson returned to The Hague for further sightseeing, followed by an evening at the embassy. Adams introduced Elkanah to the Dutch ambassador about to depart for London, Dirck Wolter van Lynden, as well as to other notable visitors.[4] As far as Elkanah could tell, John Adams was the most popular and influential ambassador in The Hague. "He is universally esteemed for his profound penetration, and extensive political knowledge." Elkanah thought America owed Adams a debt of gratitude for having defeated the attempt of the English ambassador, Sir Joseph York, to divert Dutch support from America or even transform it to hostility. Adams had also successfully negotiated the new country's boundaries. And he ensured that America's fishermen would not be impressed into the British navy. Adams, he observed, "talks but little, thinks a great deal—and what he says is always to the purposes." Elkanah's young eyes were seeing the "stern virtue of a republican genius, &c."[5]

Elkanah had all Adams' time again the next day, first visiting the medieval castle of the counts of Holland. The States General met there. Venerable but unimpressive in its lack of elegance, was Elkanah's opinion. Three drawbridges over the moat could be raised to protect the government from rioters. "The idea of thus interposing a barrier between the people and their legislators is totally repugnant to American notions of the free debates of a Republican Assembly." To discover it in liberal, peace-loving Holland was "the more extraordinary." Inside the courtyards could be found the Council of State, the Council of Nobility, the Courts of Justice, and the residence of the Stadholder—the Prince of Orange. Elkanah summarized, "In short, all public business centers here."

The Great Hall (Ridderzaal) was, he wrote, "in the antique style." By this he meant medieval, gothic style, not the classical style of Greek or Roman antiquity. The dark heights under the vast timber roof of this thirteenth-century hall were enlivened by flags and military trophies gained in battles unknown to Elkanah. Tapestries decorated the chamber of the States General, with full-length portraits of the six Stadholders. More portraits hung in other chambers. The airy room where the truce between Spain and The Netherlands had been signed in 1609 looked out on the an ornamental pond. In the middle of the water Elkanah saw "a romantic little island, crowned with shrubbery." Opposite the castle and across the pond, tall trees obscured the view to a row of palatial town houses.

But the paintings in the Council Chamber attracted the most attention, probably because

John Adams had noticed these paintings especially when he waited to hear whether American independence would be recognized by The Netherlands. Elkanah and Adams saw "a string of paintings representing the actions of Claudius Civilis by Holbein, for which Lord Bolingbrook offered £ 10,000 Sterling. This Claudius was a Batavian of royal birth, who held a principal command in the Roman army but proved a traitor in the end, & like our infamous Arnold was afterwards their most implacable enemy."

The painter was Otto van Veen, not Hans Holbein.[6] The Dutch cherished Claudius Civilis as the nation's founder—a leader of a revolt against tyranny. Elkanah's parallel with Benedict Arnold misrepresented the precedent that the artist had intended in the early seventeenth century, when the revolt against Catholic Spain was conceived by Protestants as a second revolt against Rome. To see in Claudius Civilis a forerunner of Benedict Arnold was remarkably divergent from the patriotic rhetoric that had been intended. Claudius Civilis was supposed to represent heroic opposition to Rome in the struggle for independence and freedom. Adams had mused about this depiction of rebellion against tyranny when he was waiting to find out if The Netherlands would recognize the independence of the United States of America.

Outside the courtyards of the castle itself, but still within the adjacent public square known as the Buitenhof (Outer Courtyard), Elkanah could visit the prince's collection of paintings (now called the Prince William V Gallery). Here connoisseurs admired "precious stones, fossils, minerals, petrefactions and natural curiosities, the library, pictures, and the gallery of paintings, which consist principally in sacred and historical pieces, some landscapes & portraits done by the great Masters." Elkanah called the exhibition "the greatest curiosity in The Hague." Here were no dubious paintings attributed to Rubens or Holbein; the display included pictures thought to have been painted by van Dyck and Coypel.

Leaving the square through the Prison Gate, a short walk to the north entered another square where the oligarchic republic's leaders, the brothers Johan and Cornelis de Witt, had been attacked by an Orangist mob in 1672. They were ripped to pieces, murdered by rabble calling for a military dictator to take charge and defend the country against the French invasion led by King Louis XIV. Thus Willem III (later King William III of England) rose to power at the age of twenty-one. "Mr. Adams conducted me to the spot and warmly execrated this dark event in the history of Holland." Beyond this place of gruesome memory the huge mansion of the de Witts imposed the thoughtful calm of Dutch seventeenth-century classicist architecture on the broad square in front of it. Not far away was the newer and more fanciful town house of the Count van Wassenaar-Opdam (newer, but nearly a hundred years old), designed by Daniel Marot whose ideas had changed the style of high society among the Dutch and English, even in distant echoes as far away as Williamsburg. John Wesley had talked to a select home group here just the year before, introducing piety of a sort that might be intense but would certainly be refined.[7]

A little to the right, at the beginning of the Lange Voorhout, the medieval Cloister Church displayed a wall of glass in gothic tracery. Elkanah recorded seeing the house of Prince Maurice (in fact, built for Johan Maurits, Count of Nassau-Siegen), the Jewish synagogue, the city hall, some alms houses, and a French theater.[8]

Elkanah lunched again with John Adams. That afternoon, as a diversion that permitted more informal conversation, they visited Delft, riding two miles around the city walls and ramparts. They came back to The Hague in the evening, following the course of the Vliet.

"But I must not omit to tell you," Elkanah wrote in a letter to a friend, "that If I had not exerted myself, I should probably have witnessed the unpleasant sight of seeing one of the most brilliant characters of the present age, scrambling in a muddy canal, and his wig afloat upon the surface—and all from a laudable zeal to save a child then drowning. The moment he saw the struggling infant bobbing on the top, I thought he would have darted head foremost in the canal regardless of his personal safety. But I restrained his impetuosity for a moment, as a lusty fellow had in that instant soused himself in." The flailing urchin was saved.

Leiden, the Pilgrims and Jean Luzac

On Wednesday, June 4, at nine in the morning, Elkanah left The Hague to proceed to Leiden and Amsterdam. Charles Dumas provided an introduction to Johan Luzac, described by Elkanah as "the famous lawyer at Leiden." John Adams had written letters to introduce him to the Amsterdam bankers who had provided millions of guilders of loans to finance the American revolution—De la Lande and Fyne, Willem and Jan Willinck, and Nicholas and Jacob van Staphorst.[9]

A strong gale would have discouraged a sailboat, but the canal boat to Leiden was drawn by horses and scarcely slowed in the face of the wind. Three hours for the trip meant travel had been at the rate of three miles an hour. The Vliet canal had been dug by the Romans. Its breadth was around fifty feet. Raised by dykes above the surrounding fields, some now sunk below sea level, the waterway passed through the villages of Voorburg, Leidschendam, and Voorschoten, giving slowly changing views of church towers, farms, and country estates. The ruins of Castle Boekhorst and the mansions of Duivenvoorde, Roodenburgh, and Cronenstein equaled the country houses Elkanah had seen between Rotterdam and Delft. Elkanah, intent on watching the passing scene, had to jump quickly to avoid being tripped by the shifting tow rope, especially when other boats approached.

Elkanah made the acquaintance of a passenger who pointed out places associated with

On the Vliet traveling toward Leiden (engraving and etching by Hendrik Spilman after C. Pronk, ca. 1750).

the Spanish siege of Leiden in 1573–1574. Remains of some of the siege forts could still be seen from the boat. Half the town of Leiden had died then. "They were resolved to perish with their wives and children in the flames of the city kindled by their own hands, or die with hunger, rather than submit to the tyranny of the Spaniards." Elkanah expressed intense sympathy on hearing of Leiden's sufferings. In his own experience, the blockade of Providence had done nothing to hinder supply and communication from the land side. As for Boston, he'd been on the side of the besiegers.

Leiden, second in size only to Amsterdam, grew at a point where rivers converge and disperse in the delta formation at the end of the ancient channel of the Rhine River. Rivers and canals produced a city on fifty islands connected by one hundred forty-five bridges. In 1784 the population was estimated to be around forty thousand, although Elkanah heard that, just a little over a century before, at the zenith of the city's cloth industry, the town had counted thirty thousand more. Twelve elaborate gates and a strong town wall with forty-two towers and several earthwork bastions proclaimed a defensible and important city. Rows of trees growing along the carriageway that paralleled the broad moat contradicted that memory of conflict by suggesting the quiet of Sunday promenades to view flowers and vegetables in citizens' little gardens just outside the town. An unconscious feeling of vacancy followed the visitor everywhere. Grass grew between the cobbles of small alleys. Some houses on lesser canals were empty and unrepaired. His initial impression, however, was that "the buildings are beautiful and the streets in general very spacious, and perfectly clean & white." They should have been; the town paid people to sweep up after horses and dogs. Elkanah gave particular attention to the Broad Street (Breestraat). That main street "runs quite through the City from the Hague Gate to Utrecht Gate." In contrast to other streets with a canal down the middle, the Breestraat "rises in the middle and is finely paved." Several streets with canals were ornamented with trees, "some three rows on a side, which give them all the appearance of so many alleys of a beautiful garden."

Leiden's town hall from 1597 was an "old long structure in true Dutch style." The Grand Chamber held several impressive paintings. A picture of the relief of the Siege of Leiden dominated the room. On October 3, 1574, the city's saviors brought bread and fish into the starving city by boats that could sail up to the town walls over flooded farmland. Hundreds of the starving survivors died from eating too much, he was told—"instant victims to their ravenous appetites." But the best painting, he wryly decided, was "a whimsical representation of the day of Judgment, by the famous Luke Leyden who is said to be the first modern painter who had true ideas of perspective. This painting is certainly the production of the most fertile imagination. But with what justness he has delineated the confusion of this important and awful day remains yet to be decided."

Elkanah visited the Burcht, a round castle on a man-made hill in the center of the old city. Tradition claimed that the fortress dated from the ninth century. John Milton thought it the stronghold of Horsa and Hengist, the Anglo-Saxon kings who invaded England. A flight of fifty steps brought visitors to the round walls, which were 610 feet in circumference. The view from the parapet showed the entire city spreading out around him, with village church spires and canals in the distance, ending in a horizon of dunes and the Haarlem Lake. Inside the castle, a deep well was pointed out as the place where besieged Leideners "caught a large fish which they showed in triumph from the walls to the enraged Spaniards." So he was told. He was expected also to believe that a tunnel from the bottom of the well ran all the way underground to the village of Katwijk, five miles distant in a landscape intersected by rivers and canals. This he called a pretense.

Leiden's four churches received little attention. The largest, the Pieterskerk, he described as "a vast pile," meriting "no other particular notice than to pay the tribute of homage" to "the great Physician Boerhaave, who enlightened the world with the flame of his genius." Trying to express why Boerhaave's monument was admired, he wrote that it was "for the architecture, being very simple but noble," but then he altered that to state that the monument was admired "for its noble and elegant simplicity." Finally, it was "a monument of great beauty and simplicity." There was just something about it, evidently. Later he wrote that the black marble pedestal that supports the urn "represents the four ages of life, and two of the sciences in which Boerhaave excelled." Drapery in white marble on the base included "emblems of diseases and their remedies." A relief portrait medallion and Boerhaave's motto completed the memorial, "'Simplex sigillum veri'" (Simplicity the seal of truth). Elkanah heard that during Boerhaave's life he was so internationally famous that a letter of admiration sent to him by "the Grand Turk" reached him even though it was addressed simply "To Boerhaave in Europe." This was cause for contemplation.

Monument to Hermannus Boerhaave (aquatint by Portman after a drawing by Milats, 1810).

"When we consider the extent of this idea, that his residence was known throughout Europe, it comprehended within itself a volume of flattery which I find the great men, and philosophers swallow with as much avidity as any of us.... I never met a man proof against a flattery, which gives a great advantage to a subtle fellow who can measure the dose, in proportion to his object. But it decidedly argues our weakness, in loving to hear what we know we have no claim to. Flattery in England and Holland must be spread very gently & light, but in France, there is no daubing of it on too thick."

Elkanah thought the University "well worth seeing." Why that was so, in contrast to the splendid mannerist architecture of the City Hall or the impressive gothic of the Pieterskerk, not to mention the beauty of the Hooglandsekerk (which he in fact did not mention), remains obscure. He seems to have been impressed by historical associations. The university "is the principal of the five which are in the United Provinces (Leiden, Utrecht, Franeker in Friesland, Groningen, and Harderwijk). The building is old and awkward, but the professors have been the most eminent in Europe, such as Lipsius, Scaliger, Salmasius, Heinsius, and the renowned Boerhaave.... The botanical garden, the cabinet of natural curiosities, the library, anatomy, petrefactions, and fossils are very fine and well attended." He must have been repeating what his guide told him; it is in Leiden that people recite these names, while similarly famous names can be listed for other universities from Padua to Prague, Paris to Salamanca, Oxford to Uppsala. And in every case, the professors were the most eminent in Europe.

In the Botanical Garden, Elkanah was shown the American Aloe, "which blossoms only once a century." He also saw types of tea, coffee, and "a vast variety of what I am very inadequate to say much about." Wonderful natural curiosities completed the displays.

The library, he was told, was "only open to men of letters twice a week." That might explain why the university was coasting along on the reputation of famous professors from the distant past.

Elkanah dined at the Lion d'Or. Afterward, he went out to try to find a guide, a "Don Quixote excursion." He stopped into numerous shops but had difficulty finding anyone who could speak French, much less English. "With those who did not speak French, I had like to have unhinged my underjaw in laboring, without bringing forth six words of their lingo." He imagined himself presenting the appearance of "one of their tobacco head signs, with my mouth frightfully distended." People were polite but unhelpful. He reminisced about French women "who hold a foreigner kindly by the button of his coat, and in a manner hammer words into his brain with their forefinger pressing gently upon his sleeve." Humor, he discovered, was lost on what he called "the common class of people, such as shopkeepers, etc." They were serious. They took jokes to be insults. They blushed easily. "Every generous mind," he opined, should "civilly measure his conduct in all countries by the prejudices and prevailing customs of its inhabitants," and especially by whatever peculiarities dominated their expectations.

Luckily, he found the deacon of the English Reformed Church (which he called the Presbyterian church). That man spoke French perfectly. When the deacon discovered Elkanah to be an American, he smiled with welcoming pleasure; Elkanah considered him very intelligent. He stopped work and showed Elkanah around. His church was "the identical one where the original Brownists who afterwards formed their first establishment in Plymouth, New England, the place of my nativity. The building is very old, but I viewed it with more satisfaction than a palace. The deacon assured me that Mr. Adams could not refrain from tears in contemplating this ancient structure, on account of his veneration for our forefathers." The English Reformed Church met in a ground-floor room beneath the university library, the former Béguinage Chapel. They had merged with the remnants of John Robinson's Pilgrim church in 1644.

In the evening Elkanah had supper with Johan Luzac at his imposing house on the Rapenburg Canal. Luzac, a professor of law, was internationally famous for his talents and erudition, but especially for his newspaper. The *Gazette de Leyde* was considered "the best in circulation," said Elkanah. Americans owed the rapid spread of their ideas to Luzac. He published French translations of the Declaration of Independence and other American writings and distributed them throughout Europe. John Adams had brought the Massachusetts Constitution to Luzac, whose publication of the entire text ensured that it reached his regular readers, such as King Louis XVI

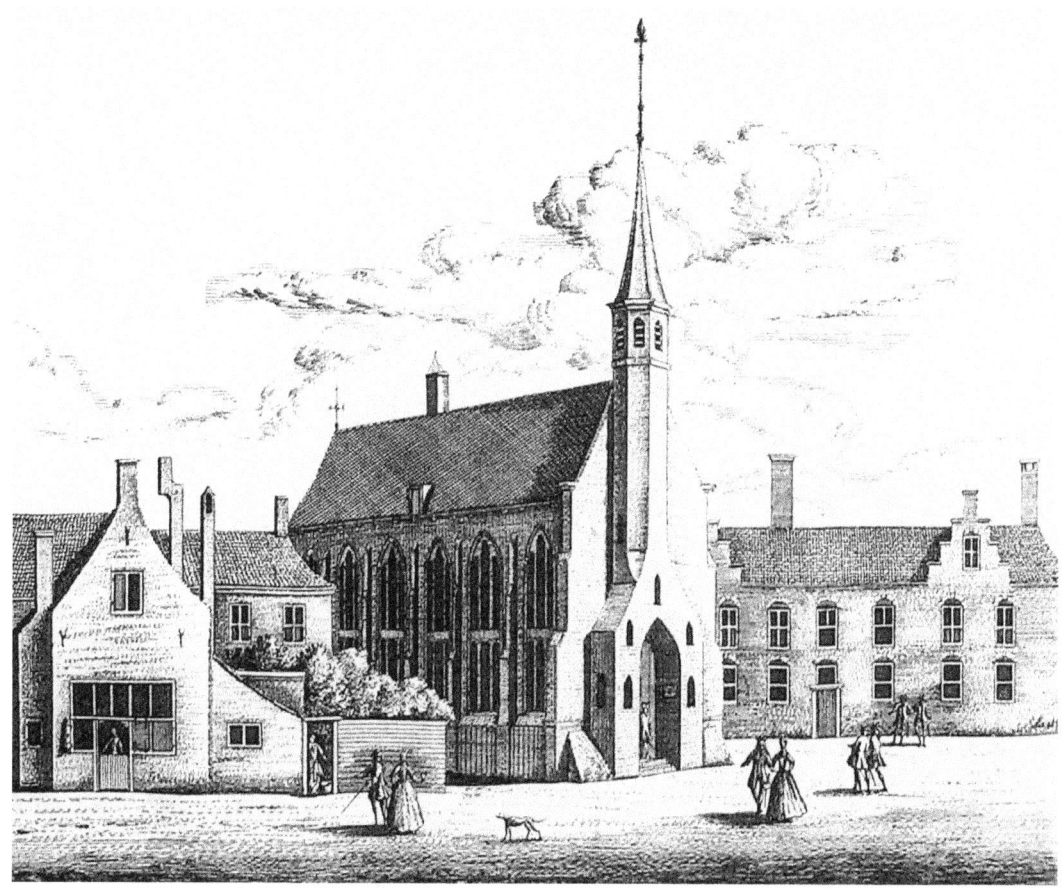

Leiden's University Library and English Reformed Church (unsigned engraving, ca. 1715).

of France and other European politicians, as well as merchants and philosophers. Luzac could converse with Elkanah in almost any language, but they spoke only in English and French.

Luzac told him Leiden's production of high quality blue and black wool cloth that had raised the city to international prominence in the seventeenth century had declined in the eighteenth. "The English woolen manufactures have given it a fatal stab," Luzac pronounced.

Elkanah left Luzac's house around eleven in the evening. Walking along the curving waters of the Rapenburg Canal on his way back to his hotel, Elkanah felt a calm isolation in the midst of the silent city, almost sensing the cool quiet of the countryside. The sky was still a darkening light blue off to the west, although fully dark behind him, as he passed the University Building on the other side of the water. Telescopes could be aimed at the night sky from platforms built on the roof.

By Canal to Haarlem and Amsterdam

Thursday morning Elkanah left his hotel—probably The Golden Ball, where most English tourists stayed, relieved to find a landlord who could speak their language. He paid

Leiden University (engraving by S. van Leeuwen, 1672).

for canal boat passage from Leiden to Haarlem, once again choosing a place on the observation roof. A Dutch naval officer traveling with him told him tales about Dutch customs. This man's credibility, Elkanah thought, could be questioned because of his grandiose claims (given without being asked) of possessing "capital connections."

The canal took them along the village of Oegstgeest northwest of Leiden out to Noordwijk. The remaining tower of Rijnsburg Abbey stood off to the left. Teylingen Castle cast bulky shadows among trees on the right. Sandy fields that in later years would be covered in the color of bulb flowers were still meadows and vegetable gardens. Elkanah noticed local habits that contrasted with the customs he'd known in America. "While we were exchanging trechschutes [canal boats] on our way the women and men were all *pissant* promiscuously *en concert*—which I find they can do, with as good a grace as Madam Ramboulet at Paris." Literature helped Elkanah experience reality. Madame de Rambouliet had invited Laurence

A canal boat at the Halfway House between Leiden and Haarlem (unsigned aquatint, 1790).

Sterne's sentimental traveler to ride with her in a coach to see the countryside. Riding back to the city, she asked him to signal the driver to stop. Sterne's hero "asked her if she wanted anything—*rien que pisser* [only to piss]," said Madame de Rambouliet.[10]

The low sandy hills marking the edge of the Haarlem Lake rose on the right. Coastal dunes formed a boundary on the left. Not far from Haarlem, the terrain changed. Forested downland opened up here and there to exhibit brick-built mansions with formal gardens coming down to gazebos at canalside. In these woods, a Haarlem alderman named Laurence Coster had absentmindedly been whittling letters in 1440. It occurred to him that with those he could set up words and begin printing. A servant, however, stole the idea and took it to Mainz. Pretending to possess magical powers, this servant, John Faustus, claimed to have invented the method of using set type. Gutenberg merely bought Coster's invention from Faustus. "This is the same Doctor Faustus so much known among the vulgar clap of people in America for his league with the devil." The Dutch thus invented printing, or so they claimed.

After lunch in Haarlem, Elkanah went to the Enschedé type foundry behind the cathedral, where he'd heard it was possible to see "the first essays Coster made with his wooden types." Despite three or four visits to ask to see these amazing antiquities of modern book production, the Coster specimens could never be found. He did get to see type casting in lead, a process he considered "very curious and expeditious." But he'd seen Baskerville's work in Birmingham, and that was "the most elegant improvement in the art of printing," as far as Elkanah was concerned.

Across the street from the type foundry and publishing house, the Great Church of Haarlem contained the finest pipe organ in the world, built in 1738 by "the ingenious Muller."

The largest of the 8000 pipes was thirty-eight feet long and sixteen inches in diameter. The sixty-eight stops could imitate the sounds of singing, either solo or in chorus, as well as "different kinds of birds, trumpets, flutes, pipes, and a kettle drum. The deep-toned flourish of trumpets is succeeded by the softer notes of gentler instruments, and then sinks into the melodious harmony peculiar to the organ itself." Two bells in the church were said to have come from Egypt, captured by Admiral Brakel, whose tomb he had seen in Rotterdam—or so Elkanah thought. In fact the bells are not even from the same century as the battle, being three hundred years or more newer. And Admiral Brakel had nothing to do with the fight in Egypt. But the three ship models suspended from arches along the aisles were fitted out with miniature saws to show how the cable across the Nile was severed by the Dutch.

Bullets were shown to Elkanah that had been fired into the church during the Spanish siege of Haarlem in 1572. After famine forced the town to surrender to the enemy, the besiegers entered the city and promptly proclaimed they were under no obligation to honor agreements made with heretics. "Two thousand people were the instant victims of Spanish fury, contrary to the express terms of the capitulation." Haarlem's example had strengthened the courage of Leiden's citizens a year later. There could be no surrender to the Spanish.

In Haarlem's City Hall, an altarpiece that had been taken out of the Great Church at the time of the Reformation was shown with its new center panel. The *Annunciation* could be seen on the wings. The *Massacre of the Innocents* replaced whatever Catholic theme had

Haarlem's St. Bavo or Great Church (etchng by J. Harrewijn, 1697).

once filled the center. Now the biblical story of the Nativity could be seen to have reached its completion in the deaths of the innocents killed by an evil political system. The Bible echoed in the lives of Haarlem's citizens. On the other hand, anyone trying to imagine an ideal time of peace and plenty, could find inspiration in a picture that appealed particularly to Elkanah. It represented *The Golden Age*.

Between thirty and forty thousand people lived within the walls of Haarlem. Eight gates led into city streets that were similar to those of Leiden. Trade was "chiefly with Amsterdam and principally in linens, ribbons, some gauzes, & tapes of which they weave 50 pieces at a time by the aid of mills." Large bleaching meadows surrounded the town, giving the impression of white fields of snow from all the linen spread out to catch the sun. Elkanah heard that in past times the Irish had sent linen to be bleached at Haarlem because of the superior quality of the water in the Haarlem Lake.

In the evening Elkanah resumed his trip toward Amsterdam, with a boat pulled along a straight canal raised above flat fields. At the settlement appropriately called Halfway, a narrow strip of land had to be crossed to take them to a boat that would continue to Amsterdam. The "stately Palace of Zwanenburg" stood here, "where the directors of the Dikes and Canals assemble." On the left was the River Het Y (which Elkanah, following English customs, called the Wye). To the right he could see the broad waters of the Haarlem Lake, fourteen miles in diameter. Seventy-two hamlets had been covered by a sudden flood that created the lake in medieval times. The Haarlem Lake (or Sea) would hardly be considered a pond in America, he thought. But the Dutchman viewed it with the admiration an American would only bestow on Lake Superior "which would embrace several republics like Holland."

From Halfway the canal went straight to the city of Amsterdam, the city steadily growing as the boat approached in the evening light. But it was June, so night's darkness would not arrive until quite late. Field followed field on either side, with nothing much of interest to relieve the repetition. This boredom was in itself enough of an annoyance, "independent of a strong funk arising from the stagnated canal water."

Amsterdam and the Dutch Bankers

Amsterdam grew around a dam on the Amstel river, near its confluence with the River Y as both emptied into the Zuider Zee. People estimated the city's population at around three hundred thousand, a figure Elkanah thought believable. Twenty-five thousand houses found safety behind a town wall with twenty-six bastions and numerous towers. A road lined with trees on each side meandered around the town's moat, past all the bastions, starting at one end of the harbor and returning in a large U-shape to the far side, with the harbor forming the north boundary. On each bastion stood a windmill. Elkanah described the air as "strongly impregnated with noxious vapours, and the stink which rises from the canals." People collected rain water for cooking and drinking.

Elkanah knew where he was going, but he didn't know where it was. His hotel was called the First Bible on the Olier Gracht, or so he thought. There's no canal called that. Perhaps it was the Looiersgracht. He complained that he had to cross a great deal of the city to find it. Because Amsterdam is laid out as a series of concentric canals, he may not have succeeded in taking the most direct route. Once arrived, tired and dirty from travel, Elkanah sent for a hairdresser and a barber-surgeon so he could have a shave. His wig went on the egg-shaped wooden stand. He would see more of the town in the morning. "Adieu! good night," he wrote.

On Saturday, June 6, Elkanah decided to devote the entire day to walking the city. The well paved streets seemed dirtier than what he'd seen in Rotterdam, and the houses were less impressive. Along some canals the mansions were palatial, like residences in Paris. But in general he thought that Rotterdam's finest houses were better. Ships' masts crowded each other for places in the harbor. The Thames had more shipping, he thought. Amsterdam had lost its dominant place in world trade. The Dutch, however, calculated their commerce as greater than that of any other port on the Continent, with at least a couple thousand ships every year from all over the world. The East India spice trade counted as the most important.

In the docks toward the northeast several new men-of-war waited at anchor, together with a number of old ones. The huge arsenal by the dockyard impressed him not only with its size but also with the quality and quantity of the naval supplies stocked there. Low-water marshes made access from the Zuider Zee difficult. At the same time, however, the marshes protected the city from naval attack. Transporting whole ships on moving dry docks of a sort called "camels" solved the problem by cradling and dragging the deep hulls up and over the obstructions.

It was Saturday evening; Elkanah had the opportunity to visit a Jewish synagogue. Strange to him as the situation was, the music enchanted him, especially "the angelic, shrill notes of a fine young Lad, and an old fellow, well-known by the name of Leonar, who accompanied him piping with his hollow grum belly, a most admirable basso." The unfamiliar sounds seemed like the notes of some instrument. Only on approaching nearer to the bimah, did he discover the cantor whose Hebrew chanting had not formed sounds he could understand. Elkanah's prejudices tinted the spectacles through which he viewed the exotic religious exercises. "As the sun verged towards the horizon the voices and agitation of the whole bowing congregation increased to such vehemence and gave them such frightful looks that I was almost apprehensive they were falling into strong convulsions, and positively stunned with their bellowing insomuch that I was glad to retreat to the open air, not only for the safety of my head—but pockets—for in fact they all looked like shabby thieves and pickpockets. The women were all in the galleries peering through lattices." (Convulsions indeed! Was he afraid of a Jewish Great Awakening?)[11]

Sunday gave little opportunity for sightseeing until the afternoon. Having observed the tomblike interiors of Dutch churches a week earlier in The Hague, Elkanah may have chosen to attend the English Reformed Church in Amsterdam. Their little chapel had been built in the fifteenth century for Béguines, but after the Reformation the mayors and magistrates had granted the building to the congregation of the English Church. "All religions are tolerated," he noted, "but Calvinism is far the most extensive and no other churches are allowed bells."

Around noon Elkanah visited the magnificent Amsterdam City Hall, whose size he indicated in an attempt to express the building's grandeur. "This is a noble structure 282 feet long, 235 wide, and 116 high; constructed with hewn stone, and is said to [have] cost two millions sterling." The entire city rested on pilings, and someone said that thirteen hundred alone were needed to support the City Hall. As the largest building in town, the City Hall appropriately looked out on the grandest square in the city, compared to which others were "very mean." From the balustraded promenade on the roof, Elkanah could see the Zuider Zee, where ships were approaching the entrance to the city from the open waters beyond. Trumpeters

Amsterdam's town hall (steel engraving and etching by A. H. Payne after W. H. Bartlett).

were stationed here at night and in church towers to keep a watch for fires. Superlatives were needed—the immense carillon was the "best in Europe." In a kind of notebook mutter, Elkanah added a comment to this repetition of second-hand reputation: "would like it played." He saw the clavier, whose pedals and keys reminded him of an organ. "A man can play on it with the same ease," he said, never having seen the exertion needed to control the counterbalanced bells with sufficient subtlety to create music instead of a loud banging din. Up on the roof, he waited until the hour struck so that he could experience the thudding vibrations of the biggest bell. Inside the civic palace, tourists might marvel at the armory, at the massively barred and vaulted bank containing bullion from far places, and at the richly impressive "burghers' hall." That chamber, one hundred twenty feet long by fifty-seven broad, was clad in sculptured marble from floor to ceiling, ninety feet above. Even the floor inspired awe. In colored marble the celestial and terrestrial globes were represented, "and the constellations in the heavens most curiously inlaid." All this noble stonework was, he thought, "really astonishing when we consider that there is scarcely a pebble to be seen in the whole country."

Chambers for the regents in charge of poor care and orphans bore ornamental sculptural reminders of civic virtues. Elkanah learned that the town administered support for twenty thousand paupers. Additionally, the City Hall displayed several fine paintings. Elkanah paid particular attention to a picture said to have been painted by van Dyck, showing the Duke of Alva conferring with Amsterdam citizens before they rejected government under the Spanish. Elkanah wrote that van Dyck "strongly paints the horrid character he exhibited to the world dark & bloody—at the same time fierce, martial, and warlike."

At two in the afternoon, Elkanah crossed the square to go visit the Exchange. Traders argued in the small arched bays of the arcaded courtyard. The activity of business and insurance deals reminded him of the beehives he'd seen in London when he met the bee-man Wildman. "The buzz was the same. The eagerness of the buzz crowding into the hive, and the industry and ardor to collect the honey of their souls was all the same." To pursue that analogy very far would require him to contemplate society's idle drones. Instead he "retired in one corner to contemplate the hive and view the bees."

He delivered the letters given to him by John Adams, including the introductions he had to the bankers, De la Lande and Fyne, Willem and Jan Willinck, and Nicholas and Jacob van Staphorst. His own business connections with Jean de Neufville and his son Leendert also brought him into the same tight circle of investors in America's future. All of them had longstanding ventures in America dating from years before the Revolution.[12] Together they created loans amounting to five million guilders in 1782—credit that allowed John Adams to coordinate America's acquisition of supplies throughout Europe.[13] Another loan came two years later, for two million guilders more.[14] Adams managed to obtain money and credit when the French loans were becoming inadequate. These Dutch loans covered bills drawn on American credit in France. They also provided the cash from which John Adams' salary as America's ambassador was paid. A typical bill, which might even be one brought along by Elkanah, read as follows:

The Hague may 14. 1784

Gentlemen

Please to pay Mr. C. W. F. Dumas Two Thousand Four Hundred fifty Three Florins Eight Sols & one denier and Charge the same to the United States of America as part of my Salary

  John Adams

Messrs. Wilhem & Jan Willink
Nicholas et Jacob van Staphorst
et de la Lande et Fynje
f. 2453. 8. 1—[15]

The bankers even paid the costs of John Adams' subscriptions to newspapers, as listed in a bill from 1783, which names *The London Courant, The Morning Post, The Morning Chronique*, and *The General Advertiser*, as well as the *Courier de l'Europe*.[16] (No doubt Johan Luzac sent Adams the *Gazette de Leyde* free of charge as a gesture of friendship.) John Adams continued to refer his accounts to the Amsterdam bankers after he moved to London in 1785. Occasionally the records show the movement of bills and money from country to country before payment finally took place. The ceremonial sword presented to Baron von Steuben in thanks for his service as a general in the American army provides an example:

Grosvenor Square Jan. 20 1786

Gentlemen

 I am &c.

on the 9th of this month I accepted a Bill of John Ledyard on me at 60 days sight for twelve Guineas in favour of Mr. Grand dated Paris decr. 29 1785. indorsed by Mr. Grand to Louis Tessier. Certified by Mr. Jefferson to be drawn by order of John Lamb expressed in a letter in Mr. Jefferson Possn. on the 18th of this Month, I drew a bill on messr. C & R Puller in favour of Coll Smith for 150 Lb st. to pay for a sword for the Baron De Steuben according to the orders of Congress and the Board of War I think I have informed you before, that I have accepted Bills of Mr Barclay as far as N. 12

Late as it is I wish you Gentlemen the Compliments of the Season and have the honour to be with much Esteem your most obedient and humble servant

    John Adams
Messieurs Wilhem & Jan Willink
Nicholas & Jacob van Staphorst

Jean de Neufville, with whom Elkanah had been doing business in France, came from a family of Amsterdam merchants and bankers whose activities extended from St. Petersburg throughout Europe and west to North and South America.[17] They had close connections (acting sometimes as partners) with the banking family van der Hope, which had helped finance the migration of Palatine refugees to Pennsylvania throughout the eighteenth century. They were trading with St. Eustatius and Curaçao in the Caribbean by the 1760s. Business with Philadelphia is documented from 1769 on.[18] By the 1770s, the firm had changed and was heavily invested in slave plantations in Suriname.[19] When the British captured Henry Laurens' diplomatic papers, the discovery of correspondence proving de Neufville's involvement of Amsterdam's government in supporting the American cause led to Britain's declaration of war against The Netherlands. Considered Amsterdam's wealthiest citizen, de Neufville became such a supporter of American ideals that he emigrated. Elkanah visited him many years later in upstate New York.

Elkanah understood and excelled in the negotiations required for long-distance investment, insurance, and delivery. For him, international trading in projects that demanded detailed knowledge of widely separated points of supply, to answer constantly shifting places of profitable demand, made the Exchange one of Amsterdam's most interesting places for a tourist to visit. He'd seen the Exchange in London, as well, which closely resembled Amsterdam's but possessed a sense of grandeur missing in Holland.

Relaxing from the tense excitement of the stock exchange, where fortunes could grow or evaporate on the strength of belief in words on scraps of paper, Elkanah spent the evening attending a play in French. The performance occurred in "a small thatched house like a barn." The acting was good, he thought, but he noticed few genteel people in the audience. He may not have been aware that many poor people in the audience belonged to Amsterdam's large population of French Huguenot refugees and their descendants. This being the "only summer amusement," Elkanah thought it strange that fewer people of quality attended, then recalled that the Dutch theater had the use of a much more elegant building. Maybe everyone of the upper classes went to see plays in Dutch—something that had not occurred to him at first.

On Monday, Elkanah decided to go on a day trip to the north, to visit Sardam and Broek-in-Waterland. In a "mixed company of English, Americans, and Germans" he crossed the River Y (now known as the IJ). Moving past the ships in the harbor, they had "a complete view of the river and a forest of masts arranged with much order." When the little ferry arrived at Sardam, "a battalion of windmills seemed to be drawn up in battle array in our front." Little houses with green-painted wooden front gables gathered together in what looked like a small village, although he heard that the group of little dwellings all next to each other had a total population of between thirty and forty thousand. It could have been another city, had there been a different social organization and the construction of a town wall. Some people said this settlement of adjacent villages formed the richest town in Holland.

The tourists visited the little cottage where Czar Peter the Great of Russia had "lived with the common workmen incognito." Peter was "the most laborious man in the yard. Afterward worked at Chatham." In his efforts to modernize Russia, the czar had decided to learn first-hand how Holland's and England's navies had become such powerful arms of political might, so he worked in shipyards to understand the construction of their men-of-war. It is impossible now to judge to what extent his participation was that of a genuine workman who depended on his labor for survival rather than consisting of the work expected of a prince showing off his condescending ordinariness. How many Dutch laborers working next to him in the yard spoke French? None spoke Russian unless he brought along some compatriots for conversation.

Ship building had made the region famous, together with the products of windmills used to grind grain, tobacco, and pigments, and to make paper and powder. Elkanah visited a sawmill where the wind worked forty saws simultaneously. Timber in stock, imported from Scandinavia and the Baltic, waited in woodyards and mill ponds to be transformed into ships. Three hundred new boats and ships left the yards here every year.

Sardam's tiled houses with their precisely tended formal gardens in front and behind reminded Elkanah of the tea pavilions he'd seen on blue-and-white Chinese porcelain. Neatness reached obsessive levels. Men returning home were even required to remove their shoes at the door, to receive slippers from a waiting servant. That happened at a side door, however, because the front door, often nicely decorated with stylish carving, remained formally shut except in the event of death or marriage. What people wore here contrasted with everything Elkanah had seen elsewhere. "The women are strangely metamorphosed and different from any other part of Holland. Their heads are bound up with broad gold or brass ridges running across their foreheads with prodigious large ear rings and amazing broad flat hats cocked up in the air—made of calico, which have a singular appearance. But with all these disadvantages I saw many beautiful faces—but vile shapes." He was told that women from Friesland did not look the same as those in Sardam. In Friesland, according to common report, they "appear to be all sisters—cast in the same mould—mere pictures."

Six miles beyond Sardam the tourists came to Broek-in-Waterland. People there were proud. "It is universally esteemed the most neat and beautiful place in the world without exception. Neither horses or carriages are suffered in the streets of this fairy village, which are finely paved with different colored stones, fancifully worked in different representations, in the mosaic taste, and strewed lightly over with sand with as much care as the inside of their houses." The glittering neatness dazzled their eyes. Rich merchants and retired insurance agents lived here.

Their guide filled their ears with tales of the isolated customs of the locals. "The common inhabitants of Broek are as little acquainted with the customs of Amsterdam as any other city in Europe." So he was told, although the construction of three hundred ships a year in the neighborhood suggests quite a lot of contact with Amsterdam's merchant investors.

In courtship the hopeful suitor had to stand beneath the window of his beloved for two or three hours every night during a period of three months. Only on completion of this formulaic demonstration of his constancy might he be allowed to visit her in the morning. From time to time the girl might soothe his anxieties "with a word of comfort," but nothing more. People in the area had become "remarkably coy of strangers and always marry within themselves. In consequence, the originality of their customs are [sic] preserved free from contamination."

A late afternoon downpour forced the travelers to go down below the hatches in the wide-bottomed sailboat that returned them to Amsterdam in the evening. Around a hundred passengers made a party of it—"a field for merriment," as Elkanah put it. "A Dutch Jew in the boat had a peculiar talent for imitating, with an empty pipe, the crying of a child." As he repeated this several times, the other passengers thought a child had fallen into the canal needing to be saved. "We hunted in vain for the sufferer." Eventually the trick was discovered, and "even Dutch phlegm ... yielded to merriment and frolic." Elkanah "squeezed in between two Dutch lasses, and in spite of the danger of dislocating my under jaw," he wrote to himself later, "I gagged out by main force a few Dutch words I had stole—but so high seasoned with French and English that I could hardly make myself understood.... I endeavored to make up in gestures and laughing what I was deficient in Dutch."

Tuesday, at an inn on the Herengracht, Elkanah joined a group of Americans for dinner, including a friend named Myers (probably Samuel or Moses Myers, both of them merchants involved in the American loans and investments). He particularly paid attention to "the lovely and killing Mrs. P."—a woman not identified further in his notes, but evidently a lively and beautiful woman. Afterward the party went for a walk "through the best streets of this wealthy City," passing many houses he described as "very noble." From a bridge over the Amstel River they could see sluices and canals, elegant barges and ships, and trees along the river's quays. Horse-drawn canal boats were moored for the night. They completed their stroll at a place called Vauxhall, where they could drink coffee in a large, smoke-filled room and join numerous parties enjoying performances by "a company of French and Italian origin."

Elkanah never heard about Amsterdam without being told of the gambling houses known as "speel houses" that were licensed by the police. Curious, he paid a policeman named Arnold to show him the way to the most famous of these. "My stars! What a scene!" He'd been told the policy of having licensed brothels rested on the fine moral foundation that to do so helped protect the virtue of proper ladies. Arnold was some species of official pimp, or perhaps merely a person who altruistically hoped to be of assistance to a visiting American. At the point of entry, Elkanah discovered he was required to buy a high-priced bottle said to be wine. But that vintage liquid was more vinegar than anything. Buying it was obligatory; drinking it was not. Pushing their way to the other end of the room, through a "gang of smoking Jack tars, boors, and vulgar citizens, ... I was ready to burst my sides with laughing to see a strapping heavy heeled Negro fellow dancing a jig with one of the speel house Ladies. And an old fellow playing upon a violin—the dancing to be sure was curious enough—they seemed to dance or rather slide heavily upon their heels, sailing about the room and turning round without the least order or animation." Looking around in the darkened hall, where candle light and oil lamps flickered vainly in an attempt at enlightenment, Elkanah felt "sickened to the heart with an idea that crossed [his] brain." Perhaps he had not given much thought to what he should expect to see in a brothel. "There was about forty or fifty of these debased wretches seated round the room. They looked like so many painted dolls, dolls stuck up for sale. It seemed like entering into a butcher's slaughter house, where the calves and sheep are hung up for the highest bidder. I could not endure the sight five minutes. I was glad to decamp after having satisfied my curiosity. Enough of speel houses!"

In the next couple of days, Elkanah and friends he had met continued to visit sites every tourist should see, such as the municipal prison called the Rasp House. He thought the idea that prisoners should be put to work deserved imitation. Here they had to rasp brazil wood as part of the process of making dye from it. "The method of rasping is nothing more than two men sawing lignum vitæ with a raspsaw." The entire time that Elkanah and his friends were in the prison, inmates followed them demanding charity, their thin naked arms stretching out from between the bars of their cell windows. He was also told of a system of punishment that he considered "curious." Anyone obstinately refusing to perform forced labor was "placed in a cistern, with water up to their chins, where they were fastened to a pump and compelled by involuntary labor to avoid drowning, as the water is made to run in as fast as it is discharged by the pump." Elkanah did not actually see this; in fact, no one did, because it was mythical. But gullible tourists believed it did exist somewhere in Amsterdam.[20]

Dinner in company was followed by attending a play in the evening.

On June 11, Elkanah was invited to dinner together with "a brilliant company" at the home of Mrs. van Staphorst, the wife of one of America's bankers. A period of two minutes' silence was observed before the meal began with soup. That custom was a novelty for Elkanah. French fashions inspired Dutch formalities of conviviality among the wealthy. Elkanah, however, left no description of the place of women in conversations here. Were they full participants, as in France? Did they retire among themselves as in England? All that he noted was that a small door from the dining room gave access to the toilet, which was thus more conveniently located than the outhouses of America or even France.

French practice intruded in a way he didn't like when he discovered his obligation to tip a servant two florins at the door when leaving. The English had abolished this "disgraceful custom" a few years earlier. At least Elkanah was not required to buy a bottle of vinegary wine.

After dinner, Elkanah attended a French play in the company of "la belle Americaine." No doubt this was Mrs. P., whom he described as "the envy of the Dutch ladies, who are, however, very elegant both in their persons and manners as they rise beyond the vulgar." Elkanah's situation pleased him, "especially as I officiated interpreter between her and a belle Hollandaise seated on my left." Afterward, they found another coffee house with a garden.

The next day, Elkanah returned to Haarlem together with two Americans and Mr. Fyne, of the banking firm, De la Lande and Fyne. Elkanah turned the Dutch name into something Irish—Finney! Their goal was an organ concert in the Great Church of Haarlem. Although hearing the largest organ in the world was in itself worthwhile, Elkanah was not entirely impressed. "The sounds were delightful, but badly executed by a bungling fellow." A thunderstorm inspired their early return to Amsterdam, traveling below decks in the canal boat. Young leaves on pollarded willows along the canals turned silvery in the wind and rain. Crossing the narrow land at Halfway put them on an isthmus in the middle of shining grey waves blown into green breakers beneath gathered dark clouds. In sodden fields beside the canal to Amsterdam, cattle disturbed by the weather started lowing, the sound of one inspiring answers from others. But the passengers were not somber. Elkanah's ludicrous attempts to speak Dutch kept the party in good spirits.

A letter waiting for him at his hotel brought an abrupt change of plans. His attorney wrote that his presence was needed immediately in London. He would have to forego his plans to travel in Germany to pay his respect for the enlightened reforms of Frederick the Great. Instead, he would now travel south to Utrecht then cut straight across the country to return through Leiden on his way to the coast.

Utrecht and Military Distraction

The canal boat to Utrecht left Amsterdam on June 13 at six o'clock in the morning. One other American, a Mr. Vanbiber, accompanied Elkanah. Many other passengers were Dutch.

Outside the city the country mansions of rich Amsterdammers bordered the Amstel River as it meandered toward the dam that had become a metropolis. A canal diverged from the river and brought them at a straight diagonal southeast, eventually bending around toward Utrecht. Country houses and a few castles came into view. "Some of them were mere palaces." The boat moored at three in the afternoon, time enough for a midday meal at the Utrecht home of a Mr. Peterson, a wealthy American merchant. Elkanah set out to explore the city immediately after lunch. The greatest monument, the old cathedral tower, stood alone at a distance from the rest of the church, ever since high winds had blown down the nave in 1674. Elkanah climbed, "460 steps or 370 feet." The view of the countryside around the city showed what looked like a vast garden. He was told that on a clear day it would be possible to see fifty cities in the distance. But it was no clear day. "The wind blew a gale and I was almost apprehensive this crazy old tower, that has resisted sieges and tempests for near on a thousand years, would at last tumble down and bury poor me in its ruins. The roaring of the wind through the hollow arches and the ruins of the old church under us naturally excited these vapours, so I hurried down." Inside the chancel of the church several monuments remained after iconoclastic destruction in the sixteenth century; but what was left was all battered to bits, with faces hacked off.

A quick visit to the university produced no list of world-famous professors, unlike Leiden. Perhaps he had no local guide. Renowned gardens belonging to Madam van Mollem were worth an hour of his time, with cascades, sculptured flower baskets, formal parks or raised beds of flowers, and two splendid grottos constructed of shells expensively gathered by Dutch traders from distant beaches. Next door he visited a silk mill. A water mill provided the driving force, powering all the machinery with a single turning motion, like the one Elkanah had seen at Derby in England. Utrecht's Mall also merited praise—three-quarters of a mile long, shaded by "four double rows of stately trees." On it, partisan citizens were gathering every day to practice formation marching and the use of arms in opposition to the Prince of Orange. A "French faction" was how these groups were named, inveterate antagonists to the English. "Military distraction beats high in every vein," Elkanah commented, "but the voice of nature and humanity shrinks at the tragic thought that these enchanting fields may be verging fast to the fatal change of Parks of bellowing murder—campments—pikes, death, and family kindred darting grins of distraction at each other."

Despite the palpable tension, he thought that "Utrecht is upon the whole an agreeable clean city." On the other hand, he also thought that Utrecht had "no particular curiosities or imposing public edifices." Elkanah had arranged to have dinner with Mr. Vanbiber, but learning that the packet boat for England would be leaving Hellevoetsluis the next day, he decided to make an effort to get to the boat on time.

Quickly Back to Leiden and Then to London

At eight in the evening he boarded the canal boat from Utrecht to Leiden. The skipper was pleasant enough, but French and English were useless here. All conversation had to be in Dutch. No one but Elkanah had paid the fare for first class, so the cabin or roof were his alone. Preferring company, he went down into the lower area where clouds of smoke assaulted the eyes. No one was able or willing "to be sociable with a poor devil who had not a word to say for himself—dam it!—stop!—I begin to be sick; but I will tell my story out in spite of the ships rolling." (He was writing his recollection of the day before in his journal on deck in a complete gale, on his way across the English Channel.)

Continuing his story of the journey from Utrecht to Hellevoetsluis, he had returned to his cabin alone, where he could sleep on a bench upholstered with cushions. The weather had cleared. Moonlight so bright that he could even read from it lit up the passing fields and farms, with a village church or two and a distant castle tower. The Utrecht canal brought them to the fortifications of Woerden and a branch of the Rhine River that flowed farther to Leiden. The river, wider than canals, had lively traffic even during the late hours. Wind was strong enough to use a sail rather than merely rely on horsepower. The river current helped boats going west. The moon lit up the fields once more, screened by rows of trees on each side of the water. Sailing through the night, the boat reached Leiden at six in the morning. Elkanah passed through the city on foot, surprised to see Leiden's militia in formation at the City Hall. "The seeds of civil war appears but too thickly scattered in this delightful country. Heaven avert the impending storm." The friends of America who helped John Adams were about to become leaders in the Dutch revolution against the House of Orange known as the Patriots' Movement. Elkanah thought Adams should deserve credit for the Patriots' revolution. "It appears probable that this country may yet have a reform in the system of their heavy moulded government principally [owing] to his active genius."

From Leiden another lumbering canal boat was dragged to Delft by nine o'clock. "Fearful of losing my passage, I dare not trust to another treckschute passage, but hired a man and chaise to drive me to Maislandsluys. [Maassluis] We rattled over the pavements and then traveled upon the edge of the canal with great expedition five miles to Maislandsluys, which I found a considerable large and agreeable fishing town.... The harbor appeared full of small vessels as I passed it. Half a mile further on, embarked aboard a ferry boat, crossed the Maas in a gale, landed upon the little Island Roozenburg, crossed the island in another chaise, ferried again to the Brille, took a rattling wagon and drove on seven miles through the mud to Helvoetsluys, where I was immediately almost stunned by the cry of 'Run! Run! The packet is just weighing anchor!' I flew to the commisaries, paid 12/6 for my pass, and the instant I arrived at the head of the quay the boat was pushing off in a pounding sea. However, I tumbled aboard—anyhow—and just saved myself to a hair ... I will venture to hazard that there has been but few instances of the same space of ground being measured in less time: everyone to whom I related it were astonished to find how expeditiously I had flew across the country."

On Saturday, June 15, the *Prince of Wales* packet boat crossed the channel in twenty-four hours of unpleasant, heaving leaden seas. (This was the same ship that had brought Elkanah across from Harwich three weeks earlier.) The only possible social contact came from the tossing of the ship when all the miserable passengers found themselves piled up together, cascading from one side to the other. Nothing would stop the motion, so it might as well be enjoyed, so far as possible. They sailed up near Yarmouth then followed the coast to Lowestoft. All fourteen passengers disembarked into a small open boat still two miles out from the shore, with a threatening squall increasing the sense of risk. Landing in surf, waves breaking over their legs as they waded to shore, they found an inn where they could refresh themselves "with a reviving dish of tea to settle our giddy heads." Tea, according to Elkanah, could provide relief as effective as that of opium. "The French use tea as a medicine; the English, Dutch, and Americans, to an extravagant extent, as a beverage." Bad teeth and consumption were supposed to be the consequences of drinking too much hot tea. (The connection of sugar and bad teeth had yet to be established.)

The first twenty-five miles on the way to London, they all had to pile onto a common horse cart, "like so many condemned criminals on their way to Tyburn" to be hanged. Rain from the skies and ridicule from villagers as they passed on their way to Saxmundham had to be endured, but the travelers, happy to be off the shifting seas, could themselves laugh at the undignified conveyance. They took rooms in a hotel. Interruptions by a crazy innkeeper, who burst into Elkanah's room around midnight, wild-eyed and fanatic, made it impossible to gain a good night's sleep, so Elkanah gave up and took a place in the stage coach just then about to depart, bound for Ipswich. The coach arrived at dawn in that large town. Elkanah found everything "exceeding flat and dirty, after leaving the magnificent and clean streets of the Dutch cities." The journey improved, however, with the addition of new passengers bound for Colchester—"two or three brisk young widows." Despite heavy-lidded eyes and the fatigue from his long and tedious journey, Elkanah had a merry time of it talking to women whose language was not restricted to Dutch.

Back in London, Elkanah stayed overnight in the George Inn on June 18. Before returning to the daily concerns of business, he decided to summarize his experience with "a few general observations respecting the United States at large, with a short sketch of each province in particular which will complete my tour to that country; and I think you will do me the Justice to confess I have not been Idle in the short space of three weeks, which has afforded me matter for a little Volume." Isaiah Thomas of Worcester, Massachusetts, published Elkanah's book in 1790: *A Tour in Holland, in MDCCLXXXIV.: By an American*. This heavily edited version of his diary notes marks the beginning of a genre—the American tourist's educational description of Europe intended to be read by countrymen unable to make such a long trip themselves.

The final section of his notes from the trip to Holland is headed "Description of the States." The prose will not excite: "The United States are composed of seven Provinces Viz. Holland, Zealand, Friesland, Guilderland, Overselle, Groningen, & Utrecht. They extend about 150 miles each way, including the Zuder & Harlem Seas which taken with their numerous canals seems to leave a doubt which of the elements, water or sea [*sic*, for land], occupies the greatest space in the area, which embraces by a late calculation 9140 square miles." The striking appearance here of the once common term "United States" as the name for The Netherlands is a reminder that the name "United States of America" originally carried a polemical intention. Everyone knew that the "United States" were the provinces of The Netherlands. The American revolt against British tyranny should be understood by a historical analogy with the famous revolt of the Dutch against Hapsburg tyranny. The new country was just as worthy of admiration as the original United States. The new creation needed to be distinguished from its model, but also connected to that great precedent, by the addition of the words "of America"—the United States of America.[21]

Besides summaries of geographical qualities, commercial activities, and population characteristics, Elkanah describes the form of government. The weaknesses of that system are enumerated as a warning in the face of the emerging forms of government in America. "Each province is independent of the rest & many cities independent of the province which of course produces a very complicated system of government. Their High Mightinesses [the States General] can neither make war or peace, nor form alliances without the consent of every state who sends deputies to the grand assembly.... One negative voice frustrates a decision upon any important point, which often occasions a most tedious delay & dogs eternally the wheels of public operations.... The power of the Stadtholder is nothing more than Generalissimo & High Admiral subservient to their High Mightinesses' directions. The legislative authority of every city is lodged in a senate of 20 or 30 persons who hold it for life. The survivors at their death choose another in his place. The representatives of the several provinces are chosen out of this body so in fact, the people have no hand in electing the persons by whom they are governed so despotically."

Elkanah became an ardent supporter of federalism when Americans debated whether or not to accept the new constitution. Federalism was intended to prevent the delays and stagnation he had observed in the original United States.

Five

America

Watson, Ignatius Sancho and Granville Sharp

In the summer of 1784, visions of unlimited opportunities beckoned Elkanah home to invest in America's growing future. The embargo on trade between England and America ceased with the end of the war. Elkanah wound up his business affairs—arranging for the shipment of his portrait from London to America, among other things. He said his farewells and discussed future trade possibilities. The last evening before his departure on August 21, he returned to the home of his friend, the surgeon William Sharp.

Several months earlier, one book in Sharp's library arrested his attention more than any other—*The Letters of the late Ignatius Sancho, An African*.[1] Sancho had died in December, 1780. His life and accomplishments stood out as proof that "an untutored African may possess abilities equal to an European," as the editor of his letters stated in her introduction to the work that came out in 1782. Twelve hundred subscribers sponsored the edition—among them two bishops, as well as Edmund Burke, Edward Gibbon, John Stedman, and Horace Walpole.

The introductory "Life" that precedes the letters informs us that Ignatius was born at sea on a slave ship making its way from the Guinea coast to the Spanish West Indies.[2] On arrival at Carthagena (in what is now Columbia), the infant was baptized and given a Christian name. His mother died soon; his father "defeated the miseries of slavery by an act of suicide." Ignatius was brought to England at age two. His master then presented him as a gift to three unmarried sisters who lived at Greenwich. They called him Sancho as a reference to Sancho Panza, the servant in Cervantes' story of Don Quixote. For these women, Ignatius was some sort of house pet. Circumstances brought him to the attention of the Duke of Montagu, whose wife supplied Ignatius with books, on learning of his interest in reading. Eventually he became the duchess's butler. When she died, he inherited some capital and an annuity, although initially he squandered his funds gambling. In a gesture later recalled to underline his sensitivity to art, he spent his last shilling on a ticket to see David Garrick perform Shakespeare at Drury Lane Theater. Giving up gambling, luckily he kept his job as a butler. He married Ann Osborne, "a very deserving young woman of West-Indian origin," and continued in service until ill health required a change in 1773.

Elkanah described Sancho as a "jet black Negro" and his wife as a "mulatto." As the biography describes it, the Sanchos were able to "settle themselves in a shop of grocery, where mutual and rigid industry decently maintained a numerous family of children, and where a life of domestic virtue engaged private patronage and merited public imitation." The shop sold Caribbean rum, molasses, and tobacco, produced far away by Africans less fortunate who remained enslaved. Lucky Ignatius!

Ignatius' outstanding accomplishments crowned these admirable virtues and the mild familial and commercial triumphs. He became a competent painter and an informed art critic. His own portrait was painted by Thomas Gainsborough when Ignatius Sancho accompanied the Duke and Duchess of Montagu to Bath in 1768. (Elkanah pasted an engraving of the portrait in his notebook.) Ignatius discussed music theory with leading experts. Ignatius's musical compositions achieved lasting notice. Many are keyboard settings of dance tunes, while a few are accompanied songs. His letters show a thoughtful and philosophical mind dispensing advice and observations cast in the mold of the wisdom of his time. To a young man, Ignatius recommended keeping a diary, so that events and sensitive reactions to them could be remembered and compared. Elkanah would have agreed with the author of the biographical notes preceding the letters, who wrote that "he who surveys the extent of intellect to which Ignatius Sancho has attained by self-education will perhaps conclude that the perfection of reasoning faculties does not depend on a peculiar conformation of the scull or the colour of a common integument." Phrenologists interested in skull bumps or shapes were just as wrong as people who discriminated on the basis of skin color, according to these sentiments. Nor was there any inherent advantage in being born in one place or another— the idea "that a luckless mortal may be born in a degree of latitude too high or too low for wisdom or for wit." For abolitionists, Ignatius Sancho formed living proof of the benefits of freedom and education.

His music may have brought Ignatius Sancho in contact with Elkanah's friend, William Sharp, who besides being a physician was an enthusiastic amateur musician. With his siblings, Sharp put on concerts in which he played organ or French horn, one brother played bassoon or serpent, sisters helped on the piano or singing, and their brother Granville played variously on flute, clarinet, oboe, or tympani. Together they went on musical excursions, performing on the deck of William Sharp's elegant yacht. We can imagine Elkanah joining in impromptu performance at the Sharp house, adding the sounds of his flute to their consort. Perhaps he even played some of Sancho's music.

Elkanah bought a copy of Sancho's *Letters*, which make frequent reference to his ardent affection for

Portrait of Ignatius Sancho (anonymous etching after a painting by Gainsborough) collected by Watson (from the Elkanah Watson Papers, courtesy New York State Library).

his wife. Elkanah wanted to visit the widow who had inspired Sancho's love. He entered the shop, but, bashful, he dithered a bit, buying this and that. He finally introduced himself as having been aroused to sympathy and curiosity by his reading. Mrs. Sancho welcomed him warmly and invited him into a parlor behind the shop, where she showed him her husband's original letters. One of the Sancho family's daughters was playing a harpsichord to accompany a singer standing next to her. Elkanah commented that the man was "white in appearance," and that some other "white persons" came in. The next hour passed in friendly conversation and music. The visitors "yielded to the females the same respectful attention that we should have extended to white ladies." Elkanah reflected on this, "'And why not?' exclaims the philanthropist." Elkanah considered himself to be such a philanthropist, eager to think generously about the equality of humanity. "The potent influence of prejudice cannot readily be subdued," he mused, before admitting how new the experience had been for him, and without noticing how powerfully prejudice dictated the terms of his contemplation of race. "A family of cultivated Africans, marked by elevated and refined feelings, was a spectacle I had never before witnessed."[3]

Elkanah's final evening before departure for America brought him for the last time in contact with Granville Sharp, who lived with his brother William. Elkanah found himself "in a manner, enchained, for several hours, by this noble enthusiast in the cause of African emancipation and colonization." Granville intensely told of the cause that had taken hold of his life—his project to provide a refuge in Africa for freed slaves. The territory he had obtained, that he gave the name Sierra Leone, still remained without such settlers, because the first ship that was bringing freed slaves had sunk with all on board. Intending to try again, Granville Sharp raised funds, bought and freed slaves, and continued to hope to establish a refuge of safety and freedom.

In the 1760s, Granville had intervened to provide medical help for a suffering black youth he came across in a street near his brother's surgery. The plight of slaves gripped him.[4] Granville investigated English law to argue before the appropriate courts that this youth could not be bought and sold and sent off to a Caribbean plantation as the property of people he'd never even heard of. In 1772 Granville Sharp's arguments triumphed when the principle was legally established that *"as soon as any slave sets his foot upon English territory, he becomes free."*[5]

Granville insisted on giving two bundles of his publications to Elkanah—books and pamphlets on emancipation and other topics. He asked Elkanah to present them as a gift to George Washington. Included were Sharp's *An Essay on Slavery: Proving from Scripture its Inconsistency with Humanity and Religion; in answer to a late publication, entitled, "The African trade for Negro Slaves Shewn to be Consistent with Principles of Humanity, and with the Laws of Revealed Religion,"* published in 1773, as well as his essay *The Just Limitation of Slavery: In the Laws of God, compared with the Unbounded Claims of the African Traders and British American Slaveholders,* from 1776.[6] The bundles might have included publications on many topics to which Sharp had given his attention, from dueling to the art of singing, but more likely is that Sharp selected writings on emancipation and representative government, that he thought should interest the great leader of the new republic. In 1776 Granville Sharp had written in support of American demands for representation in government—*The Law of Liberty: Or, Royal Law, by which All Mankind Will Certainly Be Judged!*[7] Elkanah promised to deliver the books to George Washington in person.

Returning to America and Visiting Washington at Mt. Vernon

The ship *George Washington* belonging to John Brown of Providence sailed from London on August 21, in a gale that quickly turned into a raging storm. Buoys glimpsed through driving rain guided the pilot through spray and breakers to the mouth of the Thames. Out in the English Channel, the ship made little progress for several days, blown against its course by a strong west wind. Good weather and a shift in the wind-direction at last brought movement out to open ocean. Once again, skies darkened and a hurricane threatened disaster. Despite fears of sinking, the ship cleared the terrors of the howling storm and entered a sea of heaving swells under brisk cloudless skies. Delayed by the unfavorable winds, the trip took six weeks. Reaching the coastal area of New Jersey, Captain Smith brought his ship up past Long Island and Block Island into Narraganset Bay, anchoring at Warwick Neck.

Elkanah volunteered to deliver the ship's packet of letters in Providence. Sailors rowed him to shore. Knocking on the doors of houses near the coast, he found hospitality when a farmer offered him supper of milk, baked apples, and rye and Indian bread. Elkanah, back from the world of Europe, entered into the memory of smells and tastes forgotten since his American childhood. He was welcome to stay the night. Hearing grumbling against the government and dissatisfaction with peacetime economic conditions, Elkanah couldn't refrain from telling the farmer to stop complaining. Whatever problems the cost of war had brought, he was far better off than the peasants of Europe. Freedom was worth the inflation and taxes. And Elkanah's advice was free.

Elkanah continued on to Providence the next morning, where he proceeded to John Brown's house. Brown had no reason to expect the visit and did not recognize Elkanah until the young man had re-introduced himself. Elkanah had changed beyond recognition. Several days later in Plymouth, Elkanah's own father failed to recognize him.

Re-establishing contact with old friends and family brought him new connections as well. Among those he met in Providence was General Nathanael Greene, who had fought in the siege of Newport in which Elkanah also had fought in 1778. General Greene achieved fame as George Washington's most reliable and effective commander throughout the war. His strategic success in 1782 at the Battle of Eutaw Springs effectively ended British depredations in the southern part of the war. Greene wrote Elkanah a letter of introduction to George Washington. Another letter of recommendation was provided by Colonel John Fitzgerald, who, like Elkanah's friend the deceased John Laurens, had been one of Washington's aides. Elkanah thus had the very best of references to present at the beginning of his visit to Mount Vernon some months later. He had met Washington himself a few times in the early years of the Revolution, and he had corresponded with Washington when he sent him the Masonic apron embroidered in France, but Elkanah did not presume to rely on any memory of those momentary contacts.

Just nine days after his return to America, Elkanah met the young woman who was to become his wife. His description, written many years later, is brief:

> October 12th, 1784. The most eventful, and, I may add, the most fortunate day of my life, at nine o'clock, AM, I mounted my horse at Providence, and started for Boston. My saddle-bags were dangling at his side. In Norton, Massachusetts, my kind stars conducted me to a respectable house, standing on a slight elevation, a short distance from the road. I approached the door; and, as was

customary then, cried out, "House, ahoy." A comely maiden, about seventeen years of age, came to the door, to answer my inquiries for the right road to Boston. I was at first sight, agreeably impressed by her mild and placid countenance, and the courteous manner with which she directed my route; little thinking, that I was more intently analysing her physiognomy, than attending to her directions. I was not disposed to proceed, but invented other inquiries, to prolong the conversation. I was, at the time, attired in the most gaudy trappings of a French beau; my hair, powdered and perfumed; my queue tied in a double knot; a gold-headed cane, attached to a button-hole of my scarlet coat; and my horse, caparisoned with an elegant saddle and bridle, which I had brought from London, and never used until that eventful day. Thus equipped, I dismounted, at the invitation of a matronly lady, who had also come to the door, and who invited me into the house, after a little very obvious hesitation. I will not further pursue this topic; but simply add, that, in a few weeks after this interview, the young lady became my beloved wife.[8]

(The rapid courtship that Elkanah remembered—the quick succession from being smitten with love at first sight to having so impressed both the young woman and her parents that within a few weeks he had obtained permission from her father to marry her—casts a general light on his recollections and on the numerous attempts at revision and editing that he practiced on the texts of his life. In fact, Elkanah Watson married Rachel Smith in March, 1789, four and a half years after the first exchange of smitten glances.)[9]

In early December, Elkanah traveled on a packet boat from Providence to New York with three new friends, Rufus King, Elbridge Gerry, and Judge James Sullivan. They three had all been elected to the Continental Congress, then about to meet in New York. King, having represented the interests of Newburyport in the General Court (or legislature) of Massachusetts, was at the beginning of a career in government at the national level. Elbridge Gerry already had several years of national political experience. As the official from the Continental Congress in charge of securing supplies of gun powder and other armaments for the Revolutionary army, Gerry had long been in contact with John Brown. Gerry and Brown also worked together in the development of naval power based on privateering. Many years later, at age seventy, Gerry was vice president of the United States (under Madison). James Sullivan had been a member of the Massachusetts legislature as well as a justice on the Massachusetts Supreme Court, before being chosen a delegate to the Continental Congress in 1784. But Elkanah had no such career in line himself. He was on his way to spend a month visiting an uncle who lived in New York.

Elkanah's uncle was John Sloss Hobart, former deputy to the Provincial Congress of New York in 1775–1777 and presently a judge on the bench of the New York Supreme Court, a position he held from 1777 to 1798. Perhaps Elkanah thought of studying law with his uncle, rather than starting up another import-export business. While staying with his uncle, however, he noted favorably the revival of shipping and trade in New York. The number of masts in the harbor testified to prosperity. Constantly the peaceful present contrasted with the recent violent past. A visit to Brooklyn called to mind the moments in 1776 when Washington's army found itself endangered by far superior British forces. Indecisiveness on the part of British officers allowed Washington to retreat to safety and avoid the annihilation of his army. Elkanah's new friend General Greene had first proposed the retreat that saved the army.

Elkanah found little of interest on Long Island. He observed that the soil needed continual fertilization. In the city again, he was surprised to meet the philosopher Dr. Henry Moyes, to whom he had been introduced in England at Birmingham. Moyes, whose blindness contributed to his celebrity, had arrived to begin a lecture tour of the newly independent country. His audiences in New York, Boston, Philadelphia, and Princeton eagerly sought the most recent scientific insights. Moyes asked Elkanah to describe for him what he saw from the Battery overlooking the bay and the Hudson River. The blind man directed his cane in compass directions from their vantage point, while Elkanah described in detail what could be seen. "It is the finest harbor and the most beautiful view I have ever *seen*, and it will never be effaced from my memory." Moyes may have favored other people and other places with similar expressions of sensibility. The savant had lost his sight when he was three years old, as a consequence of smallpox.

Elkanah's goal was to visit George Washington at Mount Vernon. A ferry boat across the Hudson's choppy grey water brought him to Paulus Hook, but, further on, the Hackensack and Passaic Rivers could be crossed easily on ice. Snow made travel slow; Elkanah got no farther than Newark for the night. Surveying bare trees and barren fields that gave no sign of spring and summer farming, Elkanah perceived a "general absence of that agricultural science and high tillage so characteristic of England." The next morning, a stage-sleigh took him lightly over the snow all the way to Philadelphia, arriving there after nightfall. Philadelphia was thriving, and numerous fine houses graced the straight parallel streets; but only two buildings interested Elkanah—the prison and the State House, in which the Declaration of Independence had been signed on July 4, 1776.

Elkanah was on his way to Mount Vernon to visit Washington, as he could tell the people he met. Dinner with Philadelphia's richest citizen, Robert Morris, placed Elkanah in the midst of the most refined citizens in the city's finest house, a mansion that later became the Presidential home of George Washington. Morris had managed the nation's finances during the Revolutionary War. More than once, the ability to supply the army with munitions and equipment depended on Morris's careful transfer of funds, including the contribution of his own fortune to the effort. Morris was also responsible for the resolution of problems suddenly facing Benjamin Franklin, John Adams, and private contractors such as Elkanah, when French financial structures collapsed in 1783. The promise given to Benjamin Franklin and John Laurens, that France would guarantee the ten million livres loan that America might borrow in Holland suddenly became worthless. Robert Morris organized the transfer of funds from the Dutch loans that were intended to be shipped to America, so that American credit for outstanding debts drawn on France could be salvaged and payments made.[10] Creditors in America would have to wait a while longer for hard cash. The paper money issued by Congress had become nearly worthless.

On January 18, 1785, Elkanah left Philadelphia in a stage coach that was no more than a kind of wagon with strap springs under plank seats, and with sides and top hooped over and covered with canvas. Roughly bouncing along on frozen mud roads, the landscape was sharp and inhospitable. The floating bridge constructed for the British army across the Schuylkill River served peaceful travel since the war, each section connected with hinges to the next so that the bridge could rise with the incoming tide and sink again as the flow reversed and the levels sank. The water foamed with grey fullness that seemed on the verge of freezing. Despite the chill, Elkanah surveyed pleasantly spacious farmlands, pretty little villages, and isolated farmhouses he called country seats, as if they compared favorably with mansions he had visited in England.

The Brandywine River recalled the war, as every place of past battles did; but there was also an impressive new flour mill to visit. Mechanization would increase production and reduce the number of workers needed. Elkanah saw growing profits, not unemployment. Baltimore had doubled in size since Elkanah's visit just seven years earlier, now containing around two thousand houses, with perhaps twelve thousand inhabitants. Two days out of Baltimore, the travelers reached the Potomac. The ferry across to Alexandria ran a dangerous course between floating sheets of ice. So many hours of frozen travel left Elkanah exhausted. He decided to rest for several days before venturing a little south to Mount Vernon. In that time he met a young businessman from Alexandria who knew the way to Mount Vernon and could go with him. Elkanah preferred to travel in company, especially in unfamiliar regions. Besides, the thought of visiting the great George Washington alone was more than a little daunting.

Mount Vernon presents a plain front, with classical allegiance embodied in the proportions of the gable that surmounts the central section, three windows wide, and in the visual echo below, the miniature gable over the paired pilasters flanking the central door. From the entrance driveways the distant house seems plain and massive. Up close, Elkanah saw a lack of symmetry that resulted from an attempt to unify an existing house within the overall classical design of the new additions. When Elkanah rode into the circular drive, he was met by the sight of slaves in houses, gardens, and workshops to left and right. Curving wooden colonnades connected the central house with the outbuildings, also connecting the design with the ideal of Italian palaces designed two hundred years earlier by the great architect Antonio Palladio and built of carefully hewn stone. Palladian ideas found reflections throughout Europe; enlightened members of the Masonic Order paid attention. The imitations Elkanah had seen in England had at least been built of stone like the Italian originals. Here wood, cut and painted, provided grandeur once or twice removed. The lantern cupola seems insufficient, but perhaps that is the cumulative result of the inconsequence of the hundreds of imitations built in the twentieth century, including the plastic versions on Howard Johnson's restaurants.

Elkanah and his new acquaintance Mr. Swift arrived after dinner on January 19, 1785.[11] Either Joe or Paris-boy was the slave who took their horse away to the stables. (Had Paris-boy been to France like Elkanah? The name is ambiguous.) Other slaves, Frank, or maybe Austin, took the letters of introduction from Mr. Watson to Billy who would deliver them to George Washington. (Did Billy the slave call his master "Georgey"?) Around forty slaves worked in and around the main house, together with twenty-five children, several of them old enough to work, too. Many more slaves labored in Washington's shops and farms enduring primitive conditions at no pay (beyond poor housing and a bit of their own produce for food). Drinks were brought by slaves as Elkanah explained who he was and presented the gift to Washington from the abolitionist Granville Sharp.

In 1773, having won his famous court case establishing that "Slavery is not consistent with the English constitution nor admissable in Great-Britain," Sharp wrote directly about slavery in America. How could anyone conceive or defend that slavery be "continued in the colonies, peopled by the descendants of Britain, and blessed with sentiments as truly noble and free as any of their fellow subjects in the mother country"? Referring to *Blackstone's Commentaries*, the Bible, and James Otis's *American Tracts against Slavery*, Sharp asked, "[W]hy is it that the poor sooty African meets so different a measure of justice in England and America, as to be adjudged free in the one, and in the other held in the most abject Slavery?"[12]

In 1774, Granville Sharp famously defended the rights of the Irish, mentioning also the

Mt. Vernon (lithograph by Wade, in *Views from Nature*, p. 17).

equivalent rights due to colonists in America. Because of its application to the American situation, a second edition came out in 1775. Justice demands, he wrote, that England "acknowledge their unalienable right to the same happy privileges by which the liberties of the mother-country have hitherto been maintained; the most essential of which is the privilege of paying no other taxes than what are voluntarily granted by *the people* or their *legal representatives* in general councils or parliaments."[13] But Sharp also inveighed against slavery. "The toleration of domestic Slavery in the Colonies greatly weakens the claim or *natural Right* of our American brethren to Liberty. Let them put away the accursed thing (that horrid *Oppression*) from among them, before they presume to implore the interposition of *divine Justice*; for whilst they retain their *brethren of the world* in the most shameful involuntary servitude, it is profane in them to look up to the *merciful* Lord of all, and call him *Father*!"[14]

In 1776, Sharp brought out *The Just Limitation of Slavery in the Laws of God, compared with the Unbounded Claims of the African Traders and British American Slaveholders*.[15] In his earlier writings Sharp had responded to people "who admit the indefensibility of Slavery" but who "declare it would be impolitick to emancipate those we are possessed of, and say, they generally behave ill when set at liberty." He could give many examples "of Negroes and Mulattoes, once in Slavery, who, after they have obtained their liberty (and sometimes even in a state of bondage) have given striking proofs of their integrity, ingenuity, industry, tenderness and nobility of mind." (Ignatius Sancho certainly fulfilled that role.) There would be more, said Sharp, if more slaves were set free. In 1776, he responded to claims that enlightened slave owners treated their chattel with fairness and kindness. Sharp provided an example from England of gross mistreatment. If such cruelty took place in England, where "such monstrous oppression" was "liable to severe penalties," then "how can we reasonably reject the accounts of Tyranny in America, howsoever horrid and inhuman, where the abominable plantation laws will permit a capricious or passionate master, with impunity, to deprive his wretched slave even of life?"[16]

George Washington acknowledged that he felt bad about slavery, but he discovered difficulties in the freeing of his slaves that made it more convenient, and, in his mind, even more considerate, not to free them. Some of the slaves at Mount Vernon belonged, according to Virginia's laws, to him personally, but others were his in trust as the property of his stepchildren. And the slaves from the two groups had married, so that the step-children's inheritance included a partial ownership interest in the children of such marriages. Thus, he reasoned, to free his own slaves might lead to the breaking up of families. His sensitivity was inadequate to resolve this legal riddle, so things just went on as they had been before, with the exception that the great man gave it some earnest thought. Eventually, Washington decided that his slaves should be freed after the death of his widow, stipulating that some financial aid be provided after that for some of them. Whether Elkanah upbraided him as Granville Sharp had hoped can be doubted. But it is safe to assume Washington read Sharp's publications.

On being introduced to the Washington family as they finished dinner, Elkanah remembered in later years that he "felt an unaccountable diffidence." Washington received him, he wrote, "with the native dignity and urbanity so peculiarly combined in the character of a soldier

The Washington family at home (lithograph, Currier & Ives, 1867).

and eminent private gentleman." Although Washington's manners soon put him at ease, could there have been enough urbanity for Elkanah to convey Granville Sharp's abolitionism in all its power? Could the young merchant whose military experiences had been quite limited speak prophetically on morality to the victorious Commander? The topic of slavery could not be avoided when Elkanah presented Sharp's abolitionist publications.

But Elkanah did not write about this in his memoir. Instead he remembered that Washington and he devoted hours to discussing the possibilities for commerce if a canal could be constructed that would connect the Potomac River with Lake Erie. Several locks would be needed, but the result would enrich Alexandria with the fur trade from Detroit. As Washington calculated it, the distance from Detroit to Alexandria was three hundred forty-eight miles shorter than the distance from Detroit to Montreal.

Looking out over the broad Potomac beneath the sloping lands beyond the colonnade at the grand rear of Mount Vernon, Elkanah could imagine wealth in the holds of countless sailing ships. Washington showed him his notes on how the canal company had been formed, chartered, and capitalized—how work would start that spring.

Such was the respect in which George Washington was held that what Elkanah saw was a man surrounded by servants so alert that his wishes were met almost before he spoke. "Smiling content animated and beamed on every countenance in his presence." As in France, to Elkanah it seemed that the peasants were happy. Elkanah personally experienced Washington's consideration for those around him. Severely coughing from a cold he had picked up during the days of hard travel in freezing weather, Elkanah was offered some medicines, which he declined. His coughing increased, however, after he went to bed. A little later, Washington himself drew back the curtains of Elkanah's bed and offered him a bowl of hot tea.[17]

The next morning, conversation about canals resumed. Little else occupied Washington's mind at the time, besides his garden. The Potomac canal project could be where Elkanah might build his future. Washington urged him to come settle along the river in Virginia. The prospect excited him.

According to Washington's diary, the day Watson and Swift arrived had been clear, the weather "fine." He had been working on laying out his "Serpentine road and Shrubberies adjoining." The next day, the two young men, according to Washington's journal, "went away after breakfast," and Washington resumed his work of the day before, "arranging the Walk, et cetera." The weather had turned "damp and disagreeable." Digging in the earth, setting shrubs in their place, Washington may have given some thought to the contrast between his free choice to get his hands dirty with gardening, while retaining the possibility of stopping at any time, and his slaves' labors, foreordained by overseers. Or his thoughts may have been directed to other topics entirely like the visions of canals.

At Washington's suggestion, Elkanah followed the course of the river upstream beyond Alexandria to see the major waterfalls whose roaring rapids would need to be avoided by locks and canals—the Lower Falls, Seneca, and Great and Little Falls. The Great Falls presented the most difficult hindrance to navigation—dropping twenty-three feet in the space of seventy, and a total of around eighty feet in less than a mile. The roaring sheets of water could be heard a mile away. Not a single fall but a sequence of rock-strewn rapids, the irregular boulders projected from the foaming stream to suggest tantalizingly that some kind of mills should be built across the rushing water, dropping water wheels into the current. The hydraulic power was immense. But the location was not yet built up, so a mill there would not yet serve any population. Much more profit could be imagined with the grander project of multiple canals to connect the rivers all the way to Lake Erie. What that dream needed was capital, imagination, perseverance, and an ability to achieve cooperation between the state governments of Virginia and Maryland. Washington was working to put these requirements together, but it would take time.

Elkanah returned to Providence with ideas to ponder for his future, riding twenty-four miles on horseback from Alexandria to Annapolis. At the time, the Maryland statehouse, with its cupola-topped dome was considered, as he described it, the "largest and most elegant edifice in America." Elkanah saw Charles Wilson Peale's portrait of George Washington with Lafayette and, he thought, Rochambeau (although in fact the third portrait shows Tench Tilghman, a Marylander who had served as Washington's aide).

From Philadelphia, Elkanah again took the stage-sleigh back to New York, gliding along at eight to ten miles an hour. This was even more comfortable and faster than the system of post-chaises prevailing in England. From New York, however, he again rode on horseback, stopping at Fairfield, Connecticut. He had last been in Fairfield in 1777, when he stayed with his grandmother in the beginning of his travels to Charleston, South Carolina. Now he was coming home again, after Fairfield, to Providence and Plymouth. And he needed to decide what to do next.

Touring North Carolina

Francis Cossoul, Elkanah's business partner from Nantes, joined him in America in the summer of 1786. Together they formed a plan for renewed collaboration. Cossoul would go to Haiti; Elkanah would set himself up as a farmer in North Carolina, and, at the same time, importer, exporter, and trader. Rum, sugar, rice, indigo, tobacco—somewhere the result of this commerce should be prosperity. Finding the right location would, however, take some time and travel.

Sailing along the Chesapeake by packet boat from Baltimore to Norfolk in Virginia took three days. Elkanah then hired a canoe with two men to paddle him thirty-five miles up the Nansemond to Suffolk, where he proceeded overland to Edenton. Despite inconvenience, he enjoyed the views of plantations from the canoe. His next stage was even less comfortable—riding along on a coal-cart that happened to be the only conveyance going his direction. Soaked with rain and adorned with coal dust, Elkanah stopped to ask for shelter at the plantation of someone he had visited in 1777. Presenting himself as a disheveled vagabond, Elkanah had difficulty establishing that he was in fact a gentleman worth inviting into the mansion, where a dancing party allowed guests to ignore the storm outside. Again, as in Charleston, his appearance belied his inner worth. What was the true significance of externals? Were not all men equal? But his sense of irony was gratified months later when, reappearing at the same place, this time in "a cocked hat and a blue coat, with a crimson velvet cape," and accompanied by a well equipped servant on a horse, he was welcomed with gracious hospitality.

That summer he toured the back country of North Carolina, viewing the landscape and meditating on the sites of Revolutionary War battles, such as Guildford Court house, where Generals Greene and Cornwallis had faced each other. Throughout his travels, he assessed the towns and settlements with an eye to choosing a place to live; but he also paused to examine novelties, like a layer of "perfectly defined marine shells" in a cutting on a hillside near Murfree's plantation, a settlement that later became Murfreesborough. He had letters of introduction to several social leaders whose plantations he visited. But, he thought, "no State, perhaps, had at that period performed so little, to promote the cause of education, science, and the arts, as North Carolina."[18]

Approaching the Moravian town of Salem and the Quaker community of New Garden, Elkanah noticed a great improvement in the condition of farms and cattle. Relying on their own labor rather than that of slaves, these religious enclaves were "exemplary and industrious," and their farms and houses "neat and cheerful, tidy and well furnished, abounding in plenty." Salem with its forty houses formed a central focus for several villages and separate farms, with a total Moravian population of around a thousand. All the Moravian homes in Salem had running water brought in conduits over a mile and a half long.

The farthest point in this excursion was a visit to the Catawba Indians. General Thomas Polk, who was Elkanah's host for a couple of days, showed him the way to a path that led to the Indian village on the Catawba River, midway between Charlotte and Camden. Elkanah and his servant rode into the forest, their fears turning it into a "gloomy wilderness." But it was they who brought fright when they arrived unexpected at an Indian village, alarming the women and children who had remained there while the men were out hunting. Elkanah was able to indicate that he merely wanted to meet the Catawba leader, King New-River, otherwise known as General Scott. An old woman indicated the king's log cabin. New-River spoke no English, but at his request an interpreter came from across the river, together with many Indian soldiers, called by Elkanah "savage warriors." One of them had studied at William and Mary College and could translate for Elkanah who was otherwise unable to communicate with the king except through gestures and grimaces. Elkanah indicated that he had an important message: the refusal of the English to give up military forts in the western part of the American territory, contradicting the terms of the peace treaty that ended the Revolutionary War, was likely to result in a renewal of war. King New-River lit a pipe and passed it to Elkanah. They each took three or four puffs. Elkanah offered his rum flask as a matching gesture. The council of Indians sitting around listened attentively and spoke with dignified formality, one at a time. In the village, Elkanah and the Indian interpreter "entered their cabins [and] saw several straight-limbed, handsome young girls, daubed with paint, and decorated with feathers, rings, and brooches." Elkanah withdrew to a tavern not far away, but he returned to the Indian town the next day. The king's wife herself took care of Elkanah's horse; she fed Elkanah a meal of smoked venison served in a tub on the floor. "She did all in her power to render me comfortable, if not with the grace of a Parisian lady, undoubtedly with equal kindness of heart." Despite these signs of education and gentility, Elkanah found the Indians in general to be "extremely nasty, wallowing in filth, having coarse fare and rude accomodations." The vices of their "civilized neighbors" had reduced them to insignificance. (Why was a tavern so close to the Indian village?) Elkanah could not reconcile the evidence of impoverished impotence with the sense of strength emanating from their leader. "The old chief was a hardy veteran. The lines of his face, the force of his eyes, and the expression of his countenance, commanded respect, and evinced powerful traits of mind and character."

Elkanah next visited Camden with Colonel Polk, who showed him the tomb of Baron de Kalb, the general who had come from France with Lafayette. He had fallen in battle in 1780. Here would be a monument. For common soldiers the cenotaph Elkanah found when he stopped to graze his horse in long forgotten fields of conflict consisted of bones, whitened already by the washing rain and passing wind—bones that reached out from the plowed earth or hid in grass-cast shadows. The war was still everywhere.

Around Camden, people were talking about building a canal, and he wondered whether it might be something for him. He returned, however, to Hillsborough, where he stayed for a while as a hotel lodger until bored by inactivity.

Not only the geography of imaginable canals, the potential of untilled soils, the variety of landscape and forest—also the customs of Carolina society served up novelty worth recording. Rambling on horseback one afternoon, with no set goal, he came upon a remote log-cabin, isolated in a clearing among tall pines—a tavern. Besides the landlady, the only people to be seen were some brown children playing outside by the door. Weary, Elkanah sat inside in the shadows waiting for a drink, when a "gaunt, raw-boned fellow entered ... armed with a rifle and tomahawk." Recognizing a "white savage," Elkanah made motions to leave, but, the intruder ordered him to stay a while, for he had something to say. The landlady signaled urgently that Elkanah should do as he was told. Putting on a show of joviality, Elkanah ordered "a bowl of whiskey toddy." Elkanah's uncouth companion drank more than an equal share and started singing and telling tales of rustic obscenity, demanding that the landlady come in to appreciate them. Elkanah must sing, too, he insisted, so Elkanah made up a song in fake French. Two bowls were emptied—punch bowls. The drunk demanded a dance with the landlady next, although his motions proved less graceful than energetic. This ornament of local society called for more liquor, then sank into snoring slumber. Elkanah escaped to an adjacent room before managing to leave by a window, then rush off into the forest on his horse. According to the landlady, the gentleman was wealthy, "had a lovely wife, owned forty Negroes, and a large well-stocked plantation, but spent most of his time in this lawless, vagabond life."

More elegant hospitality was offered by the planters Elkanah visited along the Roanoake River and Albemarle Sound. Friendly advice could be had without even asking. He should move to Kentucky—trains of covered wagons were forming not far away, gathering together for safety along the hundred-and-thirty-mile trek. He should plant tobacco. No, he should concentrate on rice. One plantation owner generously insisted that Elkanah come along to view a cock-fight. All classes and colors had come together from miles around, the genteel mixing casually with what Elkanah considered the "vulgar and debased." Set up in a cockpit in the middle of a square surrounded by fine houses, the vicious combat of the beautiful, steel-spurred cocks sickened Elkanah. "I was greatly astonished," he confided to his journal, "to find men of character and intelligence giving their countenance to an amusement so frivolous and scandalous, so abhorrent to every feeling of humanity, and so injurious in its moral influence, by fostering habits of gambling and drinking, in the waste of time, and often in the issues of fighting and duelling."

While he was living in North Carolina, brawling flared around political topics. Elkanah wrote articles for newspapers in North Carolina and Virginia, to urge the adoption of the proposed United States Constitution. His chief opponent, suspicious of the intentions of the federal government intended by the Constitution, was a Baptist minister and politician. Elkanah and his friends, Major Murfree and a Dr. Garvey, decided to confront him at a public meeting in a church at Woodlands, where the Baptist minister intended to inform people of the dangers of the Constitution. The "ten miles square"—the proposed capital city of Washington—was really, he said, a place that would be "walled in or fortified. Here an army of fifty thousand, or, perhaps, a hundred thousand men, will ... sally forth, and enslave the people,

The white savage (engraving by Barritt after Lossing, in *Men and Times of the Revolution*, 1861, p. 292).

who will be gradually disarmed." Elkanah and his infuriated friends stood to protest this absurdity, but the crowd rose up against them. Only Murfree's popularity saved them from attack. The meeting broke up, so to that extent Elkanah could consider their action to have been effective.

The next day he and his friend Garvey provided a caricature of the Baptist minister, depicted with a label inscribed "And lo, he brayeth!" Friends posted this on the court-house door, as voting for the election to the state convention began. A furious factional fight caused Elkanah to quit the scene hastily, perhaps recalling the election rioting he had recently seen at Covent Garden in London. The Baptist minister was elected "and the Constitution was rejected for that year, by North Carolina."

Elkanah supported himself as an entrepreneur buying and selling tobacco in the port of Edenton. He and Cossoul had laid the basis for this when they heard that America intended to use tobacco to repay war debts in Europe. They had contacted their diplomatic friends to remind them that their firm had been the importer of more American tobacco to France than any other, and they expected to participate in the next stage of that trade. Cossoul moved to Port-au-Prince to open a branch of their partnership in Haiti. Trade there was difficult. Cossoul reported that "Port-au-Prince is the worst hole in the Island. Money is so scarce that it is almost impossible to raise it." Yet he had to pay cash for "salt, molasses, and other produce of the Island," while receiving delayed payment in kind for cargoes sent by Elkanah.[19]

Elkanah's sketch of the Baptist politician (from the Elkanah Watson Papers, courtesy New York State Library).

In the spring of 1787, Elkanah bought Mount Sion, a plantation near Edenton on the Chowan River. A house, barns, and warehouses stood on six hundred forty acres. Elkanah set about improving them, while laying plans for trade with New Brunswick in Canada (where an uncle, Ben Marston, lived), with New England, and with Haiti. His uncle let him know that importing tobacco or naval stores from the "American States" was prohibited, but that "Flour & Grain of all kinds, Peas, beans, rice, Biscuit & live Stock" were allowed. Marston was about to depart for London, where he would inquire about the potential for trade there.[20] Elkanah seems to have attempted to operate a plantation without slave labor, expecting northern self-interest and enterprise to turn a profit. Unsuccessful with this project and drastically compromised by someone else's bankruptcy, Elkanah cut his losses and left the South in the spring a year later. He sold his property except for a ship, with which he sailed down the Chowan River, through the Albemarle and Pamlico Sounds, across the Ocrakoke Bar and past Cape Hatteras, where they anchored in dangerous waters during a storm. Ten days later Elkanah reached harbor in Rhode Island and could return home. Once again, his father did not recognize him until he gave his name.

Fort Stanwix and the Iroquois

Buying and selling required travel but imposed no particular schedule. In the summer of 1788, business took Elkanah, to western Massachusetts, first to Springfield and then through difficult mountain passes and gorges in the Berkshire Mountains over to Great Barrington and across to the new town of Hudson City in New York, along the river.[21] Curious to compare the Dutch settlement with what he had seen in The Netherlands, Elkanah next visited Albany. Brick houses of Dutch design, with characteristic stepped gables, recalled Holland. Nonetheless, the Dutch presence was diminishing steadily, he thought, especially because children of the old Dutch families as well as more recent settlers were attending English-language schools.

Beyond Albany, Elkanah turned west to visit the new glassworks established by John de Neufville, the former banker with whom he had done business from France, and whose associates he had met in Amsterdam. De Neufville had skillfully negotiated the treaty between the City of Amsterdam and the American Congress that led to the recognition and aid that John Adams had desired. A convinced supporter of America's war for independence, de Neufville had helped Adams negotiate the loans for millions of guilders with de Neufville's fellow Amsterdam businessmen and bankers—the loans that saved America's credit and kept supplies for the war moving across the ocean to sustain America's armies. Having spent a fortune in support of the American cause, de Neufville now lived in poverty in a small log hovel. A greater contrast with the splendor of his home in Holland could not be imagined. Here he was trying to gather sand, to cut wood, and to haul in loads of kelp brought upriver for potash, hoping to set up a flourishing glassworks that would restore his finances. America was still importing most of its window glass from England. De Neufville's hopes were well founded; a glass factory could easily succeed in diminishing the reliance on imports.[22] He died before his factory achieved the envisioned production. In 1788, at the beginning of the project, accompanied only by a moody son suspected of mental instability, Jean de Neufville appeared to Elkanah to live in disconsolate poverty. Elkanah noted that "it was Sunday, and I am sure the best sermons could not have had such an effect upon my mind as the reflections this visit excited in my heart."[23] At thirty, he contemplated his future and the unpredictable circumstances of his own old age.

Farther up the Mohawk River beyond Schenectady, Elkanah visited Colonel Silas Talbot, whose release from Mill Prison in England years before had come about through Elkanah's help. Talbot told Elkanah about the gathering for Indian treaty negotiations to be held at Fort Stanwix. Elkanah decided to extend his journey to see what would be taking place there.

Travel up the Mohawk River valley went through beautiful farmland, but the area called the Flats was sparsely settled by German immigrants who spoke no English. There were no inns. The second night out, Elkanah located a run-down log-cabin tavern—better than nothing. The road toward Fort Stanwix was nearly impassable, "obstructed by broken bridges, logs, and stumps—my horse," said Elkanah, "at every step, sinking knee-deep in the mud." The speed averaged just two miles an hour, slower than a normal walk. The next evening he slept in a barn with horses and other animals. The day before he reached Fort Stanwix, Elkanah passed through a battlefield from 1777, where General Herkimer had been ambushed and killed with half his army. Human bones still broke the surface of the earth. Just beyond this scene of defeat, Elkanah found himself surrounded by a couple hundred Mohawk Indians. Elkanah described them as "drunk as lords," and looking like "so many evil spirits, broken loose from Pandemonium." Playing up to his obvious nervousness, they "whooped, yelled, and danced round ... in such hideous attitudes," that Elkanah feared he'd be scalped. The Indians appeared "wild, frantic, almost naked, and frightfully painted." But when he made use of the only word in their language that he had learned, "Sago," which he'd been told was a "salute of friendship," the leader accepted his outstretched hand, shook it, and greeted him cordially.

Indians of several tribes were camped in the plain around Fort Stanwix. Among the women were many Elkanah considered "fantastically dressed in their best attire—in the richest silks, fine scarlet cloths, bordered with gold fringe, a profusion of brooches, rings in their noses, their ears slit, and their heads decorated with feathers." Several with "handsome countenances and fine figures" caught his eye.

Elkanah managed to find a place to sleep in the garret of the house where the government's treaty negotiators were lodging. George Clinton, the governor of New York, and eight other commissioners had come to regulate formal acquisition of eight million acres of land west of the Hudson River, "owned and chiefly inhabited by the Six Nations of Indians."[24] Elkanah commented that "many hardy pioneers have already planted themselves among the savages," without considering these interlopers to be criminals. Previous treaties with the same goal of acquiring land from the Six Nations had been negotiated in 1768 and 1773, although these applied to land east of the land in focus in 1784 (when the cession was disavowed by the tribes) and 1788. Elkanah saw the future as a positive shift toward occupation not by the Indians but instead by what he considered contrastingly "a prosperous and vigorous population."

One of the commissioners, a Dr. Taylor, wore a large, old-fashioned white wig. Many Indians, unaccustomed to such civilization, could scarcely refrain from laughing to the man's face.

Elkanah was not the only onlooker without any official function. The French Ambassador had come with the Countess de Biron, and they were provided with an impressive field tent that had been captured from General Cornwallis. Elkanah considered that the countess had exposed herself to unusual fatigue and privations to come here from New York City merely out of curiosity "to witness this great and unusual assemblage of savage tribes." For the ambassador the implications the treaty held for potential French territorial claims farther west along the Mississippi must have been of the greatest importance, regardless of the picturesque or exotic aspects of the grand gathering of tribes.

Fort Stanwix lay near Wood Creek, a small stream flowing west into Lake Oneida, from which the Oswego River emerged to empty into Lake Ontario. This could be an important link in a future canal. Elkanah left the great meeting with the idea of exploring the possible course that would connect Wood Creek with the Mohawk River, flowing down to the Hudson. Torrential rains put an end to the exploration, however, so he returned to the fort where the land cession continued to be discussed. Elkanah spent time with the commissioners attempting to inspire enthusiasm for the commercial possibilities of future canal enterprises. He also visited the Indian encampments, where he found "amusing scenes."

On his first day at the fort he had been introduced to Peter Otsequett (or Atsiquette), a young chief of the Oneidas. Otsequett had been taken to France at an early age, where his training had been arranged by the Marquis de Lafayette. Fluent in both French and English, as well as in his native language, he had become a polished European gentleman, familiar with classical music and a wide range of literature. To Elkanah, however, this was not enough; Otsequett presented a "striking instance of the moral impracticability of civilizing an Indian." Something in their nature apparently existed to prevent "their amelioration." On the last day of his ten-day visit to Fort Stanwix, Elkanah "beheld him splashing through the mud in the rain, on horseback, with a young squaw behind him, both comfortably drunk." That was proof. But proof of what—the limited vision of Elkanah's enlightenment?

In the meantime, on September 22, 1788, sober or not, Peter Otsequett had signed away the future of the Oneidas' portion of eight million acres of land between Lake Ontario and the Susquehanna River.[25] The Oneidas and Onondagas had agreed to shared use of a hundred square miles of land, retaining fishing and hunting rights everywhere, and reserving large swaths of land along the rivers to their own use. The price was "one thousand French Crowns in Money and two hundred Pounds in Cloathing" besides an annuity of "five hundred Dollars in Silver" that could be paid in that value of clothing.[26] The Indians viewed this as the terms of a lease for joint use; the New York officials pretended instead that they had bought exclusive ownership of the land from people who could be removed from it whenever that proved convenient. The annual payment characterizes the transaction as a permanent lease of mutual use, not a sale, since the obligation recognizing ownership by the Indians is permanent.

Rather than conceiving Peter Otsequett as a political leader representing his people in governmental deliberations, Elkanah saw nothing but a pitiable drunk, incapable of civilization, getting out of the way. The future of America lay in the taming of the wilderness, the construction of canals and turnpikes, and the growing prosperity of future settlements in western expansion, without these people. The United States of America, having freed itself from oppression and tyranny, could look forward to unlimited progress, free, too, of obstructions and irony.

Returning downstream from Fort Stanwix, Elkanah encountered boats loaded with families already intending to settle in the western territories. They had made their plans even before the treaty was signed as there had been no doubt what the outcome of the negotiations would be. "My curiosity satisfied," Elkanah wrote in his journal, "I sent my horse toward Albany, and embarked on board of a returning bateau [wide-bottomed canoe], and proceeded down the Mohawk to Little Falls, anxious to examine that place, with an eye to canals."

Life in Albany and the Future Erie Canal

Three years later, at the beginning of September, 1791, Elkanah began a tour of northwestern New York to explore the possible route for what was to become the series of locks and canals connecting the Hudson River with Lake Ontario, a project that would eventually emerge as the Erie Canal.

Elkanah had married Rachel Smith in March, 1789, and moved to Albany, where he opened a grocery store in his house on Market Street.[27] At the time, Albany was predominantly a town of the descendants of Dutch farmers who had established the town in the seventeenth century, when it was known as Beverwijk in the colony of New Netherland.[28] Elkanah found only four New England families there, "and perhaps twice that number of Scotch, and Irish—and a few Israelites." The Watsons joined St. Peter's Episcopal Church (the only alternative to the Dutch-language Reformed Church), where their twin daughters were baptized in March, 1790.

Relations between Albany's immigrant groups could not have been worse. The benighted Dutch, Elkanah thought, had acquired savage habits from their long commerce with the area's original inhabitants, the Indians. One of the sports of traders Elkanah called "the scum of

New England" consisted of cheating the Dutch. Because of their limited contact, the Dutch considered all Yankees to be unscrupulous and dishonest, "judging the whole people of New England by these worthless samples as we judge the Irish." New Englanders in turn demonized the Dutch. Elkanah remembered that when he was a boy, "the greatest punishment for Negroes than held in slavery in New England was to threaten to sell them 'among the Dutch at Albany.'" Elkanah found little welcome among people he considered "the most illiberal portion of the human race, sunk in ignorance, in mud, no lamps, water spouts projecting several feet in the streets, no pavements, no Library, nor a public house, or a private boarding house deserving the name." Anyone whose unlucky travels brought him to Albany left quickly, seeking lodging somewhere in the countryside rather than remaining among the dour Dutch.

Shortly after his arrival in Albany, Elkanah published an account of his travels in Holland.[29] Although he signed it merely as "an American," people soon identified him as the author. The Dutch in Albany took offense at his failure to praise their country sufficiently and consequently received his proposals for improving their town with no great friendliness. But Elkanah had concluded that Albany was destined to become a major city, and there he would live and die. He did, however, instruct his family solemnly "that I should not be buried within half a mile of any Dutchman." Whether they liked it or not, Elkanah determined that he would contribute his wisdom and experience "to elevate Albany from its then state of degradation."

Within a year, he suggested improvements to street lighting, and he accomplished the first paving of the main street. Long established residents had not been asking for outside advice, but Elkanah did not let that stop him. They, after all, were Dutch and as far as he was concerned they owed him thanks for his generosity in applying his wide international experience and superior inventiveness to the solution of inconveniences they hadn't known were problems. Drainpipes that had carried water out away from the houses to channel excess water in the center of the street had followed a design traditional in Holland, where the water flowed from the roofs into the canals. Elkanah's modern pavement included a raised center to keep the roadway dry. Rain from the gutters now flowed directly into the cellars of the old Dutch houses. In his opinion, that was not his problem, since the design of the new pavement demonstrably embodied the best and most modern way to build roads. Housewives incensed that they had to clear their houses of mud and muck washed in off the streets after a thunderstorm caught sight of Elkanah and chased him down State Street brandishing their brooms and yelling, "Here comes that infernal paving Yankee!" Elkanah insisted that he had maintained his dignity by retreating with a quickened walk, although friends were sure they'd seen him running.

A neighbor of Elkanah's, the Dutch Reformed minister Johannes Bisset, became the butt of Elkanah's anti–Dutch prejudices when he asked Elkanah to provide expert advice for the design of a new outhouse. The old clergyman assumed that, since Elkanah knew so much about every conceivable improvement, he might be capable of supplying some new insights to this ancient design problem. But Elkanah did not like Bisset, whom he described as "a large beafeated character, a notorious glutton—in course a heavy-eyed, thick lipped stupid fellow—drawling out his heavy sermons to the last sand of the hour glass, to a drowsy lead-eyed audience towards the close of which, scarcely a head was seen erect, all were most fortunately for themselves drowned in forgetfulness—snoring in a melodian concert."[30]

Smoking his long clay pipe while visiting one day in the office at the front of Elkanah's house, Bisset "placed the head of his cane very significantly under his chin, and for a moment appeared to be lost in a deep reverie, saying with an emphasis, 'Mr. Watson.'"

"Sir," replied Elkanah.

"I was reflecting, what great mechanical power you possess. Me, sir—I make no such pretention." He paused, drew in some more smoke, exhaled, then again began, "Mr. Watson."

"Sir," Elkanah repeated, "your pleasure."

"Will you do me a particular favor?"

"I will, if not too inconvenient—proceed, Sir."

"Why, my neighbor, I am about building a certain Temple [an outhouse] in the rear of my house and I shall be obliged to you to give me the best plan of one."

Elkanah couldn't tell whether Bisset was intentionally and grossly insulting him, making fun of his grandiose plans for improving all of Albany, or whether the "request emanated from shear ignorance." Bisset's face presented "a dead blank, unmeaning vacuum."

"Well, Mr. Basset, as you have been pleased to compliment me upon my great mechanical powers; and now wish a test of that fact, by furnishing you a plan, in plain French *d'une Commodité*—as a preliminary measure—I request you will proceed forthwith to your own residence;

Elkanah's engraving of Albany's old Dutch church, engraving by Henry Snyder after a drawing by Philip Hooker (from the Elkanah Watson Papers, courtesy New York State Library).

summon all your family together; and take their respective dimensions Longitude & Laditude, with great precision—your own included—and then for the plan."

The man and his entire family were "of remarkable size, square withal." The sarcastic answer "aroused him from his stupid reverie," and, mumbling, "well, well," the dominie returned home and never visited Elkanah again. "Nor did I ever hear more from the famous temple," Elkanah confided to his memoirs.

Always interested in investment possibilities, in the summer of 1790 Elkanah traveled by wagon about twenty-five miles to New Lebanon Springs, where he visited a Shaker settlement. The springs reminded him of Matlock in Derbyshire in England. Tourism by healthseekers, however, would have to wait until some sort of regular stage service had been established, so Elkanah started work on that.

The diversion of a Shaker Sunday service, he said, "disgusted and sickened" him. Elkanah considered what he saw to be a "revolting scene" of "solemn mockery," and a display of dignity and human destiny "perverted by this strange fanaticism." The Shakers' congregational dance failed to attract him as a quaint, admirably simple sectarian peculiarity. Instead he described the group's movements as most awkward—"raising their right knee high up, and dropping on the balls of their feet, the left foot performing a short up and down motion; all advancing and retiring three or four steps, and at every turn of the tune, whirling round with three steps.... Among the women were some tall oaks, some shrivelled dwarfs, and some young saplings. Their white capped heads of various heights, bobbing up and down in the mazes of the dance, had a queer and ridiculous appearance." The animated leader of the spiritual exercises was "grossly ignorant, and had a hoarse and unpleasant voice." Proud to announce himself a friend "to religious toleration in its widest latitude," this a-sexual, non-doctrinal spinning about burst the bounds of Elkanah's preconceptions of what was and what was not religion. Yet he couldn't help admiring their sincere morality and industrious productivity, however much he condemned their leader as a foolish despot.

In the fall, Elkanah tried another hot springs—Saratoga. Here would be America's elegant Bath, but as yet the amenities were primitive. A three-sided log hut gave the dozen or so bathers protection from weather and animals, but the pool was just a rude trough like a pig feeder. The spring bubbled up from a crack in a rock in the midst of a marsh. The water had the flavor of "saline ingredients, highly charged with fixed air," and its effervescence reminded Elkanah of Champagne wine. The flavor of Congress Spring, recently discovered nearby, was more heavily mineralized. Not far away Elkanah stopped at Tryon's Tavern in Ballston, where the first spring discovered by Europeans remained as a deteriorating barrel set in the mud, its staves falling outward. Men washing sores in the spring offended Elkanah, who felt that they were improperly exposed to the gaze of two or three ladies who were using a tree trunk as a bridge to reach the fountain. The tavern could serve no more than a dozen visitors at a time. Even so, Elkanah foresaw grand developments here as more and more Americans would come to take advantage of "the remarkable medicinal qualities of these springs."

These excursions, however, gave little hope for large-scale investment and development. For that, Elkanah still wanted canals. As always, he cultivated friendships and connections with important people, including the few Dutch who he thought merited his attention. For the western canal project he was looking for potential investors, and three of them joined him on the exploration trip to form a detailed idea of the possible future canal route. Among them, Jeremiah van Rensselaer belonged to the oldest of the Dutch families who had settled the region, as recalled in the name of the town Rensellaerswyck. Along with Elkanah, he had been chosen to the board of directors of the Albany Bank when it was founded at a meeting in the City Tavern on June 12, 1791.[31] The bank became heavily involved in the financial aspects of land acquisition and canal construction while van Rensselaer and Watson were directors. (The process of obtaining a charter for the bank from the state legislature brought Elkanah into close contact with yet other politicians, such as Robert Livingston, Chancellor of New York, in other words, president of the state's highest court.)

Philip van Cortlandt, another potential investor, had been a distinguished colonel of the Second New York Regiment, and retired with the rank of General in the Revolutionary Army, to become a state politician. He joined Watson in the land development projects that carved up northwestern New York State. Stephen N. Bayard, another land speculator who joined Elkanah in some projects, operated the Mohawk General Land Office in Schenectady from 1790 on.[32] He became one of the most important owners of land in the area the friends were about to explore.

Two bateaux operated by hired boatmen carried supplies for six weeks' exploration that started up the Mohawk River from Schenectady. From September first, Watson and van Rensselaer traveled by covered wagon from Albany to meet van Cortlandt and Bayard at Herkimer, when they would all continue with the boats and portage. Narrow roads through farmland along the Mohawk River carried them to Schuyler's Mills, where a new wooden bridge, seventy-five feet long with a single arch, took them across. After passing the German Flats and the Little Falls they met their bateaux at Eldridge's tavern near Fort Herkimer. The boats going upstream managed the same speed with sails and rowing as canal boats pulled by horses in Holland, about three miles an hour. But in rapids the men had to use their oars as poles, laboriously pulling the boats forward without horsepower. Fourteen miles upstream they pulled over to the shore and spent the night in a vacant log cabin. At Old Fort Schuyler Van Cortlandt and Bayard joined the party, bringing the total number to thirteen. The group's purpose was to compose detailed reports to the Western Inland Lock Navigation Company that would convince investors to become involved in the project to connect the Hudson River with Lake Ontario by a series of locks and canals to avoid rapids and other difficult passages in the rivers and to replace portages with waterways. The Mohawk River carried them as far as Fort Stanwix, although immigrants had thoughtlessly hindered passage at places by leaving branches and logs in the water where trees at riverside had been cut.

Fort Stanwix had improved slightly—Elkanah always looked for improvements. Now there was a "tolerable tavern to administer comfort to the weary traveler." But to reach Wood Creek, the beginning of rivers flowing west, the expedition had to carry and drag its baggage and its boats across two miles of land—the "Oneida Carrying Place," as it was called. Heavy rain prevented travel for a day, leaving nothing to do but go fishing. "Salmon, Oswego bass, cat-fish, chubs, trout, pike, are the fish common in this river," according to Elkanah, who mentions only having caught a large cat-fish.

The turns of the river, its reverses and loops, could be so tight that the prow of the boat stuck over the bank while the stern scraped along the mud of the same bank, when rounding a sharp bend. For this route to be convenient, low branches and brush in the stream would have to be cleared, and some channels would need dredging,. Elkanah thought a canal ignoring the twists of the natural channel could shorten the distance to just a third of the length. At a confluence the addition of the waters of a tributary widened the stream to a hundred feet and they could row again for quicker progress. Two miles farther, a blockhouse on the eastern end of Oneida Lake remained from British occupation.

Sailing smoothly on the lake, estimating it to be thirty miles long and five to eight miles wide, Elkanah imagined the future. "I saw those fertile regions, bounded west by the Mississippi, north by the great lakes, east by the Alleghany mountains, and south by the placid Ohio, overspread with millions of freemen; blessed with various climates, enjoying every variety of soil, and commanding the boldest inland navigation on this globe; clouded with sails, directing their course toward canals, alive with boats passing and repassing, giving and receiving reciprocal benefits from this wonderful country prolific in such great resources."

As yet, the region had few new settlers. Near old Fort Brewerton at the far end of the lake where the Onondaga River started, the explorers stayed with two families who had built houses there—a welcome change from their makeshift tents that had seemed fine in good weather, but proved leaky during heavy rain.

Where the Onondaga River met the Seneca River and the combination became the broad Oswego River flowing northeast to Lake Ontario, the group set up their tent together with those of a group of surveyors led by Moses De Witt. These men were laying out parcels of land to be used as payment to Revolutionary War soldiers from New York State. The settlement of the wilderness lands negotiated a few years earlier at Fort Stanwix was just beginning, but its speed was startling. Farmers would bring progress here, according to Elkanah. Onondaga Indians who visited the camp wanting rum were merely "troublesome."

The next morning, Elkanah and his friends met "old Kiadote, king of the Onondaga Indians, with several warriors and his queen." They brought "some excellent fresh salmon and eels in a basket slung on her back." Elkanah's group gave them only some rum and biscuits. Kiadote's face struck Elkanah as sensible and sedate. His wife "appeared modest and humble." Kiadote's name "means a tree with thorns, and fruit upon it." Kanastoretar, the name of the queen, meant "a good housewife."

Elkanah's party avoided the mouth of the Oswego River at Lake Ontario, where Fort Oswego was still occupied by British soldiers despite the terms of the treaty that ended the Revolutionary War. Elkanah predicted war again if the British did not leave. Instead of heading up to Lake Ontario, they launched their boats against the stream in the Seneca River, taking them to the end of the Salt Lake, where a few Indians gathered on the shore boiling water to get the salt. Elkanah found the salt works already begun by settlers "in a rude, unfinished state." But he was assured that this source could easily supply all the salt needed in America. And salt was essential for food preservation. Just poking their walking sticks into the ground produced springs of brine. The surrounding forests could be cut and burned to evaporate the water. Wind that now gave the evenings the brushing sound of branches would blow away the mist and smoke from the fires leaving nothing but salt, which could be sold far away to supply the cities and enrich the investors.

Indians in their light-weight birch bark canoes returned from fishing, "accompanied by all their families, children, dogs, cats, fowls, etc." King Kiadote and his wife glided by, paddling in a canoe that their son steered. Elkanah and his group made contact for trade, communicating by gestures, exchanging rum and biscuit for smoked eels and salmon. Elkanah had now seen seven monarchs—Little Carpenter, Chief of the Cherokees; Louis XVI, King of France; Joseph, Emperor of Germany; George III, King of Great Britain; Willem V, Stadholder of Holland; New-River, Chief of the Catawbas; and Kiadote, Chief of the Onondagas.

Elkanah meeting Kiadote (engraving by Barritt after Lossing, in *Men and Times of the Revolution*, 1861, p. 349).

"I can safely say," wrote Elkanah later, "I felt more respect for old Kiadote in the stern of his canoe than I ever did for the mighty monarchs of Europe, several of whom I have beheld with contempt, and for this plain reason that Kiadote is, probably, a blessing to his nation, whereas civilized kings, as they are called, are for the most part, a scourge to the human race, and a curse to mankind."[33]

Elkanah's shining visions of inevitable progress, of the expansion of New Englanders' civilization over an entire continent, prevented him from entertaining any alternative view of the events of his time. The disappearance of Indians from the land that had been traded for some equivalent of rum and biscuits bore the character of inevitability for which Elkanah felt no personal responsibility. That Indians might not agree, might not want to participate, could reject progress and civilization startled him. "It is surprising to observe, how tenaciously the Indians adhere to their native customs, although bordering on and intermixed with white men. They stick to the Indian to the last man, with a few exceptions; and this demonstrates a well-known fact, that they despise our customs as heartily as we do theirs. They view us, as a race of mortals degenerated into effeminacy, and unworthy the native dignity of man, in which they pride themselves."

Thoughts of these contrasting attitudes took the form of fleeting observations without any power to intrude on Elkanah's true interests—his visions of expanding agriculture, commercial development, and potential profit. And while he denounced the alcoholism of the Indians, he did not consider his own alcoholism to be a character flaw of the same sort. During this trip he became addicted to the rum that he was trading for fish, according to his own admission when he had become an advocate of temperance, recommending a moderate amount of wine, cider, or beer instead of grog.[34]

Elkanah and his friends continued west along the Seneca River, through Cross Lake, then along the river again and through salt marshes to Cayuga Lake. Here, too, they came upon new settlers' rudimentary attempts to produce salt, ineffective in the absence of long-distance transportation, but for that reason a further inspiration to believe in the need for canals. At lakeside they found shelter with pioneering farmers, but the experience of sleeping outdoors during this trip impressed on Elkanah the dangers of infection in an enclosed room, from the breath of others who might be ill. Elkanah was convinced, he said, "that the nearer we approach to the original state of savage life, the less we shall be exposed to the complicated disorders incident to a civilized state." The imagined state of savage life held inspirational attractions, whether or not the reality of native culture was incomprehensible and inevitably doomed.

Leaving one boat in the care of a single member of the crew, the party continued on the other boat from Cayuga Lake to Seneca Lake, carrying the boat overland around Seneca Falls. Sunset cast red tints on the tops of evergreen trees on the hills, surrounding the quiet blue lake with changing hues fading to grey beneath a clear, darkening sky. Elkanah felt an effusion of anticipation, looking forward to the time "when the borders of this lake will be stripped of nature's livery, and in its place will be rich enclosures, pleasant villas, numerous flocks, herds, etc.; and it will be inhabited by a happy race of people, enjoying the rich fruits of their own labors, and the luxury of sweet liberty and independence, approaching to a millennial state."

For the moment, however, they could steer toward the new town of Geneva on the northwest shore. The town had about fifteen houses, mostly log cabins. Because of nearby marshes Geneva made an unhealthy impression, but it was growing. These hovels constituted one of several new towns beginning to take possession of land and resources. Lysander, Brutus, Ovid, Romulus, eventually Troy—with such names the clusters of log cabins proclaimed the arrival of civilization reaching back to classical antiquity. The explorers found adequate lodging at Patterson's tavern, but Elkanah complained that he was kept up by gamblers and fleas—"two curses to society." The next night they could sleep again in their own tent, at the opposite end of the lake. Until about ten years earlier, this had been the main settlement of the Seneca Indians, who had remained loyal to the Crown during the Revolutionary War. In 1779 General Sullivan, Elkanah's friend, had led attacks on the Seneca that included "destroying orchards, corn, wigwams, etc." The surviving members of the Seneca nation had retreated to Canada.

Elkanah's group returned up the Cayuga Lake to Phelp's Tavern, a log cabin in the beginning of the settlement of the tract of land being used to pay old soldiers, partly through direct land grants but mostly through the proceeds of sale to investors. This marked the end-point of the expedition. Van Cortlandt and Bayard decided to return overland to the Mohawk River, riding along an old Indian path. Elkanah and Jeremiah van Rensselaer returned by boat.

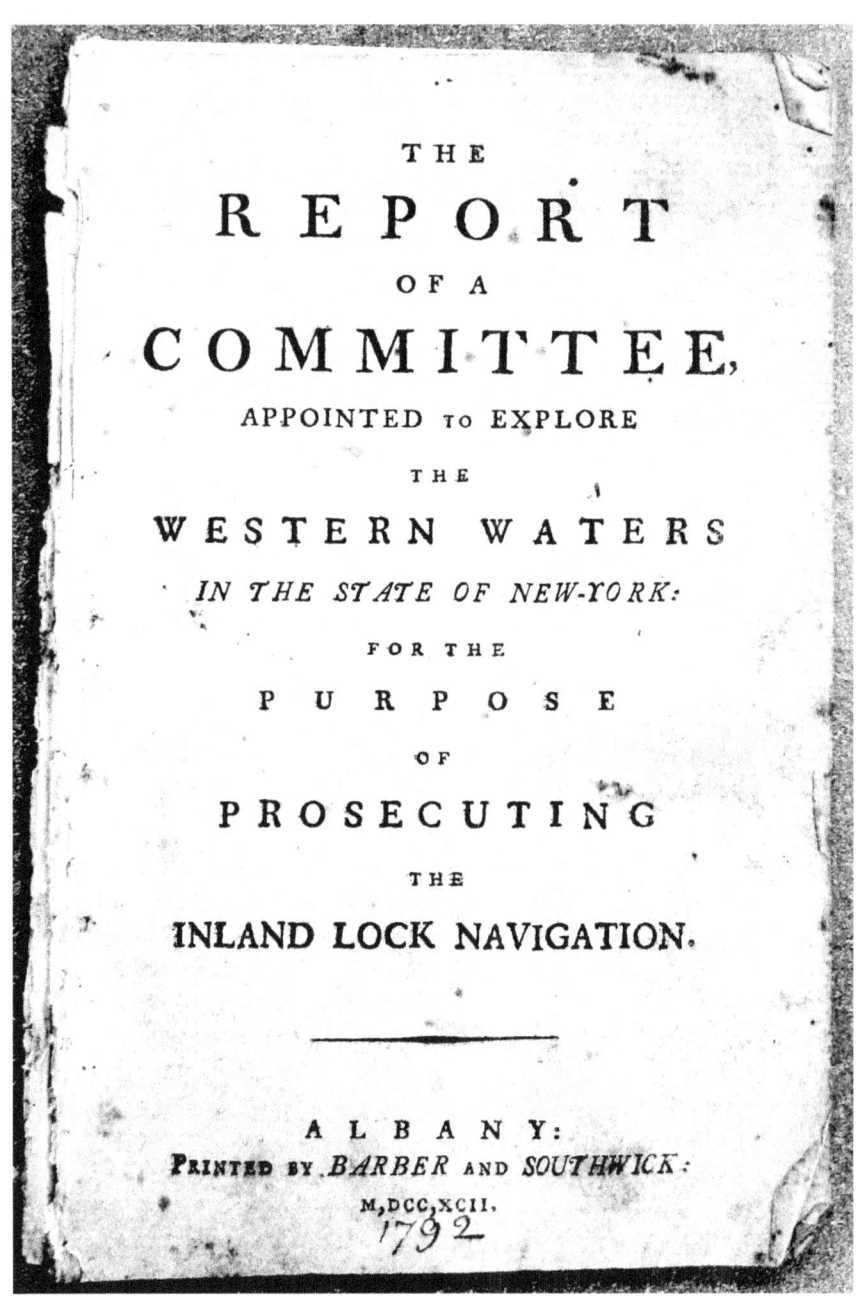

Report of a Committee ... Western Waters (from the Elkanah Watson Papers, courtesy New York State Library).

Watson and Tallyrand in Albany

King Kiadote and his family disappeared from Elkanah's meditations along with the forests cut for fuel and cleared for farmland. Watson gave little further attention to the Onondagas, the Oneidas, and the Senecas, beyond checking that the land he bought and sold was free of encumbrance. At solemn occasions, Masonic rhetoric continued to praise the brotherhood of mankind.

In 1792, Elkanah collaborated with General Philip Schuyler in the efforts needed behind the scenes to obtain passage in the state legislature of the Canal Act, resulting in state charters for two canal companies. One would connect the Hudson with Lake Ontario, and would eventually become part of the development of the Erie Canal (which took a slightly different route). Another would connect the Hudson with Lake Champlain. Eventually subsections were assigned to separate companies. Through these and other companies, Elkanah bought land where the canals and roads would be built and whose value would therefore increase, as well as joining with other investors in acquiring waterside rights along rivers where the most power could be generated by mills. Among other investments, in the mid–1790s he became part owner of Jean de Neufville's glassworks, which employed a couple hundred laborers and grew to become the state's major producer of window glass as de Neufville had hoped.

Canal investors were sought throughout America. When the shares were not selling quickly enough, Robert Morris, whom Elkanah had met in Philadelphia on his way to Mount Vernon, intervened, investing himself and publicizing the offer in Philadelphia. Among his many business projects, Morris was the chief agent in America for the Dutch bankers whose loans to finance the American Revolution were expected to be repaid in the form of income from land reserved to be sold for them in New York State—a complicated transaction organized in America as the Holland Land Company. As part of this arrangement, Morris held vast tracts of land bordering on Lake Ontario and Lake Erie at the farthest western section of the intended canal, the Robert Morris Purchase. Through faulty surveying and a lack of coherence in state policy on land distribution, these areas came into partial congruence and confusion with the administration of the so-called Military Tract.[35] The price of the lots he intended to sell there would rise greatly through the construction of the canal. The Amsterdam bankers who had provided loans to America as negotiated by John Adams were repaid with one million acres of land including and adjacent to Morris's property. They transferred this to the firm of Pieter Stadnitsky and Son, a firm that soon became known as the Holland Land Company.[36]

Elkanah's European experience became important again to him in 1794, when refugees from the French Revolution moved across the street from him in Albany. Henriette Dillon and her husband the Count de Gouvernet, Marquis de la Tour du Pin, had escaped the guillotine in disguise, fleeing Paris and taking the first ship leaving Bordeaux as Citizen De Latour and his wife. Their luggage included luxury items that they sold to raise cash on arrival in Boston—silverware, linens, books, a harpsichord. They could start afresh in the new republic. For Elkanah they brought a letter of introduction from Boston's richest merchant, Thomas Russell, who was married to Elkanah's cousin Elizabeth. Elkanah was, no doubt, also impressed by their acquaintance with the Marquis de La Fayette. At the beginning of the French Revolution, the count had been French ambassador in The Hague, and, as a reformist, he was initially continued in that post. When the violence toward aristocrats increased, he returned to France, then sought safety in America. Probably his choice of Albany indicates familiarity with the publicity in Europe about the land available through the Holland Land Company. Soon after arrival in Albany, the count bought a two-hundred-fifty acre farm near Troy, where they were joined by the Count de Tallyrand, the French diplomat who previously had been excommunicated by the pope and deposed from his office as Bishop of Autun, in retaliation for his having signed the Declaration of the Rights of Man (of which Tallyrand was also coauthor while serving in the National Constitutional Convention). Having the good fortune to be in England in an ambassadorial function, he escaped the Terror in France. Political changes in England and the suspicion he was a spy, however, forced his departure for America. While in Albany, Tallyrand speculated in land and worked in the bank of which Elkanah was director.

The first French refugees were joined in 1795 by (Count) Volney, a *philosophe* who had become a friend of Benjamin Franklin's in Paris. Although Elkanah enjoyed their civilized company, he took offense at what he considered anti–American sneers. Finally, the contact became irremediably strained when Elkanah's patriotism was affronted by their belief that Louisiana would and should provide armed French resistance to American westward expansion.

Sympathetic toward their reduced circumstances in exile, Elkanah recalled that the de la Tour du Pin's farm produce—eggs and butter stamped with their coat-of-arms—was brought to his door for his wife to buy as the aristocrats attempted to make a profit as successful peasants. The marquise, whose sentiments were of the most liberal, lamented in her diary that no competent hired hands could be found to work on the farm. They had no choice, she complained, but to buy slaves. Salving her conscience, she took care to treat them well, and on leaving America, she freed them all. In 1795 conditions in France allowed the refugees to return to their estates, where they could play the role of enlightened leaders of agricultural improvement. Elkanah no longer committed any outraged thoughts about slavery to his memoirs—that his friend and fellow canal investor Philip van Cortlandt maintained a household dependent on slave labor did not lead Elkanah to accuse him of laziness or unconscionable oppression. In fact, according to tax records, the first house of

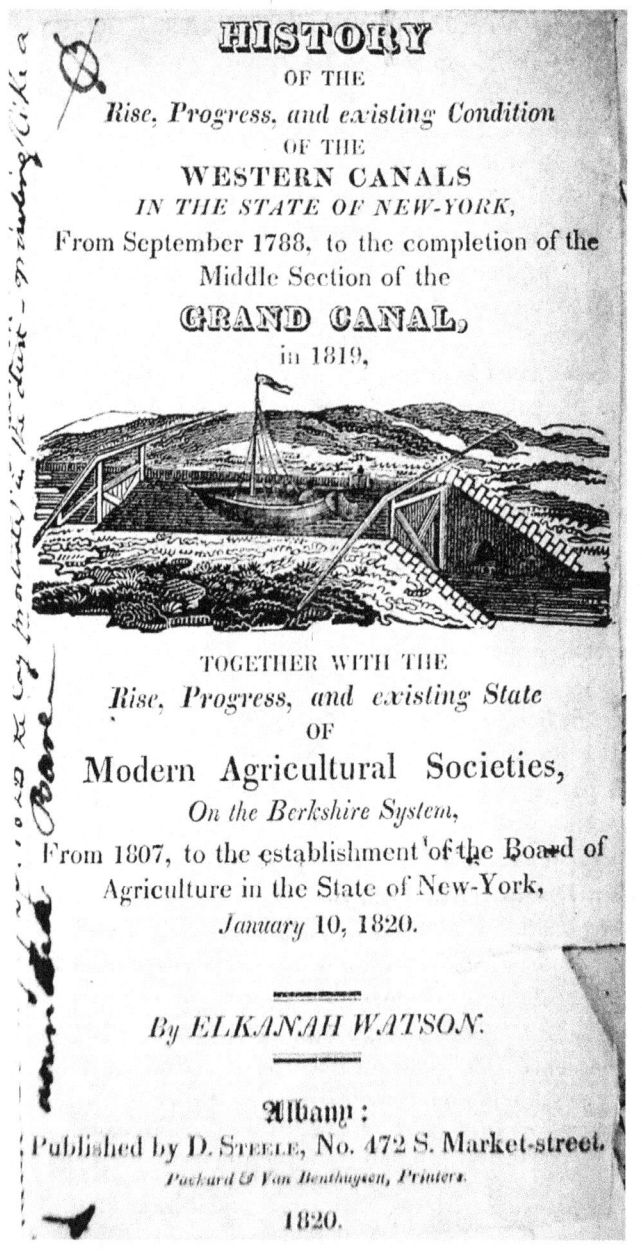

History of the Western Canals (from the Elkanah Watson Papers, courtesy New York State Library).

A vision of the future—canal boat (unsigned etching in *America Illustrated*, p. 88).

the Watsons in Albany included three slaves, but the Watsons were renters who shared the house with its owner, Simon de Witt. Who was the slave owner?[37] Like George Washington, Elkanah preferred to think about other things, to imagine the wealth that could be created by the construction of canals.

His many projects of investment and public improvement kept Elkanah busy writing essays and letters for local newspapers, besides private correspondence to political leaders he knew, such as John Adams and James Madison. Continually involved with politics and the funding of public works, Elkanah's friends included Robert Livingston, Aaron Burr, Alexander Hamilton, and Eliphelet Nott, the founder of Union College. Usually generous with his advice, he imagined improvements for the published plan of the new city of Washington, D.C., which he immediately sent off anonymously to the official town planner, Major Pierre l'Enfant, expecting his concepts for canals to be self-evidently worth incorporation in the final magnificence of the new metropolis.[38] Elkanah's interests were shared by many people, some of whom felt that he took too much credit for conceiving projects that were generally obvious and developed through wide-spread discussion, such as the need for solutions to transportation problems. De Witt Clinton and Philip Schuyler became estranged from Elkanah over contradictory claims as to who had first thought of the western canals and locks. All of them became wealthy through their knowledge and access to information about precisely what land would become significant as a consequence of future construction.

In the summer of 1805, Elkanah and his canal-prospecting friend Stephen Bayard took several weeks free for a trip to Lake George, Lake Champlain, and western Vermont. On the way he stopped at Ballston Springs and Saratoga, contrasting the grandeur of the new Hotel Sans Souci, providing a hundred apartments, with the little one-story cottage known as Tryon's Tavern that had offered isolated hospitality in 1790. "We seated ourselves at a sumptuous table, with about a hundred guests of all classes, but generally, from their appearance and deportment, of the first respectability, assembled here from every part of the Union and from Europe, in the pursuit of health or pleasure, of matrimony, or of vice."[39] The French custom of seating men and women mixed together at the table had replaced the old English and

American habit of separation—meriting Elkanah's approval, as he remembered how he had argued in favor of introducing to America this modern informality when he first came into contact with fashionable society in France. Even in the hotel's ballroom, under the chandeliers, French dances, the cotillion and quadrille, had replaced the "old-fashioned country-dances and four-hand reels of revolutionary days."

The elegantly galleried three-story hotels at Ballston and Saratoga Springs symbolized rising prosperity and progress. Elkanah saw the same virtues embodied in red clover growing in once barren fields now fertilized with gypsum, a new idea in agriculture. Everywhere he looked, nature could be seen giving way to improvement. America's future, he was sure, would surpass anyone's past. And the scenery must be acknowledged as nothing if not more grand, more picturesque, more sublime than whatever Europe could offer. Lake George's many islands standing silently in famously pure water surrounded by the high slopes of wild mountains could not simply be enjoyed—one had to be assured that "the Lake of Geneva, so vaunted by European tourists, bears no comparison to Horicon [the Indian name for Lake George, according to Elkanah], either in its quiet liveliness or imposing magnificence."

Elkanah and his friend hired four men who rowed them in a bateau to the northern end of the lake. Lunch was freshly caught trout. In the evening, they set up their tent at Sabbath Day Point. "Nothing could be more sublime than the effect of the setting sun, as its rays fell upon the piles of mountains which surrounded us." In addition, Elkanah considered ways to combine the immense potential for water-driven machinery with the timber of the region and the reports of major deposits of iron ore nearby, assisted by direct passage to Lake Champlain to the north.

Their route took them below the ruins of Fort Ticonderoga, already seeming as ancient as a European castle. Here the cannons that brought American victory at the siege of Boston in 1776 had been captured from the British by Benedict Arnold and Ethan Allan. Beyond Lake Champlain, Elkanah visited growing new towns, including one called Vergennes in honor of the French foreign minister he'd met with Benjamin Franklin. Mills along Otter Creek were already processing iron ore. The university at the village of Burlington inspired comment; it seemed to be in decline. The three-story building above the town served only thirty students, while the university's president was its sole professor. After getting as far north as Plattsburg, back into New York, they returned along the east side of the lake to Middlebury, where a college had recently been founded, still smaller than the university at Burlington. Such fledgling attempts at teaching youth brought hope of educated republican citizens, and Elkanah paid attention to them from motives of patriotic vision. Back in Albany, he involved himself in the establishment of Union College at Schenectady, founded by his old friend, the Albany minister Dr. Nott.

The trip brought new mountains, new rivers, new vistas, and new commercial possibilities within Elkanah's range of contemplation. On returning home, Albany looked constricted as well as small-minded. Improved transportation was an urgent need the locals hadn't noticed—he'd invest in regular stage-coach service. Elkanah had become wealthy through his investments in land and industry, but there was no success in entering the closed world of Albany's Dutch society. As an outsider with insistent demands for instant change, Elkanah had met resistance as well as enthusiasm. Opponents of canal investment forced him out of the bank directorship in 1795.

In the fall of 1797, antagonism in Albany convinced Elkanah to move for a while to New

Improved transportation (lithograph in *Views from Nature*, p. 79).

York City, where the Watsons lived opposite St. Paul's Church, and where, in November, their daughter Mary was born. An epidemic of yellow fever made it prudent to leave the city the following August. The Watson family returned to Albany but rented a big old farmhouse outside the town of Troy to avoid the pestilence.[40] The Watsons shared the house with the Widow van Beuren, her two grown-up daughters, and an unmarried sister. Like many Dutch farm houses in New York, a long covered porch extended the length of the front, with another porch at the rear. Elkanah was away at Albany one day, and farm hands were all out in the fields. The women were napping, Rachel Watson dozing in a rocking chair with the nine-month old baby.[41] Aroused by sounds behind her, and thinking one of her daughters was playing a joke, she turned around and "Oh GOD of Mercy—behold what! A large She bear immediately behind and near her Chair, sitting erect with her broad forepaws in a striking attitude, to seize the infant." Screaming scared the bear away. One of the other women woke up and pulled the rope of an alarm bell to call the farm-workers, while the bear heavily turned and tried to leave. A farmer grabbed a gun and ran after the bear, which was "quietly and slowly making her way up a valley in the direction of the Vermont Mountains from whence she must have come." A bear straying so far into the civilized and cultivated part of the country astonished everyone around Troy. The farmer caught up with the bear and killed her, providing dinner the next day.[42]

However odd the presence of a bear in Troy, New York, may have been, the story itself calls attention to the peculiar near absence of any references, in Elkanah's notes and published memoirs, to his wife Rachel beyond the description of his having fallen immediately in love with her when he first saw her. In extensive correspondence, however, he affectionately tells her of his adventures and experiences during his travels away from home, such as the fireworks in New York City celebrating the end of the war with Britain in 1815, but also giving homely advice on such matters as how to choose the best watermelons. Several letters describe travel by sloop or steamboat on the Hudson River.

One time, returning to Albany from New York City, Elkanah reached Troy at three in the morning. Hoping to find shelter in the rain and wind, he and a friend "found to our great joy—a light in a bar room—but as the other passengers were at our heels, we dart'd into the bar room—pell-mel—in a mass all vociferating loudly for beds—most of them pitying me more than themselves in reverence to my grey hair—but a full blood paddy who had charge of the bar room soon silenc'd our clamor by Jumping on a Chair & bawling out—'Shentlemen thur is no beds for any mothers son of you all—our beds are all full.' Profiting by my experience as an old traveler, I tip'd him a wink to follow me in a corner of the room, and then taking him by the hand saying in the Irish broug in a low tone of voice, 'and don't you Know me Pat?' 'No, by my soule I do not.' Again, 'Don't you Know that I am the Mayor of Dublin?' 'Aye, aye, that alters the case my Lord Mayor, You shall have a bed.' On which I pull'd him again by the sleeve of his coat—turning to my friend Platt, who heard what pass'd biting his lip, to restrain a laugh—'and don't you know that Gentleman is the high Sheriff of Dublin traveling in my comapny?' 'The d…l it is—he shall have a bed too.'"[43]

Rachel wrote loving notes with news of the children.[44] Children's letters to her expect their mother's attentive care—George, away at school in 1800, for example, let her know that he had "no shurts to put on" (and "had to borrow one"). "Mama," he wrote, "I wish you would send me a handsum pare of shuse my shuse that Papa brought me is verry good but I want a pare for Sunday."[45] George's older brother Joseph, on the other hand, had moved to France to learn commerce as an employee of a Mr. Lynch, the American Consul at Nantes. His letters to his father (in English and in French) report on commodity prices and French plans to invade England in 1804, but Joseph does not mention his mother.[46]

At this time the Watsons were living on Court street, in a three-story house owned by Simon de Witt, the state's Surveyor General.[47] Other government officials lived in the same street, including Elkanah's friend Jeremiah van Rennselaer, known as "Uncle Jerry." The Watson front parlor contained one of Albany's first pianos, made by George Astor. As a little boy, Elkanah's son William looked up one day while his sister Emily was playing. He remembered later seeing "an Indian decorated in all the barbaric finery they so much fancied, enter the room, another and then another until it seemed to my childhood eyes as if the whole Tribe had made their appearance, there possibly might have been half a dozen. They silently arranged themselves in a semicircle behind my sister, who with admirable calmness and bravery continued to play." William crawled under the piano. "The Indians remained until their taste was satisfied, and then left the room in the manner and silence with which they had entered it … the Aborigines are passionately fond of music … they had doubtless been attracted in passing, by the novelty and sweetness of its tones."[48]

Not willing to withdraw from finance, Elkanah became a partner in several investment companies with specific goals. Shut out of the Albany Bank, he dreamed up an unexpected response—he organized the foundation of a second bank in Albany. His new State Bank of Albany, chartered by the state legislature in 1803, competed profitably with the first which had been dominated by the old Dutch families he despised.[49] Elkanah became rich, but DeWitt

Clinton and others accused him of massive corruption because of his tactics in acquiring sufficient support in the legislature to get the bank charter passed. Not only did Elkanah provide a grand banquet for statesmen willing to support the project, it came out later that the club that would become the bank directors arranged to reserve fifteen hundred shares to become the property of politicians who voted for the measure.

Elkanah later claimed that this compensatory measure had been taken only under duress, when senators refused to vote for his bill unless they were personally rewarded. Thus he claimed innocence while admitting the bribery, and asserted that the corruption was a customary aspect of New York state politics. But a proposal by the nine bank organizers to incorporate the Onondaga salt springs into the chartered operations of the bank aroused such suspicion and opposition in the western part of the state that the plan had to be dropped before the charter passed. By this alteration the directors had expected to take over the control of the entire New York salt industry, promising increased tax revenues for the state while they envisioned immense profits for themselves. Public fury caused Elkanah to fear being lynched if he were to venture into the Onondaga region.

Pittsfield and the Gentleman Farmer

But for his restless talents he sought a larger theater; and his new bank and ongoing industrial partnerships had produced, once again, enough capital for an entirely new venture. In 1807, in their yellow carriage driven by "our coloured man Jim," Elkanah and his family moved to Pittsfield, Massachusetts, not far over the state line from Albany, where Elkanah bought a mansion situated on a large farm.[50] For the next eight years he played the part of the gentleman farmer, growing many varieties of fruit, analyzing traditional farming methods, conceiving improvements, and introducing them in the neighborhood by way of exemplary pioneering efforts. Elkanah relaxed by taking his children fishing on their twenty-acre pond.

Like the aristocrats who returned to their country chateaux in France, Elkanah judged modern farming to be his patriotic duty. His most important innovation arose from bringing a pair of Merino sheep to his farm—the first in Berkshire County, probably the first in all of Massachusetts, and certainly among the first anywhere in America. He had obtained them from Robert Livingston, who had returned from France with several Merino sheep from the flock at the Chateau of Rambouillet. Much better cloth could be woven from their strong, fine wool than had been produced from the coarser wool of common sheep.

Elkanah's contacts with Livingston had started when the Albany Bank was receiving its initial charter from the state government, but a shared interest in agriculture had grown over the years. While in Paris as Franklin's successor in the position of ambassador, Livingston negotiated the acquisition of the Louisiana Purchase. Livingston, among many American officials in Europe, responded to Elkanah's request to send him samples of the best seeds in their regions. Watson's plan was to attempt to introduce new strains that would improve American farming. Livingston was also among the people to whom Elkanah sent samples of maple syrup in the 1790s. This American product could replace cane sugar, he thought, and thus contribute to the decline of slavery—such was Elkanah's profit-seeking reaction to news of the slave rebellion in Sainte Domingue (Haiti).[51]

Several "Negros" who may have been slaves in New York accompanied the Watson family to Pittsfield, "where they were at once emancipated by the laws."[52] Black and white children played together on the lawn in front of the Pittsfield house. Elkanah liked to smoke his Turkish pipe on the front porch and preside over children's footraces. Little Winslow had fun racing around with Black Betsy, a girl his own age, "who ran with the fleetness of Atalantas."[53] Another Black child was Dick, the little boy of "a wench in the kitchen." After enjoying madeira or port with dessert, Elkanah sometimes cleared the glossy mahogany dining table and placed Dick on it, barefooted, to perform to the accompaniment of Elkanah's singing and beating time. According to Winslow, "Greatly delighted in the amusement, [Dick] danced with all a negro's spirit. It was most ludicrous and amusing, but not essentially philosophic or dignified."[54]

The kitchen was in a nearly separate wing beside the main house, providing servants' quarters. From the Black servants the Watsons heard the story behind the sudden arrival one night of a young man named Tillotson, out of breath, scared, and fearing for his life. Winslow recounted the story in his memoirs. "At that time New York was a slave state & our residence scarcely six miles from its boundary line at Most. Runaway Negros were constantly escaping along the line & taking refuge with the blacks in our neighbourhood. The masters often came to my fathers in pursuit of their slaves. On one occasion a young Tillotson from the Livingstons Manor came to us following a fugitive. Tillotson was young & green & not competent to his mission." A local innkeeper "was a reputable man & kept a reputable inn, but he also allowed it to be used by the blacks for their convivial gatherings. It happened that on the

The Pittsfield House (author's drawing).

night of Tillotson's arrival there was a negro ball at the inn & he confident of finding his slave there went from the house to reconnoiter. With more eagerness than caution or wisdom he was observed by the Blacks while he was peering into the window of the ball room. They all lashed out with wild shouts like Tam O Shanter Witches in pursuit of Tillotson. He started on the run for Father's protection at the top of his speed & the Negros in full cry after him. He reached our threshold just at the moment, as he thought, they were about seizing him; but whether they intended anything further than a healthful freight to him was doubtful. The Negros in our kitchen always laughed & looked wise, when any reference was made to Tillotson's race & fright."[55]

To show other farmers the Merino stock, Elkanah invited them to an exhibition, under an elm tree in Pittsfield's public square. Curiosity brought "many farmers and even females," to see the exotic beasts. If so many people would come to see just two unusual sheep, Elkanah considered it likely that an annual exhibition of livestock would attract a serious and numerous public from farms around the entire region.

The next year he bought a superior breed of pigs, together with a young bull "of English stock." In October, 1810, Elkanah organized the first cattle show and with his contacts made moves that resulted in a state charter the following winter to establish the Berkshire Agricultural Society, whose activities were soon imitated throughout America.

The county fair was born! Parades opened the festivities. Speeches were proclaimed. Bands played. Prizes were distributed, both for animals and for crops (which had been inspected in the fields in July), as well as for products of "domestic industry"—a move that was calculated to attract the support of the farmers' wives. Women's woven goods and other manufactures were displayed in the hall where the speeches of praise were given by Elkanah and other orators.[56] Of all his accomplishments, Elkanah said he took most pride in having nurtured the growth of the Berkshire Agricultural Society until

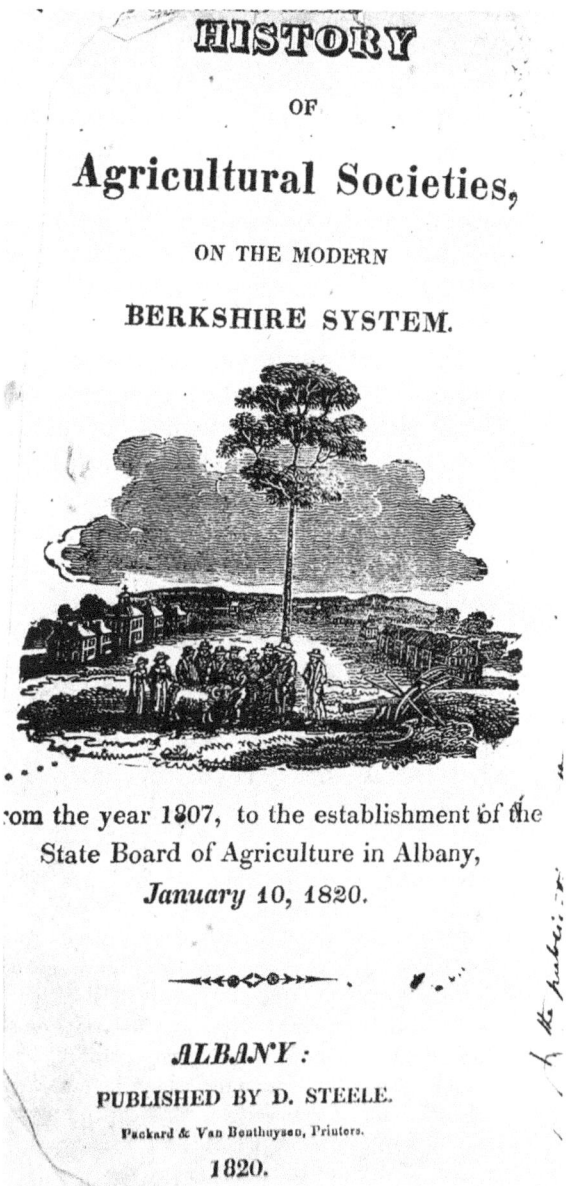

History of Agricultural Societies (from the Elkanah Watson Papers, courtesy New York State Library).

it became nationally and internationally famous as the model for communicating the best and newest improvements in farming to a wide public.

While the Berkshire society took up most of Elkanah's public time, he continued to correspond with national leaders on topics that included Merino sheep but that ranged much farther. From his old friend General William Hull, who had become the governor and Indian agent of the Michigan territory, Elkanah received details of Hull's 1807 treaty to acquire "more than five millions of acres, extending from Fort Defiance on the Miami [River], about two hundred and sixty miles upon that river, Lake Erie, the river Detroit, Lake St. Clair, the river St. Clair, and Lake Huron, comprehending all the rivers which fall into these waters, with all the islands in the same."[57] With John Adams, for example, he communicated his thoughts on the necessity of war with England, keeping in touch during the war of 1812 as America was invaded and patrols again marched through country lanes on their way to battles to ensure the nation's independence. Adams wrote in 1812 to Elkanah about General Hull's surrender of Detroit to the British, and about the danger of British invasion from Montreal that could threaten Boston, New York, and Philadelphia.[58] With Robert Fulton, Elkanah participated in experimental efforts to produce torpedoes that would offset the numerical superiority of the British navy—Elkanah providing the financing when the government turned down Fulton's request.[59]

Full of patriotic fervor, Elkanah delivered an oration to the Berkshire Society in 1814, expressing the belief that the present invasion by soldiers "from the opposite shores of the Atlantic, their hands reeking with blood," constituted "the last generation of Englishmen who will dare to assail the rights of Americans. The time is rapidly approaching, when our population will far exceed theirs. Here also is the last asylum of liberty, exiled from the corrupted countries of guilty Europe; let us cherish and embrace the fair fugitive, in this land of hope and promise, that the whole human family may eventually be blessed with our freedom." But "the whole human family" was an imaginary construction—this was not an abolitionist plea except by implication. And the Indians of Michigan had allied themselves with Britain to try to oppose American expansion into the Midwest. "It is time," said Elkanah, "to repel [the English] from our shores, and sweep from our territory, the unblushing allies of savages."

But were the Indians simply savages? A startling discovery in Pittsfield forced Elkanah to revise his assessment. His description, from a letter to Dr. Hugh Williamson, deserves to be quoted in full:

Pittsfield, November 10th, 1815.
To Hugh Williamson:
Dear Sir:—In conformity with your request to ascertain all the facts, in relation to the interesting discovery of a Jewish phylactery [*a small leather box containing Hebrew scriptures, worn during orthodox prayers*] in this village, in June last, I reply. It was ploughed up in the yard of Mr. Joseph Merrick, a respectable inhabitant who resides on the borders of the village, in the midst of rubbish, and lying some inches below the surface.

Immediately on hearing the rumor of the discovery, I repaired to the house of Mr. Merrick, where I found several clergymen, whose curiosity was greatly excited by the strange incident, and who believed with me, that the article must have found its way into this recent wilderness, by the agency of some of the descendants of Israel.

I had previously read with intense interest on the subject, and was impressed with the belief, that the Indians of America were descended from the lost tribes of Israel; and that they had been directed, by the same Almighty hand which had brought them out of the land of Egypt, to continue

Elkanah's certificate of membership in the Berkshire Agricultural Society, signed by himself, 1812 (from the Elkanah Watson Papers, courtesy New York State Library).

their journeyings in a northeasterly course, probably for many ages, and finally to reach this continent at Behring Strait; yet, retaining some knowledge of the arts and sciences, always adhering to the rites of the Jewish religion. After reaching this continent, and after the lapse of many years, and probably ages, some portions inclined to rest in the northern region, but most of them pursued a southern course, spreading in all directions, even to the southern extremity of South America, and north to the polar regions; and thus peopling the whole surface of both Americas, more or less densely, according to the varied climates. Those in the extreme north and south, became the most savage, as in the milder regions they have been found the most civilized, and in possession of arts and sciences, especially in the City of Mexico and Peru.

It is not my purpose to write a treatise on this important subject, but merely to skim the surface, with a view to account, in some measure, for this very interesting discovery. I think it must have originated from these sources. It is well known, even from Sacred Writ, that the Jews held their phylacteries, with the precious scroll enclosed, in religious reverence. This discovery forms another link, in the evidence by which our Indians are identified with the ancient Jews, who were scattered upon the face of the globe, and to this day remain a living monument to verify and establish the eternal truths of Scripture.

In order to understand the appearance of this discovery, imagine five pieces of leather or raw hide, or some composition similar to Indian rubber, and capable of resisting the ravages of time and exposure, cut into squares of two inches, sewed together with entrails. Suppose, also, a hole in the centre, half an inch in diameter, made to admit a tube, two and a half inches long, with eyelet holes at the corners to receive strings,—and you will have an idea of the article.

This tube, as described by Mr. Merrick, was of such a hard spongy substance, that it was with great difficulty he could gain an opening at one of the sloping ends; and it seemed absolutely impervious to moisture; for, although the surface was incrusted in a manner to evince its having been probably exposed for many ages, I drew out from the tube three or four scrolls of parchment, which it contained when found, inscribed with texts of Scripture, written in Hebrew, in an elegant manner,—the ink of a beautiful jet black. The parchment, writing, and ink, were all perfectly fresh."

Very respectfully,
E. Watson.

The most likely explanation of the discovery is the assumption that it was dropped by a Jewish traveler who passed by Pittsfield, or by a Jewish soldier among the British or Hessian soldiers who came through the area as prisoners during the Revolutionary War or the War of 1812.[60] These hypothetical explanations, however, were not considered by Elkanah, who welcomed proof, he thought, in support of the idea that the Indians had been sent to America by divine guidance, thus contributing to the exceptional significance of the new nation to whose development and progress he had devoted his life's efforts. The Indians were divinely special, even if those he happened to meet were oft times drunk.

A topic causing widespread regional discussion, the Pittsfield phylacteries obviously have to be reckoned among the sources that inspired Joseph Smith in the construction of Mormon views of American history based on the discovery of ancient inscriptions, that, like the Pittsfield phylacteries, have since disappeared from sight.

Elkanah Watson and his wife moved back to Albany, New York, in February, 1816, leaving the rural life of tending to field and herds as an idyllic memory. From Albany Elkanah continued his involvement in improving agriculture, helping to establish county agricultural

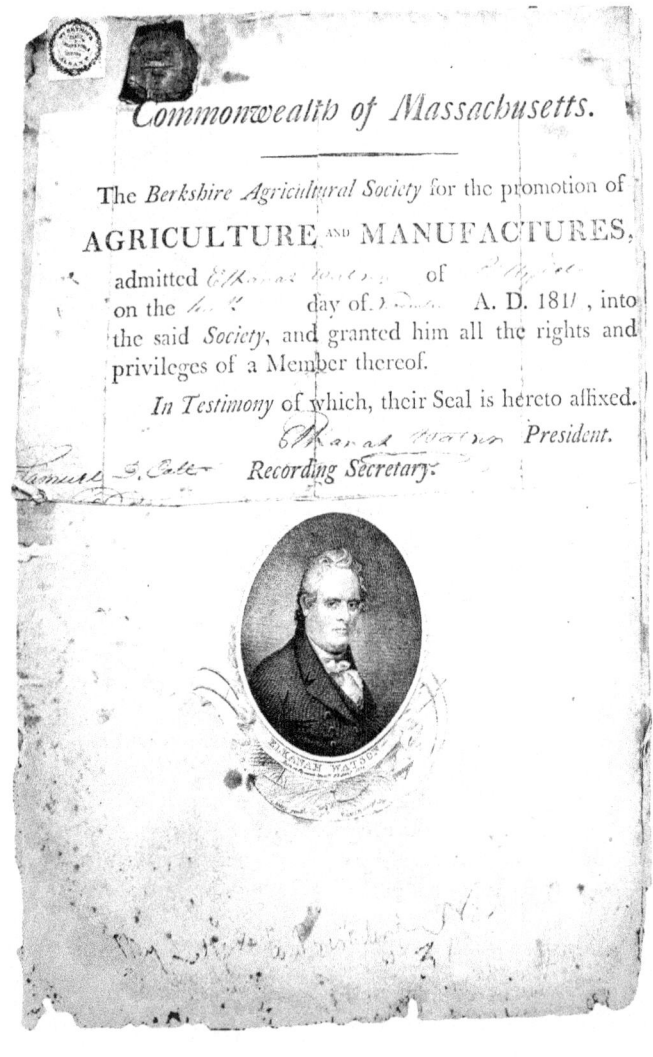

Elkanah's Testimonial, 1814? (from the Elkanah Watson Papers, courtesy New York State Library).

societies in Oneida, Schoharie, Montgomery, and Rensselaer, and attending their annual fairs. He urged the creation of a state department of agriculture, but without initial success. Through the local representative to Congress, his ideas for a national board of agriculture were proposed and debated, again without success. Jefferson and Madison responded to Elkanah's approaches with friendly and polite answers that contributed nothing. Jefferson excused himself as having retired to a life of rest and quiet, leaving politics to younger men. Madison doubted that the central government possessed constitutional powers to establish a national board of agriculture, looking instead with interest to what might be accomplished at the state level.

Elkanah and Rachel Watson had six children. Their daughter Emily had married and moved to Detroit, where she had died in 1817, just a few months after her marriage to Major George Larned. Grieving and feeling hollowness in his habitual routines, Elkanah turned once more to travel; in the summer of 1818 Elkanah undertook a trip to Detroit to pay his respects to the memory of his daughter.

Six

Final Journeys

"After a long and dreary winter, all nature was still enshrouded in mourning." In romantic pathos Elkanah projected his sorrow at the loss of his daughter onto the world. But in June, 1818, on the first day of his trip to Detroit to visit remaining family, he alluded to the forty days and forty nights of the biblical Deluge whose storms and rain Noah and his family survived on the Ark, commenting that "the dove has gone forth, and the earth appears once more glowing beneath the genial rays of grateful sunbeams."

Elkanah had been invited to be among the first passengers when a canal boat service began from the town of Manlius to Syracuse, in a segment presaging the Erie Canal. Thunderstorms drove all the passengers into the narrow boat's long cabin, but when the sky cleared, everyone moved up on the deck above, bringing up chairs and benches. There may have been a rainbow to recall the Flood. Elkanah, the only observer with any experience of canals and canal boats, noticed the approach of a bridge that looked too low for safety. None of the crew warned of the danger. At the last moment, Elkanah yelled, "Down! down! Off the deck!" Everyone fell or rolled into the spaces in front of, behind, and alongside the cabin, just in time to avoid the destruction when the chairs and benches were "crushed into atoms with a tremendous crash, the fragments flying in every direction." Astonishingly, no one was hurt. The captain had been down below drinking, while the helmsman had little if any experience with canals and their bridges.

Elkanah's carriage had continued from Manlius by turnpike and was waiting for him at Syracuse. Passing thriving villages, well established orchards, and flourishing farms, Elkanah cast his mind back thirty-seven years to his first exploration of the area, which was then, as he put it, "in its primeval condition, roamed over by savage tribes, and only occupied here and there by scattered white inhabitants." Geneva in 1791 had consisted of "a few log huts scattered along the slope of a hill, inhabited by a gang of lawless adventurers, who were prostrated by the fever and ague." Now Geneva had become "not only an elegant but a salubrious village, and distinguished for the refinement and elevated character of its society." The town of Auburn had possessed four or five log cabins and a sawmill when he first visited in 1802. Sixteen years later, the population numbered two and a half thousand, and besides their houses the town contained "several spacious churches and other public edifices."

Although fifteen hundred men were digging the Erie Canal not far from where Elkanah was traveling, modernity had not yet transformed everything. On the road to Buffalo, he was delayed for three hours behind a group of Conestoga covered wagons—huge, slow vehicles drawn by teams of six horses. There were regularly scheduled runs from Albany to Buffalo, and any traffic caught behind these wagons had no choice but to practice patience until some

Scraping under a low bridge (engraving by Barritt after Lossing, in *Men and Times,* 1861, p. 466).

widening in the narrow road might make it possible to pass. "Oh, for the completion of the canals," sighed Elkanah, "when these terrible Pennsylvania wagons will disappear."

Smaller covered wagons carrying families on the move also creaked forward slowly, as cattle and pigs were herded alongside on the way to new pastures and homesteads.

At Buffalo on June 21, for the first time Elkanah saw the ocean-like expanse of Lake Erie. Expressing Masonic emotions, he wrote that "The works of nature, in America, were arranged at creation, by the Grand Architect of the universe, on a scale of grandeur and magnificence worthy of His omnipotence." The village of Buffalo itself appeared less magnificent, being "in a depressed state; and the merchants are languishing and tottering." The canal would, he was sure, bring improvement to the economy. Even before he had ever seen the place, a year earlier, using a detailed map he had sketched improvements to the harbor. With dredging and the construction of piers the realization of his ideas might in the future enable large ships to come up to shore rather than anchoring far off. His visit suggested modifications that he made before offering his thoughts to a local committee whose task was to realize civic progress, and who, he was sure, should welcome his advice.

Before he embarked on the 23rd on a schooner to Detroit, there was time for an excursion to Niagara Falls. Crossing the Niagara River at Black Rock, Elkanah stopped in to visit his friend General Peter Buell Porter, a member of the Erie Canal Commission. Porter had fought the British in that very region during the War of 1812 and could explain the features of the nearby battlefield at Chippewa in Canada. Battle sounds ceased, but the ongoing roar of the great cataract could not be ignored; and the falls' unseen location in the distance could be guessed from a rising mist recalling the gun-smoke of battles four years past. Armament rusted in trenches and redoubts. Shattered trees spread dead limbs. Bones in the fields marked silent remains of the violence dividing soldiers and land.

Elkanah had become acquainted with the British General Phineas Riall, who had been sent as a prisoner-of-war to Pittsfield. From him, as well as from reports from the American side, Elkanah knew the view of commanders during the war. Although he looked out over Lake Ontario, Elkanah does not reflect in his memoirs on the Americans' destruction at the lakeshore town of York or their subsequent burning of a hundred houses in the Canadian town of Newark (Niagara), when hundreds of women, children, and non-military men were forced out of their homes into the merciless cold snow of December, 1813. In retaliation, the British burned the village of Black Rock, the town of Buffalo, and the government buildings in Washington, D. C., the following August. But for Elkanah, the action of war consisted of the thoughts, plans, and heroic deeds of individual leaders against a background of unfortunate but brave deaths of countless common youths. Civilian misery could be regretted without diminishing the glory of the leaders who caused it.

For accurate detail of the combat he had the first-hand information of Major Benjamin Forsyth, who now lived near the falls and acted as Elkanah's guide to the most magnificent views of the vast and overwhelming natural wonder. But fatigue from their unexpectedly long hike to reach the waterfall combined with the emotions aroused by the bloodied wastes of battle to leave Elkanah numbed: "My mind had been wrought up to such a point in anticipation, that I confess myself disappointed in the magnificence and grandeur of the spectacle." The next morning more attention was given to the patriotic drama of the deathly battlefields.

Families on the move (engraving and etching by J. W. Orr).

Six. Final Journeys

In Buffalo, Elkanah booked passage to Detroit, reserving the cabin on the schooner "Franklin." When he came on board in the evening, however, he discovered that the arrangement had not been as exclusive as he thought the price had ensured—the cabin was filled with emigrant families whose seasick children made the three-day journey to Erie through rough seas "the most trying and disagreeable" Elkanah had ever experienced. Sounds and smells close by reduced the sublimity of a storm at sea. Going ashore at Erie, he richly appreciated "the comforts of a good tavern, an excellent breakfast, a shaven face, and clean linen."

Erie had around a hundred houses and a court house laid out on a grid of streets overlooking the harbor. Here nine boats had been built which in September, 1813, the American commander Oliver Hazard Perry used to conquer a British fleet of six that had controlled Lake Erie and consequently exposed the northwest borders of the United States to invasion from Canada. Elkanah met several naval officers and sailors who recounted their experiences in the battle. Only one ship was still in use, the *Niagara*, from which Perry had sent his famous announcement of victory, "We have met the enemy, and they are ours." Elkanah visited the very cabin in which Perry had sat to write that letter. All the other ships had been sunk near the harbor. Tourists could be rowed around and over them, able to see the battle damage to the upper decks and masts just below the surface of the clear lake water.

To Elkanah and other Americans, this battle was no mere encounter of small gunboats on a lake. "What incident in history is more noble and chivalric, than that momentous and decisive crisis, when Perry left his almost conquered and disabled ship, the *Lawrence*, in an open boat, exposed to the fire of the British fleet, and passed to the Niagara, a ship fresh and uninjured, thus deciding the fortunes of the day, and capturing every vessel of a superior enemy," he exclaimed. Trying to analyze how Americans came out victorious against the world's greatest navy, Elkanah concluded that American gunners were "far more active and elastic in their habits and motions than the British," a circumstance that allowed them to get three shots off in the time it took the British to fire two. Their fire power was thus effectively superior.

Underway again on the *Franklin*, the emigrants all suffered seasickness as a gale blew them across rough waters on the long inland sea. They anchored at Cleveland on June 30. Elkanah noted with approval that the village was "inhabited by an enterprising race of full-blooded Yankees from Connecticut."

Fine weather after a night of severe storms allowed the "Franklin" to continue its voyage to the Detroit River, reached on Sunday, July 2. Landing on the Canadian side, Elkanah had a two-mile walk to a point where he could be ferried across to the American city. Although his thoughts were focused on the memory of his daughter, he could not refuse an invitation to join a select group of citizens and army officers in a dinner celebration of the Fourth of July in a field behind the house of the Governor of the Michigan Territory.

Detroit inspired dreams of prosperity the future would bring, especially when suitable harbors and canals had been built. The town was beautifully laid out, but not yet built beyond a beginning. Forests still came close to the town, and at night wolves howled close by. The Indians no longer exemplified that noble life so inspiring to Elkanah in the past that he had felt that, "the nearer we approach to the original state of savage life, the less we shall be exposed to the complicated disorders incident to a civilized state." The original state was sent back to the imaginary distant past when contradicted by present reality. "I daily notice squaws, fighting in the streets like wildcats and in conditions too revolting to describe. They lie about the city like swine, begging for cats and dogs, which they devour at the river side, half-cooked."

But the other people now living in Detroit faced a fine future, he was sure. Michigan's destiny was "to emerge from its present social and agricultural depression, into a great State, rich, populous and progressive, and enjoying all the refinements and elegancies of civilized society. Detroit will rank among the great cities of America." Elkanah aimed his telescope to visionary years ahead and invested in some Michigan land. With improved transportation—a steam boat would begin to operate on Lake Erie in the coming twelve months—Michigan would be able to send its products to the markets of the eastern states using the canals now almost complete.

After three weeks in Detroit visiting family, Elkanah returned to Albany. He made just one more major trip.[1] Yet two other trips he did not make.

In 1825, despite his published claims to have first suggested the importance of canal construction for the State of New York, he was absent from the guests invited to ride along on the first boat to traverse the Erie Canal when it opened. Irked that his own canal projects had failed to get much beyond short segments around Little Falls and across the German Flats before the 1792 company had been dissolved and absorbed in bigger projects directed by other people, his pride in having been the first to agitate for the westward canal dream drove him to complain about the attention given to DeWitt Clinton, the leader whose exertions had succeeded. After reading a pamphlet published by a friend of Watson's supporting Elkanah's pride in having initiated the canal project, John Adams had gently written to Elkanah in 1822,

Through the night by canal—The Erie Canal (steel engraving and etching by J. T. Willmore after W. H. Bartlett, 1842).

You need not wish a more ingenious, a more spirited or able vindication of your claims to the first suggestion of the canal policy in New York, and of General Schuyler's sagacious patriotism in adopting and supporting your ideas in the legislature. You both have great merit, but still I think Mr. Clinton has also great merit in supporting your plan. It is right, to preserve the memory of the first discoverers and inventors of useful improvements for the amelioration of the condition of mankind. The gentlemen who were my contemporaries at Philadelphia used to say, that the first discovery of the efficiency of lightning rods, was Ebenezer Kenneeley, a young gentleman of an ardent thirst for science, who drew lightning from the clouds, by his iron pointed kites, before Dr. Franklin had attempted any thing on the subject.... Yet all this in no degree diminishes the great merit of Dr. Franklin, in maturing, digesting, and propagating to the world his system of lightning rods. It would be well to ascertain, if it were possible, the first discoverer of the invaluable power of steam. While we should do honor to his memory, we should not withhold our admiration and gratitude from the great Fulton, whose steam navigation will be of greater benefit to mankind than Franklin's philosophy, although that is very great. While I wish to do honor to these great men, I ought to bear testimony to the merit of your long exertions, which, I think, have been very useful to our country.[2]

Elkanah, still bitter, wrote privately to a friend that the celebrations had been conceived principally to serve DeWitt Clinton's career. Everyone knew, he said, "that the whole object was intended to produce a political result to aggrandize a single individual to the exclusion of meritorious men, who conceived and projected the system many years before Clinton was known—and that he contrived and managed the celebration in all its branches, from Erie to Sandy Hook—and even the Splendid Canal ball to reflect a glow of glory around this person—these considerations deteriorate essentially from the real merits of the exhibition and place the whole scene with men of sense on the level of a *splendid farce*."[3]

A year later, in 1826, in his last major trip, Elkanah, who was now 68 years old, traveled north from Lake Champlain to Montreal. It seemed inevitable to him that Canada would happily be absorbed by the United States. "Who can reasonably doubt, that, ... in the irresistible march of events, the two Canadas [i.e., Lower and Upper Canada] and all the possessions of Great Britain in North America, will have become bright stars in the constellation of American States?"[4]

In Montreal Elkanah attended mass at the Roman Catholic cathedral, a church intended to be "of greater magnitude and splendor than any other in the Western Hemisphere." As yet, only foundations had been completed. They reminded Elkanah of "the outline of a vast castle." As Canada's commercial center, Montreal gave evidence of great wealth. Learning that Elkanah was visiting the city, the commissioners of a new canal at La Chine invited him to participate in the official opening. Out of worldly urbanity and general citizenship, Elkanah entered into the festivities with warm cordiality. But mentally he could predict the consequences of this new construction. Here was the beginning of a system connecting the sea with the Great Lakes, "that will prove a fearful rival to the Hudson and Erie Canal."[5] Out of patriotism and with expectation of personal profit, Elkanah had urged New Yorkers to build their canal in order to draw trade away from Lake Ontario, the St. Lawrence River, and Montreal down to the Hudson, Albany, and New York City.

Five years later, the Mohawk and Hudson Railway opened, its carriages drawn from Albany to Schenectady by a locomotive named the DeWitt Clinton. The forceful figure behind the triumph of the Erie Canal thus lent his name to the emergent decline of his dream. To the foresighted Elkanah, the future lay no longer with canals but with railroads. He retired to the new village of Port Kent on Lake Champlain in 1828, excited by the speed and potential of this innovation in transportation. What benefits railroads would bring to his beloved country! Commerce and migration, agriculture and settlement would increase immensely!

While awaiting time's inevitable progress, Elkanah supervised the construction of a mansion to which he and his wife could retire to live with their son Charles. Small but elegant inside and out, Elkanah's grey granite house embodied the confrontation of Old World culture with New World limitations.[6] Classically conceived as a basement, or ground floor, surmounted by a taller *piano nobile*, or main floor above, the distinction is expressed in different designs for the two levels of pillars on the two-story portico in the center of the symmetrical house. The first level porch has six square-sectioned quasi–Tuscan piers; and their capitals and bases are mere suggestions created by boards added to enlarge the pillars. Local carpenters could accomplish this simply following the line drawings Elkanah provided. The Doric columns of the upper story, as well as the ornament decorating the interior, required more sophistication. Elkanah borrowed the only copy in Albany of something called "the carpenter's book," hoping that his workmen could follow the instructions in it.[7] But inexperience resulted in structural problems: the roof leaked badly, its recessed gutters incompetently constructed. Columns could not be obtained easily. The stone balustrade proved insecure and had to be replaced with wood. The interior finish-work did not proceed according to plan. The builders dissociated themselves from the subcontractor. The rough granite of the walls was supposed to be smoothed with a coating of cement, leaving the stone visible only in the rustication at the corners and above the semi-circular windows flanking the central door (also with rustication over its lunette), as well as above the round windows on either side, known as oculi (a type of window that had never looked out before on Port Kent). But the cement failed to adhere, reducing the aesthetic effect of the contrasting parts of the structure. The square lantern above the stairs inside probably had been intended to be finished with a domed cupola; it ended up with a gabled-roof echoing that of the central two-story portico. Elkanah had to call in the help of an Albany architect, Philip Hooker, to make sure the structural attachment of one part of his design to another would in fact hold together. The builders demanded advice, shirking responsibility for failure. Much simplified, the design nevertheless reflects the classical ideas Elkanah had seen in France—Mansart's Invalides in Paris must be one very distant cousin of this small mansion sitting on five thousand acres in upstate New York, completed in 1828. But American intermediaries provided closer inspiration: similar square Tuscan piers surmounted by round Doric columns marked the portico of the Federal Hall at New York, by the French architect Pierre L'Enfant (with whom

The future arrives: the "DeWitt Clinton" Pulling America's first train (wood engraving by Jocelyn).

Elkanah had corresponded about the urban design of Washington, D.C.). That building also furnished a precedent for a square lantern cupola, although with a small octagonal dome on top.

In the end, the accomplishment had not attained the grandeur of the imagination. Elkanah's dream of a cultured America, guiding the world in agricultural and industrial progress, anticipated a possible realization sometime later—rather like the vision expressed by John Adams, who wrote to Elkanah during the War of 1812, that "two great ameliorations of terrestrial existence have already resulted [from America's independence]: the freedom of religion, and the emancipation of the Africans."[8] Napoleon's France had become delirious; England was again at war with America; prejudice compromised freedom of religion; slavery had not yet been abolished.

But both Adams and Watson could imagine a land free of bigotry and blessed with peace and freedom. To Elkanah, the nation's future required the commemoration and development of civic virtues brought to New England by the Pilgrims. The final trip he did not take was home to Plymouth. Not unexpectedly, however, he responded to an invitation to attend the Forefathers' Day celebrations in 1829 by putting his thoughts onto paper.[9] In his journal he wrote, "For many years I have been invited to attend these pious celebrations commemorative of the Landing of our forefathers at Plymouth the 22d Dec. 1620 at the same time to visit a small shattered remnant of my relatives, and the companions of my youth—above all to drop a tear over the graves of my Parents and a beloved sister and a long line of near and dear relations."

The Watsons' mansion at Port Kent (author's drawing).

Fear of illness, "the dread of Cold, and sickness on the way in so long a journey," caused him to decline, however, and instead to send the following letter.

> Port Kent on Lake Champlain
> 18 Dec. 1829
> Mr. Wm. Sullivan Eq.
> Orator of the day
>
> Sir,
> It is now 56 years since I left the place of my nativity; and such has been my rambling destiny, that I have never been gratified, in witnessing any of the anniversaries which commemorate the emigration of our pious Ancestors who landed within a few rods of the house of my nativity. This privation has been a constant source of grief to me. These jubilees will increase in value as time nods on through successive generations, and will be commemorated in tears of gratitude, & praise by millions and millions of their posterity scattered over the face of the United States. It was my settled intention to have attended the approaching exhibition, in conformity to repeated invitations, & my pledge, with my son Winslow who bears the name of his immortal ancestor, in the eighth generation; and is now in the possession of one of the wedding slippers of the Mother of Peregrine White, the first born male child in New England and the wife of Gov.: Winslow in a second marriage. But the dread of Cold in so long a journey in mid-winter, my heart has failed me on the approach of the moment of my intended departure. I can only evince my reverence and devotion to the Pilgrim Society, and these appropriate anniversaries, tending to keep alive the sacred principles of our ancestor in laying the grand work on which is established our civil and religious liberties, by offering a toast * founded on my visit at Leyden in Holland in June 1784 where Mr. Adams and myself found the church in which the Pilgrims worshiped previous to their embarkation for the wilds of America in good preservation, & nearly in the state they left it.
>
> I am &c.   E. W.
>
> * toast
> "The venerable Church at Leyden in Holland:
> In this humble edifice the pious pilgrims congregated, previous to their embarkation for America. In contemplating this sacred relic in 1784, It recalled to my mind—their virtues—their piety—and self devotion, as directed by destiny to lay the broad foundation which has blessed new England for 200 years—and will continue to bless millions & millions of a grateful posterity."

If Elkanah was not to travel again, others could visit him at Port Kent. In the summer of 1839, President Martin van Buren came north and was welcomed with three minutes' ringing of the church bells and appropriate local cer-

Silhouette of Rachel Smith Watson (from the Elkanah Watson Papers, courtesy New York State Library).

emony. Ordinary people could express their congratulations to van Buren at Hoffnagle's Hotel. Elkanah, Port Kent's most notable citizen, recorded in his diary that he had "rec[eive]d the President in Our Saloon [living room] in presence of several Ladies from Washington." Elkanah's style of address blossomed at its most flowery: "To you, Sir, we will not presume to offer the impure language of addulation—but to greet you in the Spirit of truth, in the sincerity of Our hearts. To you, Sir—thousands especially in these exposed northern frontiers and millions in the U.S. at large, without distinction of parties—but as true Americans, actuated by the pure *Amor Patria* will award the mead of a Nations praise, as the primary cause under a benign Providence in averting the dissolatons, off an unnecessary war."

Elkanah retired to Port Kent to edit his memoirs, leaving them to the future for publication. He offered his manuscript as a legacy to Rachel, his wife, "as a feint pledge of my sincere affection for her—encreasing as we advance, traveling thru this vale of years—hand in hand—heart in heart in bonds stronger than death itself. I give it also," he wrote, "as a small testimony of the deep debt of gratitude, as well for myself as our surviving children to bare witness of her exemplary deportment—for a long course of years it has pleased GOD to permit us to be one—her piety without ostentation—her liberality of sentiment—in a word in Cherishing all the essential virtues of a good wife & a good Mother—may GOD protect her, Amen."[10]

The past beckoned and demanded rhetorically useful remembrance; the future called continuously for change. The world would soon be transformed by trains. Elkanah could once more help lead the way. Port Kent might still be an outpost on the margins of greatness, but with transportation this newly founded town could achieve American success. He knew it. Elkanah had seen to it that a canal connected Lake Champlain with the Hudson River. Now there must be a railroad. Plans to connect Lake Champlain by rail with Boston continued to inflame Elkanah's spirit until the day of his death at age 85 in December, 1842. He could travel in his mind, planning the route through mountains and plains. His final words formed visions of locomotives racing to future glory: "Yonder is the track of the road, and at this point it must terminate."[11]

Elkanah Watson, the cultivator (from the Elkanah Watson Papers, courtesy New York State Library).

Chapter Notes

Introduction

1. Arthur Conan Doyle, "The Adventure of the Empty House," originally published in *The Strand Magazine* 26, no. 154 (October 1903), republished in *The Original Illustrated Sherlock Holmes, 37 Short Stories plus a Complete Novel* (Secaucus: Castle, 1978), pp. 448–462.
2. Gerard Koeppel, *Bond of Union: Building the Erie Canal and the American Empire* (Cambridge, MA: Da Capo, 2009), p. 27.
3. Mary Raddant Tomlan, ed., *A Neat, Plain Modern Stile: Philip Hooker and His Contemporaries, 1796–1836* (Hamilton, NY: Trustees of Hamilton College, distr. University of Massachusetts Press, 1993 [exhibition catalogue]), p. 212.
4. Peter L. Bernstein, *Wedding of the Waters: The Erie Canal and the Making of a Great Nation* (New York: W. W. Norton, 2005), p. 84.
5. Elkanah Watson Papers, GB12579, Box 1, Folder 2, inside the front cover is a note headed "Pittsfield, 181."

Chapter One

1. Alexander Scammel became an officer in the Continental army. At Valley Forge he became George Washington's advocate general. He was mortally wounded at Yorktown in 1781. Peleg Wadsworth survived the war, having risen to the rank of brigadier general of militia and adjutant general of Massachusetts.
2. On John Brown, see James B. Hedges, *The Browns of Providence Plantations, Colonial Years* (Cambridge: Harvard University Press, 1952).
3. Elkanah recalled his nickname in a letter to his sister Priscilla dated 12 October 1780 from Nantes, France in Elkanah Watson Papers, GB 13294, Box 1, Folder 1.
4. William T. Davis, ed. *Records of the Town of Plymouth Published by Order of the Town*, vol. III, 1743–1783 (Plymouth, MA: Memorial Press, 1903), 261–63.
5. Davis (ed.), *Records of the Town of Plymouth, III*, 280.
6. Mercy Otis Warren, *History of the Rise, Progress and Termination of the American Revolution, interspersed with Biographical, Political and Moral Observations*, Lester H. Cohen, ed. (Indianapolis: Liberty Classics, 1988) (reprint, original edition: Boston: E. Larkin, 1805), 58–61.
7. Davis, ed., *Records of the Town of Plymouth, III*, 287.
8. James Thacher describes the moving of Plymouth Rock in his *History of the Town of Plymouth, from its first Settlement in 1620, to the Present Time: With a Concise History of the Aborigines of New England, and their Wars with the English, &c.* (Salem, MA): Higginson Book Company, 1991 (reprint of the second edition: Boston, 1835), 198–99. Thacher may have had access to Elkanah Watson's report; cf. Winslow C. Watson, ed., *Men and Times of the Revolution; or Memoirs of Elkanah Watson* (New York: D. Appleton, 1861), 23–4. See also John Seelye, *Memory's Nation: The Place of Plymouth Rock* (Chapel Hill: University of North Carolina Press, 1998), 23–32. For other interpretations and an earlier depiction of Plymouth Rock than those discussed by Seelye, see Jeremy Dupertuis Bangs, "Commemorating Colonial New England's First Families: The Triumph of the Pilgrims," in D. Brenton Simons and Peter Benes, eds., *The Art of Family, Genealogical Artifacts in New England* (Boston: New England Historic Genealogical Society, 2002), 222–244.
9. William Gordon, "An Account of the Commencement of Hostilities between Great-Britain and America, in the Province of Massachusetts," in Nathanael Low, *An Astronomical Diary, or Almanack, For the Year of Christian Æra, 1776* (Worcester, MA: I. Thomas; Watertown: B. Edes; Cambridge, MA: S. & E. Hall, 1775).
10. R. A. Lovell, Jr., *Sandwich, A Cape Cod Town* (Sandwich, MA: Sandwich Archives and Historical Center, 19960, 207.
11. Davis, ed., *Records of the Town of Plymouth, III*, 297, 302–3 (28 April 1775), 305–6, 309.
12. "Pleafant Weather to work In the forenoon Dind upon turkey to day It being thanksgiving Last night had a verry Grand Supper upon Turkey & geefe" [Thirsdy nov. 23, 1775: diary of Moses Sleeper, transcribed by Frances Dickerson Ackerly, Friends of Longfellow House, who attempted to represent the long S by typing "f"].
13. Friday, April 5, 1776. Diary of Moses Sleep (see note 12).
14. For example, Scituate, Massachusetts, June 4, 1776; Samuel Deane, *History of Scituate, Massachusetts, From its first Settlement to 1831* (Boston: James Loring, 1831), 135–6. These instructions were in response to a request to all towns from the Massachusetts legislature, so presumably most towns issued similar responses at that time.
15. Warren, *History of the Rise, Progress and Termination of the American Revolution*, I, 170.
16. Hedges, *The Browns of Providence Plantations*, 243–244.
17. Hedges, *The Browns of Providence Plantations*, 357, n. 25 cites Watson's receipt for the amount entrusted to him. Elkanah may have included in his total an additional unspecified amount he was supposed to pick up en route

for the Browns from the company of Wiley & Seixas (perhaps Moses Seixas).

18. GB 13294, Box 5, Folder "Letters to Wm.Goodwin, etc.": Old Friend, 14 Aug. 1777.

19. Hedges, *The Browns of Providence Plantations*, 237, n. 25.

20. Founding Families: Digital Editions of the Papers of the Winthrops and the Adamses, ed. C. James Taylor (Boston: Massachusetts Historical Society, 2007) 50, the case *Watson vs. Caesar* (1771). John Adams represented Elkanah Watson, Sr.; reference to SCJ Rec 1771, fol. 51; SF 142381 (Suffolk Files). Available online at http://www.masshist.org/ff/.

21. The positive report on the oranges is from Elkanah Watson Papers, GB 12579, Box 1, Folder 1. It contrasts with the published version: "The fruit proved rather bitter to the taste, but was exceedingly beautiful."

22. Elkanah Watson Papers, GB 13294, Box 9, letter from Charleston to John Brown, 18 January 1778.

23. From the letter to John Brown, 18 January 1778 (see preceding note).

24. Elkanah misspells the horse's name as Rozinante and Rosonanta, so he may not have been aware that this was the name of Don Quixote's horse. On the other hand, his spelling was never dogmatic, and he might have decided to call the horse by this literary name as a humorous gesture towards his own quest. "Mr. Clark" was probably Jonas Clark; see p. 33.

25. The ms. has "squaw"; the published version has "queen."

26. In the published version, comments are added that are not found in the diary: "The painful scene illustrates a remark I often heard at the South, that Northern overseers were the hardest task-masters, and foreign owners the most cruel masters. The relation between the native master and his slave seems generally to be of the fondest and most affectionate character." This may have been added by the publisher in 1854.

27. This and the following quotations are from Zubly's sermon before the Provincial Congress of Georgia, 1775, with the title "The Law of Liberty." John J. Zubly, *The Law of Liberty. A Sermon on American Affairs, Preached at the Opening of the Provincial Congress of Georgia. Addressed to the Right Honourable The Earl of Dartmouth. With an Appendix, Giving a Concise Account of the Struggles of Swisserland [sic] to Recover their Liberty* (Philadelphia: Printed and Sold by Henry Miller, 1775).

28. This poem appeared in *The Scots Magazine*, James Boswell, ed., no. 35 (1773), 92.

29. Essex Record Office Level: Category Estate and Family Records Level: Fonds BARRINGTON FAMILY OF HATFIELD BROAD OAK Level: Sub-Fonds LEGAL Level: Series Papers re arbitration between Lady Huntingdon and Rev. Piercy by Thomas Day Level: Item Copy letter from Rev Piercy to Lady Huntingdon. Level: Item Reference Code **D/DBa L97/6** Dates of Creation 29 October 1773 Extent 1 item Title [Copy letter from Rev Piercy to Lady Huntingdon].

30. In another place, Elkanah recalled that he first met General Varnum when Elkanah was sixteen years old and attended an oration Varnum delivered "before the free Masons in the episcopalean Church in Providence." GF 12579, Box 3, Folder 2, p. 529. Thus he was at least aware of the Masons at that age.

31. The slave auction is briefly described in *Men and Times*; Elkanah's more extensive letter is found in Elkanah Watson Papers, GB 12579, Box 1, Folder 2. Jonas Clarke was probably the son of the minister of the same name from Lexington, Massachusetts, a friend of Paul Revere and Samuel Adams.

32. Hedges, *The Browns of Providence Plantations*, 237, n. 25.

33. Elkanah adds the following as a footnote: "The above paragraphs, marked as a quotation, were first published in *Morse's Geography*, in 1789, as an extract from my Journal; and after being republished in other works, in 1829 I read it in Dr. Hosack's *Memoir of De Witt Clinton*, extracted from 'Tatham on Island Navigation,' an English work, where it appeared as original. I notice the fact, as an evidence of unjust plagiarism" [p. 78 of printed version, 2d ed.]. That his own work appeared thus in a panegyric of Clinton, whom Elkanah accused of stealing his glory for conceiving the Erie Canal, added to the insult.

34. Elkanah's father's trade is documented in the Watson Family Papers, among the collections of the Pilgrim Society, Plymouth, Massachusetts. Additional references occur in other papers in the same collections.

35. The published version says that Elkanah "proceeded by sea to Boston." The original notebook contradicts that.

36. Edward Winslow is quoted in, "Plymouth in the Revolution," part of the Pilgrim Hall Museum website, viewed 3 June 2015, http://www.pilgrimhallmuseum.orgpdf/Military_Officers_Continental_British_Armies.pdf.

37. GB 13294, Box 5, Folder "Letters to Wm. Goodwin etc.": 21 Sept. 1778, 4 Nov. 1778 (2), 16 Nov. 1778, 29 Nov. 1778.

Chapter Two

1. Elkanah describes his plans in letters to his friend, William Goodwin: GB 13294, Box 5, Folder "Letters to Wm. Goodwin, etc.": D[ea]r Will, 15 Dec. 1778, 4 May 1779, 29 May 1779.

2. Massachusetts Historical Society, Docno: PJA09d 024. Author: Watson, Elkanah Jr., Recipient: JA. Date: 1780-03-10.

3. Elkanah Watson Papers, GB 12579, Box 1, Folder 3, pp. 1–2. This material amounts to 191 pp. and is the source of the information and quotations in this chapter, especially where there are differences from the published version.

4. The interpreter was Mr. Schweighauser, a correspondent of Benjamin Franklin's.

5. The school was no longer run by Jesuits in 1779, but instead by Fathers of Christian Doctrine.

6. The order of events given in the two versions in the mss. differs from the published version. I have tried to make sense of the three.

7. The notebooks are contradictory about whether Elkanah did in fact visit the Madrid Palace. P. 89: "this Chateau was built by Francis I upon his return from his Imprisonment in Spain, after the model of the Palace at Madrid; this Edifice has nothing particular, therefore we made no stop." But on p. 38, he gives a description of the contents of the chapel. Perhaps he visited the chapel but nothing further in the palace.

8. Tobias Smollett, *The Adventures of Roderick Random*, Paul-Gabriel Boucé, ed., intro. (Oxford: Oxford University Press, 1979), pp. 117–138.

9. On Bancroft, see CIA article: CIA Home > Library > Center for the Study of Intelligence > Studies Archive Indexes > vol5no1 > html > Edward Bancroft (@ Edwd. Edwards), Estimable Spy.

10. Laurence Sterne, *A Sentimental Journey through*

Notes—Chapter Three

France and Italy (New York: Three Sirens Press, 1930), pp. 31–43.

11. Elkanah Watson Papers, GB 13294, Box 1, Folder 1: Dear Sister, 25 Dec. 1779. See also: GB 13294, Box 5, Folder "Letters to William Goodwin etc.": Dear Friend, 20 Dec. 1779.

12. Elkanah Watson Papers, GB 12579, Box 1, Folder 3, p. 155: Hon.d Father, Ancenis 20 Dec. 1779.

13. Elkanah Watson Papers, GB 12579, Box 1, Folder 3, p. 156. Dear Sister Ancenis 20th Jan.y 1780

14. Elkanah Watson Papers, GB 12579, Box 1, Folder 3, p. 158: Dr. Cossoul, Ancenis Febry. 10,th, 1780.

15. Elkanah Watson Papers, GB 12579, Box 1, Folder 3, p. 170: Ancenis 24th April 1780, Mr. Jos Gridley, Nantes.

16. Elkanah Watson Papers, GB 12579, Box 1, Folder 3, p. 163: Ancenis, 24th March 1780, My Dear Patty.

17. Elkanah Watson Papers, GB 12579, Box 1, Folder 3, p. 161: Nantes ... Ancenis, 10th March 1780, His Excellency John Adams Esq. Ambassador extraordinary from the United States of America at Paris.

18. Elkanah Watson Papers, GB 12579, Box 1, Folder 3, p. 172: Copy of his Excellency John Adams Esqrs letter Verbatim.

19. Elkanah Watson Papers, GB 12579, Box 1, Folder 3, p. 167: Chateauso 5 miles from Ancenis, on the Borders of the Loire, 16th April 1780, Dr. Casey at Angers.

20. Elkanah Watson Papers, GB 12579, Box 1, Folder 3, p. 184: Coast of St. Sebastians 1 Sept. 1780, Dr. Casey At Angers.

21. GB 13294, Box 1, Folder 1 (family correspondence, 1775–1782), letter to Priscilla, 6 June 1780; letter to Priscilla, 12 Oct. 1780.

22. Elkanah Watson Papers, GB 12579, Box 1, Folder 3, p. 186: Paris 18th Sept. 1780, Dear Cossoul.

23. Elkanah Watson Papers, GB 12579, Box 1, Folder 3, p. 186: Sketch of a Journal of Occurrences from Paris to Nantes via Orleans, viz. Sept. 23 1780.

24. Elkanah Watson Papers, GB 13294, Box 1 Folder 1: Dear Sister, 12 Oct. 1780, p.s. 1 Nov. 1780. Priscilla added a note to this letter that she read it for the last time in Plymouth on 3 March 1846.

25. Elkanah Watson Papers, GB 12579, Box 1, Folder 3, p. 188: Nantes 27th Dec. 1780, John Brown Esqr., Providence.

26. Edmund S. Morgan, *Benjamin Franklin* (New Haven: Yale University Press, 2002), pp. 25–26.

27. Elkanah Watson Papers, GB 12579, Box 1, Folder 3, pp. 189–191 [last letter] Nantes 27th Dec.r 1780, Dear Patty.

28. Later, Elkanah placed his daughter Mary in "one of the best female schools or academies in America." GB 13294, Box 4, Folder 12, letter to his wife "27th May" [no year].

29. *Men and Times,* 127. The 1781 visit to France is mentioned in biographies of Paine, for example: Audrey Williamson, *Thomas Paine, His Life, Work and Times* (London: George Allen & Unwin, 1973), pp. 54, 95–96; Eric Foner, *Tom Paine and Revolutionary America* (New York: Oxford University Press, 1976), p. 189; John Keane, *Tom Paine, A Political Life* (Boston: Little, Brown, 1995), pp. 208–213.

30. The published version *Men and Times* has the ellipsis. The ms. has "scotch fiddle" a term for skin ailments called "the itch," but, judging from the treatment, Watson was referring probably to syphilis.

31. Morgan, *Benjamin Franklin*, pp. 268–271; Keane, *Tom Paine*, pp. 211–213.

32. GF 12579, Box 9, Folder 2, pp. 415–422.

33. American Philosophical Society, Elkanah Watson, Jr. to William Temple Franklin (unpublished), Nantes 25 December 1782. Although in writing to his friend Billy (William Temple Franklin), Elkanah referred to Franklin as Billy's grandfather, Mrs. Wright had told him that Franklin was Billy's father, and that the mother had been Franklin's London washerwoman.

34. Elkanah added in the published version: "Many years afterward, the head was broken in Albany, and the clothes I presented to the Historical Society of Massachusetts." *Men and Times,* p. 140. The Massachusetts Historical Society presented this suit to the Smithsonian Institution in 1963; see: http://www.smithsonianmag.si.edu/smithsonian/issues06/jan06/small.html

35. American Philosophical Society, Elkanah Watson, Jr., to William Temple Franklin (unpublished), London. 19th. Apl. 1783.

36. An overview of the sorts of shipments can be derived from Benjamin Franklin's correspondence in the collections of the University of Pennsylvania, in letters to and from Jonathan Williams, Jr.

37. Elkanah Watson Papers, GB13294, Box 20, Letter book, English & French, No. 2, 1780, p. 2: Nantes, 12th Oct. 1780, Messrs. John de Neufville & Son, Amsterdam, p.12. For de Neufville's contact with Franklin, see, for example, his letter mentioning the arrival in Amsterdam of John Paul Jones: John de Neufville and Son. Amsterdam to Benjamin Franklin, 1779 October 7, A.L.S. 2p. XVI, 9. Arrival of John Paul Jones, whose orders they have carried out to the best of their ability (Franklin correspondence, University of Pennsylvania). There are around one hundred fifty notarial acts mentioning John de Neufville preserved in the Amsterdam Archives.

38. Elkanah Watson Papers, GB 13294, Box 20, Letter book, English & French No. 2, Copy Letters relating to mercantile affairs begun Oct. 1780, p.12: Nantes, 1st Nov. 1780, Messrs. John de Neufville & son, Amsterdam.

39. The Honble. Benj. Franklin Esqr. Passi, *Notation:* 28 Mar 81 Chr, *Addressed:* A Monsieur / Monsieur Franklin / Ministre Plénipotentiaire des / Etats unis en Son Hotel / a / Passi / pres Paris [636154=035–047a.html] Am. Phil. Soc. Franklin correspondence; The Honbl. Benja. Franklin Esqr. Passy, *Addressed:* The Honbl. Benja. Franklin / Esqr. American Ambassador / at / Passy, *Notation:* E Watson & Cossoul May 20 1781 [636192 =035–087a.html]. Am. Phil. Soc.

40. The letter is reproduced in *Men and Times,* p. 158.

41. Elkanah Watson Papers, GB 13294, Box 1, Folder 1, fragment: My brother Marston's letter ...; GB13294, Box 20, Letter book, English & French No. 2, Copy Letters relating to mercantile affairs begun Oct. 1780, p. 72 Nantes, 3rd March 1781, Mr. Winslow Warren, Amsterdam.

42. Elkanah Watson Papers, GB13294, Box 20, Letter book, English & French No. 2, Copy Letters relating to mercantile affairs begun Oct. 1780, p. 73: Nantes 5th March 1781, Messrs. John de Neufville & son, Amsterdam.

43. No copy in the Library of Congress or in the libraries of Brown, Yale, Columbia, Harvard, Princeton, or Chicago. The text may never have been published.

Chapter Three

1. Elkanah's map, drawn later, imprecisely shows the locations with respect to each other of Compiègne, St. Quentin, and Amiens. The map also indicates a route from Senlis to St. Quentin that does not go through Compiègne, although that town name is included on the map. Such a route does not appear possible.

2. Difficulty with the dialect he was hearing must account for Elkanah's writing that he entered the Hapsburg Netherlands on the way to Ostende, north of Lille at "Manheim." This has to refer to Menin (or Menen).

3. Elkanah Watson Papers, GB12579, Box 2, Folder 3, 192.

4. Elkanah Watson Papers, GB12579, Box 2, Folder 3, pp. 194–5.

5. For Deane in Ghent, see George L. Clark, *Silas Deane: A Connecticut Leader in the American Revolution* (New York: G. P. Putnam's Sons, 1913), ch. 12, 192–214.

6. Mercy Otis Warren, *History of the Rise, Progress and Termination of the American Revolution, interspersed with Biographical, Political and Moral Observations*, Lester H. Cohen, ed. (Indianapolis: Liberty Classics, 1988) (reprint, original edition: Boston: E. Larkin, 1805), pp. 289–292.

7. Later, when editing his memoirs, the scene he encountered brought to mind an engraving: David Martin's portrait of Franklin, published in *The Portfolio*, Philadelphia, Oct. 1819; also as frontispiece of *The Works of Benjamin Franklin*, 1817, ed. William Temple Franklin.

8. The eyewitness account on which the description of the battle of Yorktown is based is part of a journal of the voyage of De Grasse's fleet, written in Dutch and French: Nationaal Archief, The Hague, Admiraliteits colleges, II, XL, nr. 33 "Stukken betreffende zee- en admiraliteitswezen, aanwezig in de verzameling De Jonge," the description of the battle of Yorktown (in Dutch), is on pp. 24–32. This account is not mentioned in most histories.

9. The Masonic apron is now owned by the Alexandria Washington Lodge No. 22.

10. Elkanah Watson Papers, GB13294, Box 21, Folder 2: small book labeled: Journal of travels from Nantes to Paris and from Paris to Calais by way of Abbeville, Amiens, Namport, Montrieul, & Boulogne, from Calais across to Dover, from thence to London, Oxford, Birmingham, Liverpool, Warrington, Manchester, Halifax, Leeds, Sheffield, Bristol, Bath, in all about Eighteen hundred miles out & home. At the end of the book are essays on Genius, Courage, Virtue & Vice, Beauty, Misery, etc.

11. Elkanah Watson Papers, GB13294, Box 21, Folder 2, Journal of travels, pp. 2–3.

12. Elkanah Watson Papers, GB13294, Box 21, Folder 2, Journal of travels, p. 4, Fryday Sept. 6.

13. Archibald Duncan, *The Mariner's Chronicle, being a Collection of the Most Interesting Narratives of Shipwrecks, Fires, Famines, and other Calamities incident to a Life of Maritime Enterprise ...* (London: James Cundee, 1804), pp. 236–240: The Loss of the Royal George, at Spithead, August the 19th, 1782. See also: *The Gentleman's Magazine by Sylvanus Urban* 9, New Series, May 1838, p. 506 (published in London), reports that the ship sank because large parts of the hull were rotten, as indicated in testimony at the court martial afterwards—thus not merely because the ship had been heeled for repairs.

14. Watson, *Men and Times*, 164–165.

15. It now houses the Wallace Collection, comprising major paintings by many artists highly esteemed in the nineteenth century, including Rembrandt, Rubens, Titian, Fragonard, and Watteau, with eighteenth-century French furniture of similar quality.

16. London: T. Cadell, in the Strand, 1776.

17. Douglas Adair, John A. Schutz, *Peter Oliver's Origins & Progress of the American Rebellion: A Tory View* (Stanford: Stanford University Press, 1961).

18. GF 12579, Box 3, Folder 2, pp. 565–568, "Religion."

19. Besides Watson's *Men and Times*, p. 184, see also p. 31 of S. G. Howe, "The Education of the Blind," pp. 20–58, in Jared Sparks, Edward Everett, James Russell Lowell and Henry Cabot Lodge, eds., *The North American Review* 37 (Boston: Charles Bowen, 1833). About Moyes this quotes "Memoir on Blindness, by Mr. Bew, of the Philosophical Society of Manchester": "Though he lost his sight in early infancy, he made rapid progress in different sciences; he acquired not only the fundamental principles of physics, music, and languages, but he plunged deeply into the most abstract sciences, and displayed a minute knowledge of geometry, of optics, of algebra, of astronomy, of chemistry, and in a word of most of the branches of the Newtonian philosophy. Every time he entered into society, he first passed some minutes in silence: the sound enabled him to judge of the dimensions of the apartment, and the different voices of the number of persons present. His calculations in this respect were very exact, and his memory was so faithful that he was seldom mistaken. I have known him recognise a person the instant he heard him speak, although more than two years had elapsed since they had met. He could ascertain with precision the stature of persons by the direction of their voices; and he made tolerable hits at their character and disposition by the tone of their conversation.

20. GB 12579, Box 5, Folder 2, pp. 120–124.

21. *Monody on Major André By Miss Seward (Author of the Elegy on Capt. Cook) To Which are Added, Letters Addressed to Her by Major André, in the year 1769* (Lichfield: J. Jackson for the author, 1781).

22. Watson, *Men and Times*, 204–5.

23. Elkanah Watson Papers, GB 13294, Box 4, Folder 6, letter from Charles Watson to Luther Bradish, 18 May 1858.

24. It seems that when poetically necessary the sun could rise in the west.

25. Elkanah Watson Papers, GB 12579, Box 5, Folder 3: Agricultural note book [going the other way:] Copy of private letters. p.3: Nantes 10th Feb. 1783. Hon'd Father. Much later, Elkanah received a letter from his father dated 18 May 1782, gently reproving him for thinking his father had not written. Several letters had been intercepted or lost at sea. This one, sent with Elkanah's brother Marston on his way to London, reached Elkanah over a year later. Elkanah Watson Papers, GB 13294, Box 1, Folder 1.

26. Copies of both notices are in Elkanah Watson Papers, GB 13294, Box 20, Folder 4.

27. GB 13494, Box 5, Folder 2, 18 April 1783.

28. GB 13294, Box 1, Folder 2, 18 May 1783, Dear Elk.

29. GB 12579, Box 5, Folder 3: My dear Lucia, 21 Aug. 1783.

30. Elkanah Watson Papers, GB 12579, Box 5, Folder 3, pp. 47–50.

31. Elkanah Watson Papers, GB 13294, Box 22, Folder 2: A three weeks tour in Holland by an American in June 1784, [p. 4].

Chapter Four

1. Elkanah Watson Papers, GB 13294, Box 22, Folder 2: A three-week tour in Holland by an American in June 1784. The information is in the form of copies of letters that Elkanah wrote during the trip and addressed to "Thos. Reeves Esqr. Esher Surry." This ms. is more complete than the version Elkanah edited and had published: *A Tour in Holland, in MDCCLXXXIV. By an American* (Worcester, MA: Isaiah Thomas, 1790). The 1790 version is included with no significant changes in *Men and Times*.

2. Rotterdam Municipal Archives, Notarial Archives, no. 3466. acts no. 475, 512 (March 22, 1784).

Notes—Chapter Five

3. The phrase "my best dudds" is in the ms. (page 37) but was not included in the published versions of 1790 and 1854.

4. O. Schutte, *Repertorium der Nederlandse Vertegenwoordigers, Residerende in het Buitenland, 1584–1810* (The Hague: Martinus Nijhoff, 1976), p. 119: Van Lynden left The Hague for London on October 15, 1784.

5. At least those are words that came to him at some point, and which he added to his journal copy of the letters he wrote about his trip.

6. On this painting, see my article, "A Window Into Holland's Heroic Golden Age," *New England Ancestors* 5, no. 4 (Fall 2004), pp. 55–56.

7. William Stephen Gunter and Johannes van den Berg, *John Wesley and The Netherlands* (Nashville: Kingswood Books, 2002).

8. The house of Johan Maurits, Count of Nassau-Siegen, is now the Mauritshuis Museum.

9. Elkanah Watson Papers, GB 13294, Box 22, Folder 3: Journal: Tour of Holland, vol. 2 [in fact, rough draft of vol. "1"], Written on the inside of the back cover.

10. Sterne, *A Sentimental Journey*, p. 99.

11. Elkanah regretfully noted his own inadvertent expression of common anti–Jewish prejudice in 1786 when he met Moses Hays, described by Thomas Russell (Elkanah's cousin Betsy's husband and a leading merchant of Boston) as "the most respectable and gentlemanly Jew he had ever known." Elkanah, trying to be agreeable to Hays' negative opinion of another businessman, replied, "Sir, I considered him a d—m'd old Jew." Realizing his offense, Elkanah felt "mortified into irredeemable confusion." Elkanah Watson Papers, GF 12579, Box 3, pp. 557–559.

12. In the Amsterdam Municipal Archives, Notarial Archives, there are more than a two thousand acts concerning American investments for the Revolutionary War loans, with the names De Neufville, Willink, Morris, Staphorst, van Eeghen, van Vollenhoven, Schimmelpennink, and Stadnitski. Over three hundred of these name Rutger Jan Schimmelpennink. Around six hundred are for the firm of the Van Staphorsts. Around two hundred fifty concern the Van Eeghen investments, some of which are in company with the Van Staphorsts, et al.

13. The loans are documented in the Amsterdam Municipal Archives, Notarial Archives: NA 16335/243, 244, 245, 246, 247, 248 (P.G. v. Hole) 1782 juni 11; NA 16336/355, 356 (P.G. v. Hole) 1782 aug. 13; NA 16336/351 (P.G. v. Hole) 1782 aug. 15.

14. Amsterdam Municipal Archives, Notarial Archives, NA 16343/ 273 (P.G. v. Hole) 1784 juni 4; NA 16343/ 283 (P.G. v. Hole) 1784 juni 9.

15. Amsterdam Municipal Archives, Notarial Archives, NA 16743/ 34 (Petrus Cornelis Nahuys).

16. Amsterdam Municipal Archives, Notarial Archives, NA 16743/ 23 (18 August 1783): six months' subscriptions totalled ƒ 177.10.

17. Amsterdam Municipal Archives, Notarial Archives, N.A. 5931 (J. Hoekeback) 1714, sept. 24.

18. Amsterdam Municipal Archives, Notarial Archives, NA 11481/33 (T.D. de Marolles).

19. See, for example, Amsterdam Municipal Archives, Notarial Archives, NA 16323/316 (Pieter Galenus van Hole), 1779-08-24; NA 16323/369 (PG van Hole) 1779-09-27; NA 16324/500 (PG van Hole) 1779-12-14.

20. Simon Schama is ambivalent about whether it actually existed, despite the lack of historical evidence and the obvious physical impossibility of any prisoner succeeding in keeping his head above water. See Simon Schama, *The Embarrassment of Riches, An Interpretation of Dutch Culture in the Golden Age* (Berkeley: University of California Press, 1988, p. 23: "Was the drowning cell a bizarre fable, a sadistic fantasy, concocted from half-digested gobbets of hearsay? ... the possibility of this cold-blooded experiment in behaviorist persuasion having functioned at some time cannot be altogether dismissed."

21. Jeremy Dupertuis Bangs, "What's in a Name?" *New England Ancestors* 3, nos. 5–6 (Holiday 2002), pp. 56–58.

Chapter Five

1. Ignatius Sancho, *Letters of the late Ignatius Sancho, an African, In two volumes, To which are prefixed, memoirs of his life,* Frances Crewe, ed. (London: printed by J. Nichols, and sold by J. Dodsley in Pall Mall; J. Robson in New Bond Street; J. Walter, Charing Cross; R. Baldwin in Paternoster Row; and J. Sewell, Cornhill, 1782). The "Life" (from which the quotations are taken) is by Joseph Jekyll.

2. Brycchan Carey thinks that, because Joseph Jekyll's information about Sancho's early life is not confirmed by other sources (although also not contradicted by any), the fact that Carey can perceive the use of sentimental literary language in Jekyll's text is sufficient reason to doubt the veracity of otherwise unconfirmed information, such as the statement that Sancho was born on a slave ship. The use of literary analysis to establish unilaterally whether or not an event should be considered to have in fact taken place seems to me flimsy, whatever might be said about the literary form of the description of an occurrence. It is possible, however, that Sancho did not know exactly in what year he was born. Many people before the nineteenth century were unsure of the exact year of their birth. See Brycchan Carey, "'The extraordinary Negro': Ignatius Sancho, Joseph Jekyll, and the Problem of Biography," *British Journal for Eighteenth-Century Studies* 26 (2003), pp. 1–14.

3. Watson, *Men and Times*, 268.

4. Gloucestershire Record Office, Ms D3549/13/3/ 28, Reel 70; excerpted online.

5. In R v Knowles, ex parte Somersett, 1772: 20 State Tr. 1.

6. Granville Sharp. *The just limitation of slavery: In the laws of God, compared with the unbounded claims of the African traders and British American slaveholders* (London: printed for B. White, and E. and C. Dilly, 1776). The second part, with separate title page, pagination and register, contains the following: 'Appendix (No. I) An essay on slavery, ... By Granville Sharp...', with the imprint: "Burlington: West Jersey, printed, M.DCC.LXXIII.

7. Granville Sharp, *The law of liberty: Or, royal law, by which all mankind will certainly be judged!* (London: printed for B. White; and E. and C. Dilly, 1776).

8. Watson, *Men and Times*, 304–305.

9. Marriage date is given by Stefan Bielinski, in his lemmas on Elkanah Watson and Rachel Smith Watson, New York State Archives, CAP biography number 6835 and 6830[?].

10. Around two dozen documents in Amsterdam's archives record direct participation by Robert Morris as Superintendent of Finances, besides those having to do with the Robert Morris Purchase in northwest New York State. For example: NA 12470/ 779 (C. V. Homrigh) 1783-12-08.

11. George Washington's diary for January 19, 1785. Elkanah's memoir, written later, dates the visit to January 23.

12. Granville Sharp, *An Essay on Slavery, Proving from*

Scripture its Inconsistency with Humanity and Religion ... (Burlington: Isaac Collins, 1773).

13. Sharp's italics. Granville Sharp, *A Declaration of the People's Natural Right to a Share in the Legislature, which is the Fundamental Principle of the British Constitution of State* (London: printed for B. White, at Horace's Head in Fleet Street, 1774); second printing, 1775. This quotation is on p. 35 from the second edition.

14. p. 28, n. 25.

15. Granville Sharp, *The Just Limitation of Slavery in the Laws of God, compared with the Unbounded Claims of the African Traders and British American Slaveholders* ... (London: printed for B. White in Fleet-Street, and E. and C. Dilly, in the Poultry, 1776).

16. Sharp, *Just Limitation*, p. 36.

17. In the eighteenth century, tea was served in small cups without handles. The best tea bowls were Chinese porcelain.

18. *Men and Times*, 290.

19. Elkanah Watson Papers, GB 13294, Box 9, Folder 5.

20. GB 13294, Box 1, Folder 2, 28 June 1787, Dear Elk.

21. The trip is described in a small notebook: GB 12579, Box 5, Folder 1.

22. Several Europeans had asked for financial backing from the United States government to guarantee their investment if they were to come set up glass production in America. See Morgan, *Benjamin Franklin*, p. 295.

23. Elkanah Watson Papers, GB12579, Box 5, Folder 1, from the loose notebook pages (50 pp., starting 10th Aug. 1788), p. 9.

24. The origins of the Iroquois Confederacy and the history of land dispossession lie beyond the scope of this book. Among many articles and books, William N. Fenton's "Problems in the Authentication of the League of the Iroquois," published in *Neighbors and Intruders: An Ethnohistorical Exploration of the Indians of Hudson's River*, Laurence M. Hauptman and Jack Campisi, eds. (Ottawa: National Museums of Canada, 1978), pp. 261–268, remains important.

25. http://microformguides.gale.com/Data/Index/203000a.htm.

26. The treaty quotations are from Laurence M. Hauptman, *Seven Generations of Iroquois Leadership, The Six Nations since 1800* (Syracuse: Syracuse University Press, 2008), pp. 52–53.

27. Marriage date is given by Stefan Bielinski, in his lemmas on Elkanah Watson and Rachel Smith Watson, CAP biography number 6835 and 6830[?]. He reports that Watson offered "fish, liquor, cookeryware" for sale in newspaper advertisements. Watson was also shipping fish, tea, and rice to be sold in New York City. GB 13294, Box 9, Folder 5.

28. The following remarks are taken from: Elkanah Watson Papers, GB12579, Box 3, Folder 2: Journal "E" Mixt Medley Letters, copies letters essays, projects Anecdotes &c. 7c. and Journal, pp. 48–49.

29. *A Tour in Holland in MDCCLXXXIV. / by an American*. (MA: Printed by Isaiah Thomas, sold at his bookstore in Worcester, and by him and company in Boston, 1790). Noticed extensively in the *Monthly Review of New American Books*, the book's style is praised as "easy, gay, and familiar," and its author called "a second Yorick." "We could have wished that some details of innocent gallantry had not been painted with so strong a glow of colouring," the reviewer frowned.

30. Elkanah Watson Papers, GB12579, Box 3, Folder 2: Journal "E" Mixt Medley Letters, copies letters essays, projects Anecdotes &c. 7c. and Journal, pp., pp. 50–52

31. Joel. F. Munsell, *The Annals of Albany* (1852), III (Albany: J. Munsell, arranged chronologically, sub 1791).

32. Munsell, *The Annals of Albany*, p.617: Gazetter of the State of New York, embracing a comprehensive view of the geography, geology, and general history of the state ... J. H. French, 1859.

33. Elkanah Watson, *History of the Rise, Progress, and Existing Condition of the Western Canals, in the State of New York, from September, 1788, to the completion of the Middle Section of the Grand Canal in 1819, together with the Rise, Progress, and Existing State of Modern Agricultural Societies on the Berkshire System, from 1807 to the establishment of the Board of Agriculture in the State of New York, January 10, 1820* (Albany: D. Steele, 1820), p. 45; see also Martin Hunt, "Elkanah Watson—A Man of Vision," publication of the Massachusetts Department of Agriculture, Division of Plant, Pest Control and Fairs (undated).

34. Watson, *Men and Times*, pp. 517–518.

35. Walter Gable, "The Military Tract," http//www.co.seneca.ny.us/history/chap%207—The%20Military%20Tract.doc. Marian S. Henry, "Bounty Lands in the Military Tract in Post-Revolutionary War New York State," New England Historic Genealogical Society, http://www.newenglandancestors.org/research/services/articles_bounty_lands_military_tract.asp.

36. The transfer is documented in Amsterdam Municipal Archives, Notarial Archives, nr. 16743 (Petrus Cornelis Nahuys) [fol. 1:] nr. 1. Acte van executeurschap. 5 Jan. 1793, Willem Willink named as his executors: Nicolaas van Staphorst, Christiaan van Eeghen, Hendrik Vollenhoven, Mr. Rutger Jan Schimmelpenninck, and Pieter Stadnitski ... te stellen tot Executeurs zijner natelatene actien of Effecten in de fondsen ten lasten van de Vereenigde Staaten van America midtsgaders Landerijen Huizen en Gebouwen in America, voor zo verre die dan staan op de naam van hem Heer Comparant met en nevens de Heeren [as above]; [fol. 5] nr. 2. Identical, from Nicolas van Staphorst, to the others; [fol. 9:] nr. 3. Identical, from Christiaan van Eeghen, to the others; [fol. 13:] nr. 4. Identical, from Hendrik Vollenhoven, to the others; [fol. 17:] nr. 5. Identical, from Rutger Jan Schimmelpenninck, to the others; [fol. 21:] nr. 6. Identical, from Pieter Stadnitski; [fol. 26:] nr. 7. Sale Contract. 9 Jan. 1793. the partners on the one side and Pieter Stadnitski and Arent van Halmael, Jr., trading under the Firm of Stadnitski & Zoon ... having become owners of one million acres in the State of New York, Ontario County, belonging to that part of the lands known as the Genesee lands, beginning in the north on Lake Ontario and going southerly to the Pennsylvania line across and west of the Genessee River, further going westwards across the "Algany" River to Lake Erie just before one reaches Presqu'isle, going northwards to Lake Erie and following along the lake and the possessions of his Great British Majesty northeastwards up to Lake Ontario, acknowledge that they have received one million eight hundred thousand guilders in full payment, besides the transfer of one million two hundred thousand guilders in "effecten ten lasten van het Congres der Vereenigde Staaten van America rentende vyf procento sjaars" (effects due from the Congress of the United States of America at five percent annual interest). This is the payment and transfer of the American debt, resulting in the property of the Holland Land Company, to be sold to recover cash. For the records of that company, see Wilhelmina C. Pieterse, *Inventory of the Archives of the Holland Land Company, including the related Amsterdam companies and negotiations dealing with the purchase of land and state funds in the United States of America, 1789–1869*, Amsterdam Municipal Printing Office, 1976. See further, Paul Demund Evans,

The Holland Land Company (Buffalo: Buffalo Historical Society, 1924) (Buffalo Historical Society Publications 28); William Chazanof, *Joseph Ellicott and the Holland Land Company, The Opening of Western New York* (Syracuse: Syracuse University Press, 1970).

37. According to Stefan Bielinski's lemma on Rachel Smith.

38. Elkanah Watson Papers, GB12579, Box 4: Commonplace Book. Includes Watson's proposal for the plan of Washington: "Plan of the City of Columbia, About being erected on the Powtamac."

39. Watson, *Men and Times*, 402–403.

40. Elkanah Watson Papers, GB12579, Box 3, Folder 3: Memoirs continued (1837 included) p. 65: Mrs. Watson and the bear.

41. Marginal note: 1838, Now Mrs. Wood, the Mother of 10 children, only one whom is a son, but Alas!! An Idiot—.

42. Elkanah completed his recollection of these events with a certificate of authenticity: "Least this extraordinary incident, may hereafter be considered partaking a tendency of the fabulous, I have requested my son Col. Charles M. W., to attach the following Certificate. No[vembe]r 1838: Having read to my Mother the above story in all its detail, she distinctly recollects all the facts as related, to be correct, altho' written by my Father from recollection after a lapse of 40 years. Port Kent, Nov[embe]r. 26th 1838. [signed:] Charles M. Watson."

43. GB 12579, Box 3, Folder 3, Memoire, p. 34.

44. GB 13294, Box 1, Folder 6, 15 June 180[4?], My dear.

45. GB 13294, Box 1, Folder 5, March 1800.

46. GB 13294, Box 1,Folder 6, 5 April 1803, 26 March 1804, 23 July 1804.

47. GB 12579, Box 11, Folder 1: Recollections of the Life of Winslow C. Watson, pp. 1–2.

48. GB 12579, Box 11, Folder 1: Recollections of the Life of Winslow C. Watson, pp. 18–19.

49. *Collections on the History of Albany: From its Discovery to the Present Time; with Notices of its Public Institutions, and Biographical Sketches of Citizens Deceased* (Albany: J. Munsell, 1857), vol. 2, pp. 398–401: STATE BANK: ELKANAH WATSON'S ACCOUNT OF ITS ORIGIN.

50. GB 12579, Box 11, Folder 1: Recollections of the Life of Winslow C. Watson, p. 35. The house was built in 1785 by Henry van Schaick (or Schaak). It is now the main part of the clubhouse of the Country Club of Pittsfield.

51. Watson, *Men and Times*, p. 391.

52. GA 12579, Box 11, Folder 1: Recollections of the Life of Winslow C. Watson, p. 35. Winslow Watson, a young boy in 1807, added to his memoirs written more than sixty years later, the peculiar comment that he thought "no one took advantage of the circumstance."

53. GA 12579, Box 11, Folder 1: Recollections of the Life of Winslow C. Watson, p. 38.

54. GA 12579, Box 11, Folder 1: Recollections of the Life of Winslow C. Watson, p. 73.

55. GA 12579, Box 11, Folder 1: Recollections of the Life of Winslow C. Watson, pp. 88–89.

56. A proposed schedule for the 1812 festivities is in GB 13294, Box 6, Folder 5.

57. William Hull's letter is published in Watson, *Men and Times*, pp. 441–442.

58. John Adams' letter is published in Watson, *Men and Times*, p. 439.

59. Robert Fulton's letter is published in Watson, *Men and Times*, pp. 443–444.

60. Lee M. Friedman, "The Phylacteries Found at Pittsfield, Massachusetts," *American Jewish Historical Quarterly* 25 (1917), pp. 81–85.

Chapter Six

1. Besides long journeys, Elkanah attended the wedding of his son Winslow to Frances Skinner, May 28, 1829, at Manchester, Vermont. In 1831, he travelled to Montpelier, Vermont, for a meeting of investors interested in his project for establishing a railroad from Boston to Lake Champlain.

2. Watson, *Men and Times*, pp. 378–379. On pp. 329–330, Watson commented, "A great estrangement existed between Dr. Franklin and Mr. Adams, which it was painful to observe in personages so worthy and so distinguished." Adams must have felt the same about Watson and Clinton.

3. Elkanah's letter is quoted in Gerard Koeppel, *Bond of Union, Building the Erie Canal and the American Empire* (Cambridge, MA: Da Capo, 2009), p. 383. I have corrected a couple of misspellings in the original retained by Koeppel.

4. Watson, *Men and Times*, pp. 507–508.

5. Watson, *Men and Times*, p. 506.

6. The house is described and documented in Mary Raddant Lomlan, *A Neat, Plain Modern Stile: Philip Hooker and His Contemporaries, 1796–1836* (Hamilton, NY: Hamilton College/University of Massachusetts Press, 1993) (exhibition catalogue: catalogue raisonné by W. Richard Wheeler), cat. no. 62, Country Seat for Elkanah Watson, Port Kent, N.Y., designed c. 1826, built 1826–1828, by Sheldon & Merritt, mason John York. Later in the nineteenth century, the pillars were modified and a porch was added extending around the house; in front it extended forward to include a porte-cochère. These were demolished ca. 1970. A photograph taken in 1963 shows that the square columns of the later additions were fluted, and that the four columns inserted in the 1828 portico matched them. The present columns are a restoration to the six column design seen in original plans.

7. The book could have been any of several pattern books then available, such as William Pain's *The Builder's Companion*, published in London in 1762, and known to have been used in America. Besides standard information on the Tuscan, Doric, Ionic, and Corinthian orders, with diagrams of columns, bases, and capitals, the book had portico designs and instructions on "the manner of Rusticating Windows" including oculi.

8. *Men and Times*, p. 437.

9. Elkanah Watson Papers, GB12579, Box 3, Folder 2: Journal "E" Mixt Medley Letters, copies, letters, essays, projects Anecdotes &c. 7c. and Journal—Includes, pp. 98–99: Pilgrims anniversary at Plymouth Mass.ts 22d Dec. 1829.

10. Elkanah Watson Papers, GB 12579, Box 3, Folder 2 (inside back cover).

11. Watson, *Men and Times*, p. 526.

Bibliography

Adair, Douglas, and John A. Schutz. *Peter Oliver's Origins & Progress of the American Rebellion: A Tory View.* Stanford: Stanford University Press, 1961.

Bangs, Jeremy Dupertuis. "Commemorating Colonial New England's First Families: The Triumph of the Pilgrims." In D. Brenton Simons and Peter Benes, eds., *The Art of Family, Genealogical Artifacts in New England.* Boston: New England Historic Genealogical Society, 2002, 222–244.

———. "What's in a Name?" *New England Ancestors* 3, nos. 5–6 (Holiday 2002), pp. 56–58.

———. "A Window Into Holland's Heroic Golden Age." *New England Ancestors* 5, no. 4 (Fall 2004), pp. 55–56.

Carey, Brycchan, "'The extraordinary Negro': Ignatius Sancho, Joseph Jekyll, and the Problem of Biography," *British Journal for Eighteenth-Century Studies* 26 (2003), pp. 1–14.

Chazanof, William. *Joseph Ellicott and the Holland Land Company, The Opening of Western New York.* Syracuse: Syracuse University Press, 1970.

Clark, George L. *Silas Deane: A Connecticut Leader in the American Revolution.* New York: G. P. Putnam's Sons, 1913.

Crewe, Frances. *Letters of the late Ignatius Sancho, an African, In two volumes, To which are prefixed, memoirs of his life.* London: printed by J. Nichols, and sold by J. Dodsley in Pall Mall; J. Robson in New Bond Street; J. Walter, Charing Cross; R. Baldwin in Paternoster Row; and J. Sewell, Cornhill, 1782.

Davis, William T., ed., *Records of the Town of Plymouth Published by Order of the Town, vol. III, 1743–1783.* Plymouth, MA: Memorial Press, 1903.

Deane, Samuel. *History of Scituate, Massachusetts, From its first Settlement to 1831.* Boston: James Loring, 1831.

Deane, William Reed. *A Biographical Sketch of Elkanah Watson, Founder of Agricultural Societies in America, and the Projector of Canal Communication in New York State ...* Albany: J. Munsell, 1864.

Duncan, Archibald. *The Mariner's Chronicle, being a Collection of the Most Interesting Narratives of Shipwrecks, Fires, Famines, and other Calamities incident to a Life of Maritime Enterprise ...* London: James Cundee, 1804.

Evans, Paul Demund. *The Holland Land Company.* Buffalo: Buffalo Historical Society, 1924 (Buffalo Historical Society Publications 28).

Fenton, William N. "Problems in the Authentication of the League of the Iroquois." In Laurence M. Hauptman and Jack Campisi, eds., *Neighbors and Intruders: An Ethnohistorical Exploration of the Indians of Hudson's River.* Ottawa: National Museums of Canada, 1978.

Flick, Hugh Meredith. "Elkanah Watson, Gentleman-Promotor, 1758–1842." Ph.D. diss., Columbia University, 1958.

———. "Elkanah Watson's Activities on Behalf of Agriculture." *Agricultural History* 21 (1947), pp. 193–198.

Foner, Eric. *Tom Paine and Revolutionary America.* New York: Oxford University Press, 1976.

Franklin, William Temple, ed. *The Works of Dr. Benjamin Franklin ...* Philadephia: W. Duane, 1808–1818.

Friedman, Lee M. "The Phylacteries Found at Pittsfield, Massachusetts." *American Jewish Historical Quarterly* 25 (1917), pp. 81–85.

Furstenberg, François. "George Washington, Slavery, and Transatlantic Abolitionist Networks." *The William and Mary Quarterly* 68 (2011), pp. 247–286.

Gordon, William. "An Account of the Commencement of Hostilities between Great-Britain and America, in the Province of Massachusetts," in Nathanael Low, *An Astronomical Diary, or Almanack, For the Year of Christian Æra, 1776.* Worcester, Massachusetts: I. Thomas; Watertown: B. Edes; Cambridge, Massachusetts: S. & E. Hall, 1775.

Gunter, William Stephen, and Johannes van den Berg. *John Wesley and The Netherlands.* Nashville: Kingswood Books, 2002.

Hauptman, Laurence M. *Seven Generations of Iroquois Leadership, The Six Nations since 1800.* Syracuse: Syracuse University Press, 2008.

Hedges, James B. *The Browns of Providence Plantations, Colonial Years.* Cambridge: Harvard University Press, 1952.

Henry, Marian S. "Bounty Lands in the Military Tract in Post-Revolutionary War New York State." New England Historic Genealogical Society, http://www.newenglandancestors.org/research/services/articles_bounty_lands_military_tract.asp.

Howe, S. G. "The Education of the Blind." In Jared Sparks, Edward Everett, James Russell Lowell and Henry Cabot Lodge, eds., *The North American Review*, Vol. III, pp. 20–58. Boston: Charles Bowen, July 1833.

Hunt, Martin. "Elkanah Watson—A Man of Vision." Publication of the Massachusetts Department of Agriculture, Division of Plant, Pest Control and Fairs undated.

Keane, John. *Tom Paine: A Political Life*. Boston: Little, Brown, 1995

Koeppel, Gerard. *Bond of Union, Building the Erie Canal and the American Empire*. Cambridge, MA: Da Capo, 2009.

Lomlan, Mary Raddant. *A Neat, Plain Modern Stile: Philip Hooker and His Contemporaries, 1796–1836*. Hamilton, NY: Hamilton College/University of Massachusetts Press, 1993 (exhibition catalogue: catalogue raisonné by W. Richard Wheeler).

Lord, Clifford L. "Elkanah Watson and New York's First County Fair." *New York History* 23 (1942), pp. 437–448.

Lovell, Jr., R. A. *Sandwich: A Cape Cod Town*. Sandwich, MA: Sandwich Archives and Historical Center, 1996.

Mastromarino, Mark A. "Fair Visions: Elkanah Watson (1758–1842) and the Modern American Agricultural Fair." College of William and Mary, Ph.D. diss., 2002

Morgan, Edmund S. *Benjamin Franklin*. New Haven: Yale University Press, 2002.

Munsell, Joel. F. *The Annals of Albany*, III. Albany: J. Munsell, 1852.

"State Bank: Elkanah Watson's Account of its Origin." In *Collections on the History of Albany: From its Discovery to the Present Time; with Notices of its Public Institutions, and Biographical Sketches of Citizens Deceased*. Albany: J. Munsell, 1857, vol. 2, pp. 398–401.

Pain, William. *The Builder's Companion, and Workman's General Assistant....* London: Robert Sayer, 1758, 1762, 1765, 1769.

Parramore, Thomas C. "A Year in Hertford County with Elkanah Watson," *The North Carolina Historical Review* 41 (1964), pp. 448–463.

Pieterse, Wilhelmina C. *Inventory of the Archives of the Holland Land Company, including the related Amsterdam companies and negotiations dealing with the purchase of land and state funds in the United States of America, 1789–1869*. Amsterdam Municipal Printing Office, 1976.

Pound, Arthur. *Native Stock: The Rise of the American Spirit Seen in Six Lives*. New York: Macmillan, 1931.

Schama, Simon. *The Embarrassment of Riches: An Interpretation of Dutch Culture in the Golden Age*. Berkeley: University of California Press, 1988.

Schutte, Otto. *Repertorium der Nederlandse Vertegenwoordigers, Residerende in het Buitenland, 1584–1810*. The Hague: Martinus Nijhoff, 1976.

Seelye, John. *Memory's Nation: The Place of Plymouth Rock*. Chapel Hill: University of North Carolina Press, 1998

Seward, Anna, *Monody on Major André By Miss Seward (Author of the Elegy on Capt. Cook) To Which are Added, Letters Addressed to Her by Major André, in the year 1769*. Lichfield: J. Jackson for the author, 1781.

Sharp, Granville. *A Declaration of the People's Natural Right to a Share in the Legislature, which is the Fundamental Principle of the British Constitution of State*. London: Printed for B. White, at Horace's Head in Fleet Street, 1774; second printing, 1775.

Sharp, Granville. *The just limitation of slavery : In the laws of God, compared with the unbounded claims of the African traders and British American slaveholders*. London: printed for B. White, and E. and C. Dilly, 1776. The second part, with separate title page, pagination and register, contains: 'Appendix (No. I) An essay on slavery, .. By Granville Sharp...', with the imprint: "Burlington: West Jersey, printed, M.DCC.LXXIII.

Sharp, Granville. *The law of liberty: Or, royal law, by which all mankind will certainly be judged! ...* London: Printed for B. White; and E. and C. Dilly, 1776.

Shaw, Ronald E. *Erie Water West, A History of the Erie Canal, 1792–1854*. Lexington: University Press of Kentucky, 1966.

Smollett, Tobias. *The Adventures of Roderick Random*. Ed. and intro. Paul-Gabriel Boucé. Oxford: Oxford University Press, 1979,

Snow, Dean R., Charles T. Gehring, and William Starna, eds. *In Mohawk Country: Early Narratives about a Native People*. Syracuse: Syracuse University Press, 1996.

Sterne, Laurence. *A Sentimental Journey through France and Italy*. New York: Three Sirens Press, 1930.

Taylor, C. James, ed. *Founding Families: Digital Editions of the Papers of the Winthrops and the Adamses*. Boston: Massachusetts Historical Society, 2007. http://www.masshist.org/ff/.

Thacher, James. *History of the Town of Plymouth, From its first Settlement in 1620, to the Present Time: With a Concise History of the Aborigines of New England, and their Wars with the English, &c.*. Salem, MA: Higginson Book Company, 1991 (reprint of the second edition, Boston, 1835).

Troup, Robert. *Vindication of the Claim of Elkanah Watson, Esq., to the Merit of Projecting the Lake Canal Policy, as created by the Canal Act of March, 1792, and also, a Vindication of the Claim of the late General Schuyler, to the Merit of Drawing that Act, and Procuring its Passage through the Legislature*. Geneva, NY: J. Bogert, 1821.

Warren, Mercy Otis. *History of the Rise, Progress and Termination of the American Revolution, interspersed with Biographical, Political and Moral Observations*. Ed. Lester H. Cohen. Indianapolis: Liberty Classics, 1988 (reprint, original edition: Boston, Massachusetts: E. Larkin, 1805).

Watson, Elkanah, *History of the Rise, Progress, and Existing Condition of the Western Canals, in the State of New York, from September, 1788, to the completion of the Middle Section of the Grand Canal in 1819, together with the Rise, Progress, and Existing State of Modern Agricultural Societies on the Berkshire System, from 1807 to the establishment of the Board of Agriculture in the State of New York, January 10, 1820*. Albany: D. Steele, 1820.

_____. *A Tour in Holland, in MDCCLXXXIV, By an American.* Worcester, Massachusetts: Isaiah Thomas, 1790.

_____, et al., *The Report of a Committee appointed to Explore the Western Waters in the State of New-York: For the Purpose of Prosecuting the Inland Lock Navigation.* Albany: Barber and Southwick, 1792.

_____. *History of the Rise, Progress, and Existing State of the Berkshire Agricultural Society in Massachusetts* ... Albany: E. & E. Hosford, 1819.

Watson, Winslow C., ed. *Men and Times of the Revolution; or Memoirs of Elkanah Watson.* New York: Dana, 1856; 2d, enlarged ed., New York: D. Appleton, 1861.

Williamson, Audrey. *Thomas Paine, His Life, Work and Times.* London: George Allen & Unwin, 1973.

Zubly, John J. *The Law of Liberty. A Sermon on American Affairs, Preached at the Opening of the Provincial Congress of Georgia. Addressed to the Right Honourable The Earl of Dartmouth. With an Appendix, Giving a Concise Account of the Struggles of Swisserland to Recover their Liberty.* Philadelphia: Printed and Sold by Henry Miller, 1775.

Index

Abbéville 85
Abbott, Jacob 5
Adam, Robert 90
Adams, Abigail 41
Adams, John 4, 41, 61, 62, 71, 84, 85, 93, 105, 117, 118, 120–125, 128, 136, 137, 142, 150, 171, 173, 180, 188, 189, 191, 192
Adams, Samuel 8, 9, 10
Adamson, Mrs. 26, 27
Africa 145
Aire River 96
Albany, New York 3, 4, 72, 160, 162–164, 171–177, 182, 184, 188, 189, 190
Albemarle Sound 20, 157, 159
Alexander, William 48, 50
Alexandria, Virginia 34, 151, 154, 155
Allan, Ethan 13, 174
Allegheny Mountains 167
Alston, William 22
Alva, Duke of 135
Amalia, von Solms Braunfels, Princess of Orange 121
American Tracts Against Slavery 151
Amiens 85
Amstel River 141
Amsterdam 71, 72, 105, 113, 116, 125, 126, 129, 133–138, 160
Ancenis 58, 59, 60
André, John 94, 99
Angers 44, 58, 62
Annapolis 155
Anne, Princess Royal of England 118
Aquidneck Island *see* Rhode Island
Arnold (policeman and pimp) 139
Arnold, Benedict 13, 94, 124, 174
Arras 75
Ashepo 25
Ashford 87
Ashley River 25
Astor, George 176
Atlantic Coast, Ocean 5, 21, 38, 42, 58, 76, 95
Atsequette *see* Otsequett, Peter
Attakullakulla (Little Carpenter) 25, 26, 167

Austin 151
Austria 64

Baker, Miss 30
Ballston Springs 165, 173, 174
Baltimore, Maryland 151, 155
Bancroft, Edward 50, 52, 82
Barclay, Mr. 136
Barkley, Thomas 85
Baskerville, John 131
Bath 100, 146
Bath, North Carolina 21
Bay of Biscay 57
Bayard, Stephen N. 166, 169, 173
Belgium 4, 5, 74–110
Belle Ile, Governor of 65
Bering Strait 181
Berkshire Agricultural Association 4, 179–181, 182
Berkshire County 177
Berkshire Mountains 160
Bethesda Orphanage 29, 30, 31
Bethlehem, Pennsylvania 17, 18, 35, 36
Beverwijk, New Netherland, New York 162
Billy 151
Birmingham 85, 92, 93, 99, 101, 131, 149
Birmingham Canal 93
Biron, Countess de 161
Bisset, Johannes 163–165
Black Betsy 178
Black Rock 186
Blackheath 89
Blackstone's Commentary 151
Blanchard, Monsieur 47
Blenheim Palace 91
Blois 57
Blount, Colonel 21
Boerhaave, Hermannus 127
Bolingbrook, Henry St. John, Lord 124
Bologne, Joseph, Chevalier de St. George 68
Bonn 72
Boston, Massachusetts 8–13, 25, 38, 40, 41, 43, 61, 72, 102, 148–150, 171, 180, 193
Botetourt, Norborne Berkeley, Baron de 20

Bouchez, Monsieur 62, 63
Boulton, Matthew 93
Bourbon, de, family 47
Bowen, Oliver 29
Bradford, Samuel 72
Brakel, Johan van 113, 114, 132
Brandywine Creek 17, 18, 150
Bray 90
Bridgewater, Francis Egerton, Duke of 94, 96
Brielle, Den 142
Bristol 93, 99, 100
Britain *see* Great Britain
Brittany 60
Brittany, Duchess of 64, 65
Broek-in-Waterland 137, 138
Bromfield, Henry 25, 33
Brooklyn 149
Brown, John 3, 4, 7, 9, 11, 12, 15, 19, 22, 25, 34, 37–39, 41, 63, 72, 77, 92, 103, 148, 149
Brown, Moses 12, 19
Brown, Nicholas 15, 17, 19, 22, 34, 41
Bruges 77, 78, 79
Brunswick 21
Brussels 79, 115
Brutus, New York 169
Buffalo 184, 185, 186, 187
Bunker Hill 38
Burgoyne, John 21, 39
Burke, Edmund 4, 85, 101, 103, 145
Burlington, New Jersey 17
Burlington, Vermont 174
Burr, Aaron 4, 173

Caesar (slave, freedman) 19
Calais 56, 85
Cambrai 75, 80
Cambridge, Massachusetts 13
Camden, North Carolina 156, 157
Canada 13, 104, 159, 186, 187, 189
canal boats 114, 115, 129, 130, 137, 138, 140, 142, 166, 173
canal, Duke of Bridgewater's 94
canals 3, 4, 94, 154, 162, 170, 173, 188, 189
Canterbury 87
Cape Cod 11, 12, 38
Cape Fear, Cape Fear River 14, 21
Cape Hatteras 159

Index

Caribbean 7, 11, 64, 100, 137, 145, 147
Casey, Wanton 60, 61, 62, 63
Castries, Charles de La Croix, Marquis de 67
Catawba Indians 156, 167
Catawba River 156
Cathagena 145
Cayuga Lake 169
Cervantes, Miguel de
Chambers, William 90
Chantilly 74, 75, 85
Charles I 87
Charleston 4, 11, 14, 15, 17, 18, 20–25, 31–33, 44, 84, 100, 155
Charlotte, North Carolina 156
Charlotte of Mecklenburg-Strelitz, Queen of England 69
Chartres, Duc de 68
Chatham 87, 88, 137
Chenais 55
Cherbourg 72
Cherokees 25, 26, 167
Chesapeake Bay 83, 155
Chesterfield, Lord Philip Stanhope 118
Cheveloup 55
Child, Robert 90
Child, Sarah 90
China 84
Chippewa 186
Chowan River 159
Civilis, Claudius 124
Clark, Jonas 33
Cleveland, Ohio 187
Clinton, DeWitt 173, 176, 177, 188, 189
Clinton, George 161
Clinton, Sir Henry 13, 14, 40
Colchester 110, 143
Columbia 145
Combee River 26
Common Sense 65, 66
Compiègne 74
Conan Doyle, Arthur 3
Concord 10–12
Congress 4, 12–15, 19, 28, 39, 41, 46, 65, 68, 80, 149, 150, 160, 183
Connecticut 15, 16, 23, 155, 187
Connecticut River 16
Conway, Henry Seymour 103
Copley, John Singleton 4, 102, 103
Cork 14
Cornwall 93
Cornwallis, Charles, Earl 67, 82, 83, 101, 155, 161
Cossoul, François 59, 60, 71, 73, 83, 84, 98, 105, 106, 155, 158
Cossoul, Louis 105
Cossoul, Moriseau 105
Coster, Laurens 131
county fairs 3, 4, 179
Cowes 107
Coypel, Antoine 124
Cross Lake 169
Curaçao 137

Danbury, Connecticut 17
Dartford 87

Dawes, William 10
Deane, Silas 39, 80, 81
Declaration of the Rights of Man 171
De Kalb *see* Kalb, Baron de Johann von Robais
De la Lande and Fyne 125, 136, 140
Delaware River 17, 34
Delfshaven 111, 112
Delft 113–117, 124, 125, 142
Den Briel 111–113
Derby 99, 141
Derbyshire 165
Derwent River 99
Dessein, Monsieur 86, 87
Detroit 5, 154, 180, 183–185, 187, 188
Deule canal 76
Devizes 100
De Witt, Moses 167
De Witt, Simon 173, 176
De Witt Clinton (railway engine) 189
Dick 178
Digby, Robert 83
Dillon, Henriette 171
Dorchester, Massachusetts 10, 41
Dordrecht 113
Douai 75, 80
Dover 87
Dracut 38
Dreux 71
Dumas, Charles 121, 125, 136
Dunkers 18, 19
Dunmore, John Murray, Earl of 20

Easton 36
Edenton 20, 155, 158, 159
Effingham 101
Effingham, Thomas Howard, Earl of 101
Egypt 95, 113, 132, 180
Elizabeth Islands 11
England 4, 5, 39, 63, 68, 71, 77, 82, 85, 96, 116, 123, 145, 149, 150, 153, 180
English Channel 148
Ephrata, Pennsylvania 18, 19
Erie, Pennsylvania 187
Erie Canal 3, 162, 171, 184, 188, 189
Ermenonville 81
An Essay on Slavery 147
Estaing, Jean Baptiste, Count d' 39, 50, 57, 64
Europe 4, 12, 37, 39, 61, 63, 66, 72, 76, 78, 79, 148, 173
Eutaw Springs, Battle 148

Fairfield 17, 155
Falagan, Father 60
Falmouth (Portland, Maine) 13
farming 3
Farnham 107
Faustus, John 131
Fénelon, François 75
Ferrers, Robert Shirley, Earl of 92, 99, 101

Fitzgerald, John 148
Flanders 77
Florida 25
Floris V, Count of Holland 117
Forsyth, Benjamin 186
Fort Defiance 180
Fort Herkimer 166
Fort Johnston 21
Fort Oswego 167
Fort Stanwix 6, 159–162, 166
Fort Ticonderoga 13, 174
Fox, Charles James 103, 109
France 4, 5, 15, 39, 41–73, 77, 80, 82, 87, 89, 90, 95, 101, 103, 104, 136, 140, 150, 154, 167, 174, 176, 177, 190, 191
Franeker 128
Frank 151
Franklin 187
Franklin, Benjamin 3–5, 39, 41, 43, 45–48, 50–52, 64, 67–70, 72, 73, 80–83, 85, 88, 92, 93, 101, 104, 150, 172, 174, 177, 189
Frederick Hendrick, Prince of Orange 121
Frederick the Great 140
Fredericksburg 19, 20, 34
Freemasons 32, 33, 68, 75, 80, 83, 84, 92, 98, 148, 151, 170, 185
Freetown 105
French Revolution 108
Fulton, Robert 180

Gage, Thomas 10
Gainsborough, Thomas 146
Garrick, David (and sister) 94, 145
Garvey, Dr. 157, 158
Gaspée 9, 11, 12
General Scott *see* New River
Geneva, New York 169, 184
George II 118
George III, King 4, 69, 90, 101–104, 118, 167
George Washington (ship) 72, 148
Georgetown 22
Georgia 25, 28, 29
Gérard, Conrad 41
Gerards, Balthasar 116
German Flats 166, 188
Germantown 18
Germany 140
Gerry, Elbridge 149
Ghent 79, 80
Gibbon, Edward 145
Gibbs, Mr. 33
Gibraltar 102
Gloucester 99
Gloucester, Virginia 82, 83
Gouvernet, Count de; Marquis de la Tour du Pin 171, 172
Grand, Mr. 136
Grasse, François Joseph de 67, 68, 81–83, 93
Graves, Thomas 82
Gravesend 87
Great Barrington 160
Great Britain 13, 39, 176, 189
Great Dismal Swamp 20
Great Lakes 189

Green, Joseph 92, 94, 99
Greene, Nathaniel 40, 148, 149, 155
Greenwich 87, 88, 89, 145
Grenada 50, 57, 64
Gridley, Joseph 72
Groningen 128
Grotius, Hugo 117
Guildford Court House 155

Haarlem 129, 130, 131, 132, 133, 140
Haarlem Lake 126, 131
Hackensack River 150
Hackney 85, 89
The Hague 113, 117–124
Haiti 6, 158, 177
Hale, Nathan 17, 99
Halfway (Halfweg) 133, 140
Halifax 96
Halifax, Nova Scotia 13
Halifax, Virginia 33
Hall, George 31
Hamburg 7
Hamilton, Alexander 4, 173
Hancock, John 9, 10, 40
Hanover Court House 34
Hapsburgs 64
Harderwijk 128
Hartford, Connecticut 16
Harvard College 38
Harwich 109, 110, 111
Harwood, Captain 20, 22
Hearn, Captain 111
Hein, Piet 117
Heinsius, Daniel 128
Hellevoetsluis 111, 142
Hengist 126
Henley 90, 101
Henri IV 44
Henry, Mr. 55
Henry, Patrick 20
Herkimer, Nicholas 160
Herkimer, New York 166
Hillsborough 157
Hobart, John Sloss 149
Holbein, Hans 124
Holland 65, 72, 77, 109, 111–144, 150, 160, 192
Holland Land Company 171
Holmes, Sherlock 3
Hood, Viscount Samuel 109
Hoogland, Jeronemus 17
Hooker, Philip 164, 190
Hope, van der, family 137
Horsa 126
Howe, Sir William 13, 102
Hudson City 160, 189
Hudson River 4, 17, 34, 150, 166, 171, 176, 189, 193
Hull, William 180
Hull, Massachusetts 41
Hungary 64
Hungerford 101
Huntington, Countess of *see* Shirley, Selina, Countess of Huntington
Hussey, Paul 33, 35
Hutchinson, Thomas 9, 10, 92

Ile de Rhé 43
Indians 9, 25, 30, 59, 60, 68, 109, 156, 159, 160–162, 167–170, 176, 180, 187
influenza 84
Ipswich 143
Ireland 14
Iris 83
Iroquois 159, 161
Irving, Washington 5
Isle of Wight 107, 108
Israel, Lost Tribes 180, 181
Italy 123

Jamaica 93
Jamaica Plain 10
James II 48
James, Henry 5
James River 20, 33, 34, 82
Jamestown 20
Jay, John 62, 85
Jefferson, Thomas 4, 136, 183
Jim 177
Johan Maurits, Count of Nassau-Siegen 124
Jones, John Paul 72
Jones River 46
Jordaens, Jacob 121
Joseph II 71, 77
The Just Limitation of Slavery 147, 152

Kalb, Johann von Robais, Baron de 156
Kanastoretar, wife of Kiadote 167
Katwijk 127
Kenneeley, Ebenezer 189
Kiadote, King of the Onondaga Indians 167–170
King, Rufus 149
King's Ferry 17
Knox, Henry 13, 43
Knox, William 43, 46

LaChine 189
Lafayette, Marquis de 18, 40, 73, 82, 155, 156
La Flèche 44, 71
La Fleur 60, 74, 79, 84, 94, 105
Lake Champlain 4, 13, 170, 173, 174, 189, 192, 193
Lake Erie 4, 154, 155, 180, 185, 188
Lake George 173, 174
Lake Huron 180
Lake Ontario 4, 162, 166, 167, 171, 186, 189
Lake St. Clair 180
Lamb, John 136
Lancaster, Pennsylvania 17, 18, 19
Larned, George 183
La Rochelle 43
La Trappe 71
Laurens, Henry 4, 72, 84, 88, 100, 101, 104, 137
Laurens, John 65, 68, 100, 148, 150
Lausan, Duc de 82
The Law of Liberty 147
Ledyard, John 136
Lee, Arthur 39, 80

Lee, Charles 12
Leeds 96, 97
Leesburg 19
Leeuwenhoek, Anthony van 117
Lehigh River 18
Leiden 4, 112, 118, 125–130, 133, 141, 142, 192
Leidschendam 125
Le Mans 44
L'Enfant, Pierre 4, 173, 190
Lens 76
Le Ray de Chaumont, Monsieur 52
The Letters of the late Ignatius Sancho, An African 145, 146
Lexington 10, 11, 12, 38, 39, 103
Leyden, Lucas van 126
Lichfield 94
Lille 76
Lipsius, Justus 128
Little Carpenter *see* Attakullakulla
Littlepage, Louis 62
Live Oak 15
Liverpool 7, 93, 94, 95
Livingston, Robert 47, 166, 173, 177
Livingston Manor 178
Locke, John 90
Lockwood's Folly 33
Loire 44, 60, 63, 73, 83, 84
London 4, 9, 20, 25, 51, 68, 69, 73, 82, 84, 87–89, 99, 101, 104–107, 109, 121, 123, 136, 137, 141, 143, 145, 148, 158, 159
Long Bay 21
Long Island 14, 15, 148, 149
Louis XIV 75, 124
Louis XVI 47, 68, 105, 128, 167
Louisiana 172, 177
Lucieno 55
Luzac, Johan 125, 128, 129, 136
Lynch, Mr. 176
Lynden, Dirck Wolter van 123
Lynn, Mr. 32
Lynn's Tavern 32
Lys River 79
Lysander, New York 169

Maas River 112
Maassluis 142
Madison, James 4, 149, 173, 183
Madrid 62
Maidenhead 90
Maidstone 87
Manchester 93, 95, 96
Manchester, George Montagu, Duke of 88, 89
Manhattan Island 15
Manlius, New York 184
Manningtree 110
Mansart, François 190
Marblehead 23, 38
Margate 106, 107
Maria Theresia 64
Marie Antoinette 45, 47, 64
Marlborough 101
Marlborough, John Churchill, Duke of 91
Marly 54, 55
Marot, Daniel 124

Index

Mars 63
Marshfield 10
Marston, Ben 159
Martha's Vineyard 11
Martin, Robert 81
Mary Stuart, Queen with William III 121
Maryland 19, 155
masonry *see* freemasons
Massachusetts 3, 8, 23, 40, 92, 128, 149, 177
Matlock 99, 165
Maurice, Prince of Orange 117, 121
Mayflower 7
Mazarin, Jules Raymond, Cardinal 48
McCrea's Inn 25, 32
McGraw's Inn 26
McIntosh, Lachlan 21
Medford 13
Médicis, Marie de 44
Mediterranean Sea 72
Medway River 114
Men and Times of the Revolution 5
Menin 77
Mercury 41–43
Merrick, Mr. 180
Merrimac River 38
Mersey River 94
Mexico City 181
Miami River 180
Michelangelo 79
Michigan 5, 180, 187, 188
Middlebury, Vermont 174
Milford, Connecticut 16, 17
Mill Prison *see* Plymouth, England
Milton, John 91, 126
Milton, Massachusetts 38
Minus, Mrs. 29
Mississippi River 161, 167
Mohawk and Hudson Railway 189
Mohawk Indians 160
Mohawk River 160, 161, 166, 169
Mollem, Mme. (David) van 141
Montague, Duke and Duchess of 145, 146
Montgomery, New York 183
Montreal 5, 154, 189
Montreuil 85
Moravians 35, 156
Mormons 182
Morris, Robert 4, 150, 171
Morristown 17
Moudon 46
Mount Vernon 4, 150–154, 171
Mowat, Henry 13
Moyes, Henry 92, 93, 149, 150
Müller, Christiaan 131
Murfree, Hardy 157, 158
Murfreesborough 156
Murray, John 92
Myers, Samuel or Moses 139
Mystic 13

Namptwich 94
Nansemond River 155
Nantasket 41
Nantes 4, 34, 44, 47, 55–59, 61–67, 70–72, 83, 84, 98, 100, 104–106, 155, 176
Nantucket 7
Napoleon 191
Naragansett River, Naragansett Bay 15, 37, 39, 148
Netherlands 4, 5, 84, 104, 109, 111–144, 160
Neufville, Jean de 71, 72, 73, 136, 137, 160, 171
Neufville, Leendert de 72, 136
Neuse River 21
New Brunswick 159
New Castle 20
New England 9, 11, 15, 18, 20, 21, 27, 31, 33, 54, 64, 95, 159, 163, 191, 192
New Garden 156
New Hampshire 38
New Haven 16
New Jersey 14, 15, 36, 68
New Lebanon Springs 165
New Netherland *see* New York State
New River 21
New River, King of the Catawba Indians (General Scott) 156, 167
New York City 8, 14, 17, 39, 40, 98, 149, 150, 155, 161, 174–176, 180, 189, 190
New York State 3, 5, 13, 21, 137, 160–162, 167, 174–178, 188, 190
Newark, New Jersey 150
Newark, Niagara 186
Newbern 21
Newburyport 149
Newcastle under Lyme 94
Newport 4, 11, 12, 15, 38, 39, 40, 104, 105
Niagara 186, 187
Niagara (ship) 187
Nile River 132
Nonetter River 74
Noordwijk 130
Norfolk, Virginia 155
North Africa 84
North Carolina 14, 20, 105, 155–158
North Sea 110, 120
Norton, Massachusetts 148
Nott, Eliphelet 173
Nova Scotia 13, 39

Observations on Civil Liberty 89, 90
O'Burne, Irish giant 90
Ocrakoke Bar 159
Oegstgeest 130
Ogeechee River 30
Ohio River 167
Old Sarum 108
Oliver, Peter 4, 92, 93
Oneida, New York 183
Oneida Carrying Place 166
Oneida Indians 162, 170
Oneida Lake 167
Onondaga Indians 162, 170
Onondaga River 167, 177
Orange *see* Frederick Hendrick, Prince of Orange; Maurice, Prince of Orange; William of Orange; William III; William V, Prince of Orange
l'Orient 65
Orléans 56, 57
Ostende 77, 78
Oswego River 167
Otis, James 40, 151
Otsequett, Peter 161, 162
Otter Creek 174
Ovid, New York 169
Oxford 90, 91, 93, 128

"P.," Mrs. 139, 140
Padua 128
Paine, Robert 41
Paine, Tom 4, 63, 65–68
Palatine refugees 137
Pamlico, Pamtico 21, 159
Paris 4, 41, 44, 45, 47–52, 55–58, 61, 62, 65, 68–72, 74, 79–85, 89, 104, 105, 107, 128, 130, 134, 177, 190
Paris Boy 151
Passaic River 150
Passy 45, 69, 70, 81, 85, 101
Patriots' Movement (Patriotten) 142
Paulus Hook 150
Pawtucket 15
Peak District 98
Peale, Charles Wilson 155
Peekskill 17
Pennell, Joseph 5
Pennsylvania 33, 73, 137, 185
Peronne 75
Perry, Oliver Hazard 187
Peru 181
Peter the Great 137
Peterson, Mr. 141
Philadelphia 4, 8, 17–19, 28, 33, 39, 150, 155, 171, 180
Philip II 116
Piercy, Mrs. 30
Piercy, William 29, 30, 31
Pigot, Robert 40
Pilgrims 3, 4, 191, 192
Piquet de la Motte, Toussaint-Guillaume 64
Pitt, William, the Elder 69
Pitt, William, the Younger 103
Pittsfield, Massachusetts 177–180, 182
Pittsfield phylactery 180–182
Plattsburg 174
Pliarne, Penet, & Co. 34, 52
Plymouth, England 72, 109
Plymouth, Massachusetts; Plymouth Colony 3, 4, 7–10, 12, 14, 38, 39, 41, 46, 61, 63, 77, 92, 105, 148, 155, 191
Pocahantas 20
Pocotaligo 31
Poland, King of 62
Polk, William 156
Port-au-Prince 158
Port Kent 189, 190, 192, 193
Port Royal Island 26
Porter, Peter Buell 186
Portsmouth, Maine 13

Index

Portugal 95
Potomac River 34, 151, 154
Poussin, Nicolas 48
Prague 128
Price, Richard 4, 85, 89, 90
Priestley, Joseph 4, 85, 92, 93, 99
Prince of Wales 111, 142
Princeton 17, 150
Providence, Rhode Island 3, 4, 9–13, 15, 19, 22, 25, 33, 37–40, 48, 55, 67, 73, 77, 84, 148, 149, 155
Puk, Mrs. 16
Puller, C. and R. 136
Purisburg 28

Quimper 60

Rambouillet, Chateau de 177
Rambouliet, Mme. de 130, 131
Random, Roderick 4
Reading 101
Reading, Pennsylvania 17
Reed, Joseph 73
Rennes 63, 64
Rennes, Governor of 65
Rennselaer, New York 183
Rennselaerswyck 166
Revere, Paul 10
Revolutionary War 3, 4, 6, 7–40
Rhine River 126, 142
Rhode Island 3, 7, 9, 12, 15, 22, 35, 37, 39, 40, 83, 104, 105, 159
Riall, Phineas 186
Richelieu, Armand-Jean du Plessis, Cardinal 51
Richmond 90
Richmond 83
Rigby, Richard 110
Rijnsburg 130
Rijswijk 117, 122, 123
Roanoake River 157
Robbins, Chandnler 14
Rochambeau, Count de 82, 83, 155
Rochdale 96
Rochester 87, 88
Rome 47, 48, 71
Romulus, New York 169
Roozenburg Island 142
Roquencourt 55
Ross, Mr. 46, 47
Rotterdam 111–114, 116, 125, 134
Rousseau, Jean Jaques 81
Rowlandson, Thomas 109
Roxbury 38
Royal George 85, 107
Rubens 121, 124
Russell, Elizabeth 171
Russell, Nathaniel 15, 22
Russell, Thomas 171
Russia 84, 137, 138
Rutledge, John 24, 33

St. Cloud 46
St. Cosme 44
St. Denis 74, 85
St. Eustatius 137
St. Germain 47, 50, 67
St. Lawrence River 189
St. Martin 43

St. Petersburg 7, 72, 137
St. Quentin 74
St. Simon, Marquis de 82
Salamanca 128
Salem, Massachusetts 38
Salem, North Carolina 156
Salisbury 108, 109
Salmasius, Claudius 128
Sampson, Simeon 41, 43, 58, 63, 72
Sancho, Ignatius 4, 68, 145, 146, 152; wife and daughters 147
Sandy Hook 39
Saratoga Springs 121, 39, 165, 173, 174
Sardam 137, 138
Savannah, Savannah River 28, 29
Saxmundham 143
Scaliger, Josephus Justus 128
Scammel, Alexander 7
Scheldt River 79
Scheveningen 120
Schnectady 166, 174, 189
Schoharie 183
Schuyler, Philip 171, 173
Schuyler's Mills 166
Schuylkill River 35
Scituate, Massachusetts 109
Scotland 98
Scott, Mr. 19
Seine 48
Seine-Loire canal 57
Seneca Falls 169
Seneca Indians 170
Seneca River 167, 169
Senlis 74, 81
La Sensible 41
A Sentimental Journey 86, 87
Seward, Anna 99
Shaftsbury 109
Shakers 165
Shakespeare, William 91
Sharp, Granville 4, 145, 146, 147, 151, 152, 153, 154
Sharp, William 145, 146
Sheffield 98
Shelburne, William, Earl of 85, 88, 89
Sheldon, Captain 24
Sherborn 109
Sheridan, Richard Brinsley 103
Shirley, Selina, Countess of Huntington 29, 31
Silas (Old Silas) 27, 28, 33
Silliman, Gold 17
slavery, slaves 4, 6, 7, 14, 19, 20, 22, 24, 26–28, 30, 31, 33, 34, 37, 39, 58, 65, 72, 100, 137, 145, 147, 151, 152, 156, 157, 163, 172, 173, 177
small pox 14
Smeadley, Captain 72
Smith, Captain 148
Smith, Joseph 182
Smith, Rachel 148, 149, 162; *see also* Watson, Rachel
Smollett, Tobias 4, 5, 50
Socinians 4, 85, 89, 90, 92
Somme Valley 75
South Carolina 4, 14, 15, 17, 22, 100, 155

Southampton 108
Spain 85, 116, 123, 124
Speedy 114
Springfield, Massachusetts 159
Stadnitsky, Pieter 171
Stafford 94
Staffordshire Canal 93
Staphorst, Jacob van 125, 136, 137
Staphorst, Mrs. van 140
Staphorst, Nicholas 125, 136, 137
Staten Island 15
Stedman, John 145
Sterne, Laurence 5, 56, 60, 86
Steuben, Friedrich Wilhelm, Baron von 136
Stony Creek 26
Stony River 25
Stour River 110
Stratford-on-Avon 91
Suffolk, Virginia 155
Sullivan, James 149
Sullivan, John 39, 40, 169
Sullivan's Island 14
Surinam 7, 72, 137
Susquehanna River 162
Swift, Mr. 151, 154
Syracuse, New York 184

Talbot, Silas 72
Tallyrand-Périgord, Charles Maurice de 4, 170, 171, 172
Taunton, Massachusetts 38
Taylor, Dr. 161
Terrible 82
Tessier, Louis 136
Tewkesbury 99
Thames River 88, 90, 134, 148
Thomas, Isaiah 143
Tilghman, Tench 155
Tillotson 178, 179
Tom (servant of Elkanah Watson) 19
A Tour in Holland in MDCCLXXXIV 5, 143, 163
Tours 58
Town Brook 46
Towsend, Mr. 22, 25
trekschuit *see* canal boats
Trenton 17
Trianon 55
Tromp, Maerten Harpertsz. 111, 117
Troy, New York 169, 171, 175, 176
Trumbull, John 81
Tryon's Tavern 165, 173
Twain, Mark 5

Union College 173, 174
United States (The Netherlands) 143, 144
Uppsala 128
Utrecht 128, 140, 141, 142

Valley Forge 19, 35, 36, 37
Valton, Mrs. 116
Van Beuren, Widow 175
Vanbiber, Mr. 140, 141
Vanbiber's Tavern 31
Van Buren, Martin 192, 193

Van Cortlandt, Philip 166, 169, 172
Van der Werff, Adriaen 121
Van Dyke, Anthony 79, 124, 135
Van Rennselaer, Jeremiah 165, 169, 176
Vaughan, Benjamin 85, 101
Veen, Otto van 124
Velsen, Gerard van 117
Vergennes, Charles Gravier, Count de 4, 39, 46, 47, 82
Vergennes, Vermont 174
Vermont 173
Vernon River 30
Versailles 44, 47, 55, 56, 74, 104, 105, 122, 123
Vienna 64
Virginia 13, 19, 20, 33, 82, 155, 157
Vliet 124, 125
Volney 172
Voltaire 48
Voorburg 125
Voorschoten 125
Vouet, Simon 48

Wadsworth, Peleg 7
Wales 100
Wales, Prince of 4, 101
Walpole, Horace 145
Walton, George 29
War of 1812 6, 104, 180, 186, 191
Warren, James 41, 72
Warren, Mrs. James 41
Warren, Mercy Otis 4, 9, 40, 72, 81
Warren, Winslow 72, 73
Warrington 94, 95
Warwick Neck 148
Washington, George 4, 12–15, 17–19, 21, 35–37, 45, 52, 71, 80, 82–84, 92, 98, 114, 117, 147–155, 173; mother 34

Washington, D.C. 4, 157, 173, 186, 191, 193
Wassenaar-Opdam, Johan Hendrik, Count van 124
Watch, dog 25, 33
Watson, Charles 190
Watson, Elkanah, Sr. 4, 7, 11, 12, 15, 38, 41, 61, 95, 104
Watson, Emily 176, 183
Watson, George 176
Watson, John 3
Watson, Joseph 176
Watson, Marston 105, 106
Watson, Patty 64
Watson, Priscilla 63
Watson, Rachel 175, 183, 192, 193
Watson, William (Elkanah's son) 176
Watson, William (Elkanah's uncle) 9
Watson, Winslow 178, 192
Watt, James 4, 92, 93, 99
wax sculptures 3
Wesley, John 124
West, Benjamin 102
West Indies 12, 19, 22
West Point 94
Western Inland Lock Navigation Company 166
Wharton, Samuel 46, 48–51, 56
Whitefield, George 29
Wildman, Thomas 109
William and Mary College 20, 156
William of Orange 114, 116, 117, 121
William III 121, 123, 124
William V, Prince of Orange 118, 121, 123, 167
Williams, Jonathan, Jr. 47, 61, 65, 67
Williams, Mr. (Port Royal Island) 26

Williamsburg 20, 33, 34, 124
Williamson, Hugh 180
Willinck, Jan 125, 136, 137
Willinck, Willem 125, 136, 137
Wilmington 21, 33
Wilton 109
Windsor Castle 103, 104
Winslow, Edward (Pilgrim) 7, 39, 192
Winslow, Edward (18th c.) 9, 38, 39
Winslow, Edward, Jr. (18th c.) 10, 39
Winslow (family) 4
Winyaw Bay 22
Witt, Johan and Cornelis 124
Woerden 142
Wood Creek 161
Woodlands, North Carolina 157
Woolwich 87, 88
Worcester 99
Worcester, Massachusetts 143
Worcestershire Canal 93
Worsley Mills 96
Wray, Cecil 109
Wren, Christopher 89
Wright, Joseph 71
Wright, Patience Lovell 4, 63, 68, 69, 71, 73, 107

Y (IJ) River 133, 137
Yarmouth 142
Yeovil 109
York, Joseph 123
York, Ontario 186
York, Pennsylvania 17, 19
Yorktown 5, 67, 82, 83

Zubly, John Joachim 28
Zuider Zee 133, 134
Zwanenburg 133

www.ingramcontent.com/pod-product-compliance
Lightning Source LLC
Chambersburg PA
CBHW081555300426
44116CB00015B/2894